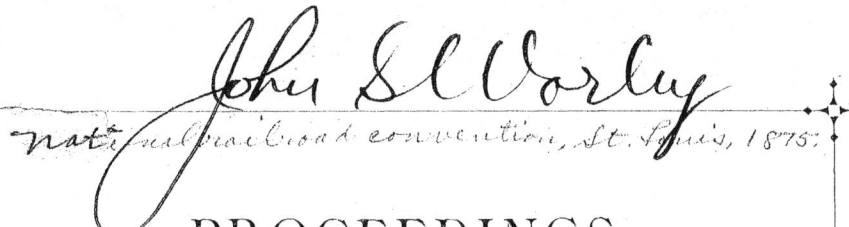

John M Vorley
National railroad convention, St. Louis, 1875.

PROCEEDINGS

OF THE

National Railroad Convention

AT ST. LOUIS, MO.,

NOVEMBER 23 & 24, 1875,

IN REGARD TO THE CONSTRUCTION OF THE TEXAS & PACIFIC RAILWAY AS A SOUTHERN TRANS-CONTINENTAL LINE FROM THE

MISSISSIPPI VALLEY TO THE PACIFIC OCEAN

ON THE

THIRTY-SECOND PARALLEL OF LATITUDE.

PUBLISHED BY ORDER OF THE CONVENTION,
JOHN M. HARRELL, of Arkansas, Secretary.

ST. LOUIS
WOODWARD, TIERNAN & HALE, PRINTERS AND BINDERS.
1875.

Transportation
Library

[*Resolution authorizing publication of Proceedings. Page* 149.]

Resolved, That the Secretary of the Executive Committee appointed by the citizens of St. Louis, together with the Secretary of this Convention, be instructed to prepare, under the direction of said committee, the proceedings of this Convention for publication in pamphlet form, and to publish such number of copies as they may deem advisable.

INDEX.

ADDRESSES—

By the Chairman of Executive Committee	viii
By the Memorial Committee	11
By Col. James O. Broadhead, (temporary organization)	26
By Gen. Anderson, (temporary organization)	38
By Mayor Britton, of St. Louis, (temporary organization)	41
By Judge Stanley Mathews, (permanent organization)	60
By Judge Stanley Mathews, (response to vote of thanks)	150
By Gen. Preston, (permanent organization)	63
By Gen. Preston, (response to vote of thanks)	151
By Hon. R. W. Thompson, of Ind., (by invitation)	135
By E. N. Hill, of Ark.	110
By Robertson Topp	135

COMMITTEE—

On Credentials	40
On Permanent Organization	43
On Resolutions	70
Of Arrangements, request of	74

COMMUNICATIONS—

From R. C. Clowry, Sup't Western Union Telegraph	44
From Gov. Dingley, of Maine	47
From E. C. Pike	48
From J. N. Dyer, Librarian Mercantile Library	58
From Hon. Erastus Wells, of St. Louis	74
From Frank Ogden, of Texas	78
From J. H. Simpson, Col. U. S. A	79
From Col. Thomas A. Scott, of Pa	81
From Citizens of El Paso	93
From Citizens of Grant County, New Mexico	97
From California, Arizona and Nevada delegates	200
From Prof. Waterhouse	202

CONVENTION—

Origin of	vii

DISCUSSION—

On Temporary Organization	39
On Invitation to Jefferson Davis	45
On Committee on Resolutions	69
On Report of Committee on Resolutions	108

INDEX.

DELEGATES—
List of 48

MEMORIAL COMMITTEE—
Meeting of 155
Address of 11

ORGANIZATION—
Opening prayer by Rev. Dr. Eliot 26
Temporary Officers 39
Permanent Officers .... 59—67

SPEECHES—
By Mr. Hill, of Ark 110
By Hon. R. W. Thompson, of Indiana 135
By Col. Robertson Topp, of Tenn 139
By Hon. Stanley Mathews, (in response to vote of thanks) 150
By Gen. Preston, of Kentucky, (same) 151
By Mr. Marshall, of Miss 120
By Mr. Harrison, of Texas .... 121—125
By Mr. Hale, of Texas 124
By Mr. McCarty, of Miss 126
By Mr. Topp, of Tenn 126
By Mr. Turner, of Cal 126
By Mr. Higgins, of Texas 127
By Mr. Snowden, of Pa 128
By Mr. Jones, of Kentucky 129
By Mr. Stemmon, of Ky 129
By Gen. Preston, of Ky 131
By Mr. Pierce, of Ind 131
By Mr. Kidd, of Texas 132
By Mr. Thompson, of Texas 132
By Mr. Sumner, of Texas, ... 132
By Mr. West, of Texas 132
By Mr. Soussy, of Ga 133

REPORTS—
From Committee on Credentials 47
From Committee on Permanent Organization 57
From Committee on Resolutions 102

RESOLUTIONS AND MOTIONS—
By Mr. Burwell, (of instruction) 46
By California Delegation 72
By Mr. Smith, of Tenn., of Memphis Convention 75
By Mr Halliday, of Kansas, (Atchison, Topeka & Santa Fe R. R.) 76
By Mr. Palmer, of S. Carolina, (basis of action) 77
In reference to communication of Col. T. A. Scott 92
By Mr. Barlow, of Illinois, (of thanks) 92
By Mr. Tatum, (extending courtesies) 97
By Mr. J. T. Trezevant, of Ark., (branch lines) 102
By Mr. E. N. Hill, of Ark., (courtesies) 102
By Mr. Smoot, (to print Mr. Hill's speech) 110
By Mr. Broadhead, (printing proceedings) 149
By Mr. Haven, of La., (thanks to Hon. R. W. Thompson) 149

INDEX.

RESOLUTIONS AND MOTIONS—*Continued.*
    By Mr. Haven, of La., (thanks to R. R. Companies)........................ 149
    By Mr. Stearns, of Col., (relating to official proceedings).................. 149
    By Mr. Bowman, of Ky., (thanks)... 150
    By Mr. St. Gem, of Mo., (invitation to Hon. R. W. Thompson)............ 134

APPENDIX—
    Banquet at Masonic Hall... 157
    Speech of Hon. T. L. Jones.. 158
    Speech of Gen. Preston.. 161
    Speech of Col. Thos. A. Scott... 164
    Speech of Mayor Fox, of Philadelphia....................................... 166
    Speech of Gen. Hodge... 168
    Speech of Judge Turner... 169
    Speech of Judge Kennard... 171
    Speech of Judge Wilson... 172
    Speech of Mr. Claiborne.. 173
    Speech of Mr. Pierce.. 174
    Steamboat Excursion.. 176
    Communication from Delegates.. 200
    Merits of the Texas & Pacific Railroad (by Prof. Waterhouse)............. 202

ORIGIN OF THE NATIONAL RAILROAD CONVENTION.

The largest Convention of representative men ever held in the West owed its origin and great success, not to individual or local influences, but to a national impulse or movement in favor of an enterprise which commands the assent or warm support of a vast majority of the American people. In obedience to the evident wishes of the people, and in response to a call signed by Col. J. O. Broadhead, Hon. Isaac H. Sturgeon, and many other leading citizens, a meeting was held at the Southern Hotel, St. Louis, on the night of the 15th of September, to take the initiatory steps in this matter. Hon. Henry Overstolz was called to the chair, and J. L. Tracy appointed Secretary. Col. James O. Broadhead explained the purpose of the meeting, and after a number of speeches, all advocating the measure, the following resolution by Col. Broadhead was unanimously adopted:

Resolved, That a National Railroad Convention be held in St. Louis on the 23d day of November next for the purpose indicated in the call for this meeting, and that the Chairman appoint an Executive Committee of fifteen, who shall have power to appoint sub-committees to carry out the objects of this meeting.

The Chairman appointed the following gentlemen on the Executive Committee, called for in the above resolution:

James O. Broadhead, John B. Maude, E. O. Stanard, Web. M. Samuel, Jas. E. Yeatman, Edwin Harrison, Chas. P. Chouteau, D. P. Rowland, O. Garrison, S. H. Laflin, Isaac M. Mason, Giles F. Filley, Charles Speck, Isaac H. Sturgeon, Silas Bent.

The following names were subsequently added to this committee:

Jno. P. Meyer, T. J. Bartholow, W. S. Stewart, Jno. H. Maxon, George Bain, Miles Sells, W. G. Eliot, Chauncey I. Filley, Henry Hitchcock, Wm. Senter, Carl Schurz, T. T. Gantt, Albert Todd, D. M. Frost, A. W. Slayback, Robt. Campbell, E. C. Cabell, D. T. Jewett, W. S. Bartley, L. L. Ashbrook, Andrew McKinley, C. B. Bray, Jas. T. Howenstein, J. H. Beach, Chas. E. Barney, Ben. Stickney, Jun., W. H. Scudder, T. R. Allen, Isaac Cook, Wm. Nichols, T. Pakers, Geo. Knapp, John M. Gilkeson, Geo. I. Barnett, Joseph Bogy, Michael Heller, R. P. Tansey, H. C. Brockmeyer, Thos. Richeson, J. N. Booth, N. Mulliken, A. A. Mellier, E. C. Simmons, M. Collins, D. B. Gould, D. G. Taylor, J. H. Terry, Abram Nave, Wm. Taussig, Jno. Knapp, J. B. C. Lucas, G. W. Chadbourne, W. C. Kinney, C. Minnegerode, J. A. Wherry, R. B. Brown, W. McMillan, J. T. Davis, S. M. Dodd, E. C. Quimby, P. Behr, H. C. Yaeger, J. E. Shorb, Geo. H. Heafford, Geo. T. Hull, D. G. Tutt.

At the first meeting of the Executive Committee, held September 20th, Col. Broadhead was elected Chairman and J. L. Tracy Permanent Secretary.

The following resolution was unanimously adopted:

Resolved, That the Chairman of this Committee be authorized to issue an address setting forth the action and objects of the people in calling a National Railroad Convention to be held in St. Louis on the 23d of November, 1875, and requesting the co-operation of Governors of States and Territories and of the various trade associations in the cities of the United States.

This beginning resulted in the assemblage of about eight hundred delegates from thirty States and Territories, including representatives from seventy-six cities, twenty-two trade organizations, the National Grange, and four State Granges.

At a subsequent meeting the following resolution, offered by Col. Broadhead, was unanimously adopted:

Resolved, That the city of St. Louis does not ask or claim that she shall be made the eastern terminus of the proposed Southern Trans-continental Railroad. What she asks is, that the building of the road shall be secured to some suitable point in the Mississippi Valley, within the territorial limits of Texas, Louisiana, Arkansas, Missouri or the Indian Territory, and she will trust to her geographical and commercial position, and to the intelligence and enterprise of her citizens, to secure such connection therewith as may be desirable.

J. L. TRACY,
Secretary Executive Committee.

In obedience to the above resolution, Col. Broadhead, Chairman of the Executive Committee, issued the following address to the people of the United States, in regard to a Southwestern Pacific Railroad:

ADDRESS.

The Executive Committee appointed by a mass meeting of the citizens of St. Louis, to make arrangements for calling a National Convention to consider the subject of the construction of a Pacific Railroad through the States and Territories of the Southwest, and to take such action in its favor as might seem fit, hereby announce that such a Convention will be held in St. Louis, on the 23d of November next; and we formally and cordially invite the people of the several States and Territories, through their Governors and Boards of Trade, Chambers of Commerce, Cotton Exchanges, and other commercial or municipal organizations, whose action can be conveniently had, to appoint delegates to attend and participate in its proceedings.

It is made a National Convention, because the enterprise is thoroughly national in its scope and influence. While it will be of vital importance to a vast region of rich territory, three times as large as the thirteen original States of this Republic, and now almost destitute of railroad facilities, the completion of such a work will yield great benefits to every section of the country.

The proposed railroad will have at least seven Eastern terminal points on the Mississippi or the Gulf—these radiating branches meeting at some convenient point in Western Texas, and thence constituting one grand trunk line to the Pacific Ocean. The States of Texas, Louisiana, Arkansas, California and Missouri, also Mississippi, Tennessee and Illinois, with the Territories of New Mexico, Arizona, and the Indian Territory, and the Northern States of Old Mexico will be directly on the main line or its branches.

The road may be considered as completed to Fort Worth in Northwestern Texas, to which point the exertions of the Company will carry it during the coming year. From this point to San Diego on the Pacific coast, a distance of 1,457 miles, the work is beyond the reach of individual enterprise.

Some of the immediate and legitimate results of the inauguration and vigorous prosecution of this work may be briefly stated as follows:

It will bring many millions of foreign capital into the country, to be distributed amongst iron-masters, contractors and laborers, thus contributing largely to the relief of the financial pressure throughout the country.

It will rekindle the fires and start the machinery in furnaces and foundries East and West, giving profitable employment to an army of idle men, either in the construction of the work or in the preparation of material.

It will aid in the rapid development of many millions of acres of good farming land in Texas, the Indian Territory, New Mexico and Arizona, and in the successful working of the rich silver, gold and copper mines of the two last-named Territories, and of the Northern States of Old Mexico.

It will bring into those regions a multitude of industrious emigrants from the older States, and from Europe, to build up mining towns, and transform a wild waste into productive farms.

It will do much towards the solution of the Indian question, by reason of the more rapid advance of the great army of civilization, which it will inevitably secure, thus saving to the Government millions annually in the single item of border protection. [It was estimated by a committee of the last Congress that it costs the Government annually $10,000,000 to maintain an available force sufficient to protect the lives and property of the white inhabitants of the country traversed by this line of road.]

It will save to the Government in the diminished cost of transporting military stores, Indian supplies, and the mails, more annually than the interest on the bonds proposed to be issued for the construction of the road.

It will carry the industries of civilization into the Northern States of Mexico, a country containing nearly ten millions of people, and secure to us an immense trade that is now being diverted into other and foreign markets.

It will secure to us a highway from the Mississippi to the Pacific Ocean, on the shortest, best and most economical route—a line free from the obstructions of high mountains, deep snows, and the annual floods which beset the present route.

It will aid largely to secure cheap transportation by creating a healthy competition with the only other line of trans-continental railway.

It will bring increased revenue to the Government, by substituting industrious, productive communities in the place of savage hordes, now a source of enormous expense and perpetual annoyance.

It will resurrect and rehabilitate the South, by pouring through that fertile but distracted region of our country a perpetual tide of the world's commerce, vitalizing its railroad system, and reviving its paralyzed industries.

It will bring more immediate, substantial and permanent benefits to the West and South than any enterprise that has yet been inaugurated.

This rich territory, covering an area of nearly one million of square miles, which has been practically ignored in the legislation of Congress whilst it is entitled, equally with any other section, to such favors as the Government may legitimately bestow, will add by its prosperity to the wealth and glory of the whole country.

The Union and Central Pacific roads have received magnificent donations of money and lands, and now have the monopoly of the transportation to and from the Pacific coast. The Southwest must have a road to counteract this influence, and give accommodations to the people of the whole country by the competition which its construction will produce.

What is asked from the Government to consummate this great national enterprise? Not money, not subsidies, not loans or lands. The companies having this enterprise in charge simply ask for a guaranty of five per cent. interest on construction bonds, and offer to indemnify the Government for its indorsement by a first lien on all their property, by the surrender of 30,000,000 acres of land already granted, and the transportation of the mails, troops, and supplies; also by depositing in the U. S. Treasury $5,000 in bonds for each mile of road, to be sold by the Government if necessary to meet any possible deficiency during the period of constructing the road.

In view of the facts we have mentioned, and the importance of this movement to the people of this whole country, we earnestly invite your co-operation. We hope that delegates may be sent from every part of the country, in order that the will of the people may be ascertained, and such expression given to their wishes as will insure their being carried out by their representatives at Washington.

JAS. O. BROADHEAD,
Chairman Executive Committee.

ISAAC M. MASON,
President Board of Trade.

OLIVER GARRISON,
E. O. STANARD,
ISAAC H. STURGEON,
SILAS BENT,
HENRY OVERSTOLZ,
GILES F. FILLEY,
JAS. E. YEATMAN,

JAS. H. BRITTON,
Mayor of St. Louis.

D. P. ROWLAND,
President Merchants' Exchange.

CHARLES SPECK,
EDWIN HARRISON,
S. H. LAFLIN,
WEB. M. SAMUEL,
CHAS. P. CHOUTEAU,
JNO. B. MAUDE,
J. L. TRACY, *Secretary.*

JNO. P. MEYER,
T. J. BARTHOLOW,
JNO. N. BOFINGER,
W. S. STEWART,
JNO. H. MAXON,
} *Committee of Merchants' Exchange.*

ADDRESS

TO THE

PEOPLE OF THE UNITED STATES.

The National Convention, which held its sessions in the city of St. Louis on the 23d and 24th days of November, 1875, to consider the subject of the construction of a railroad from the Mississippi river to the Pacific Ocean, through the States and Territories of the Southwest, directed the preparation and publication of an address to the people of the United States, embodying the views set forth in the preamble and resolutions adopted by it.

The propriety of such an appeal is justified by the character and composition of the Convention itself, and by the nature of the great enterprise it recommends.

The Convention consisted of delegates duly appointed from thirty-one States and Territories, many cities and boards of trade, merchants' exchanges and other commercial bodies, constituting a body of 869 members, representing not only a large proportion of the people of the United States, but of the active, producing, business capital of the country. Speaking to their fellow-citizens of the entire Union on a subject of common national interest, there is not even the appearance of presumption in the attitude of such a body representing such a constituency. On the contrary, the fact of its speaking constitutes its title to be heard.

The motive for addressing the people at large grows out of a deep conviction, entertained by the Convention, that the enterprise recommended by them is one in which every citizen of the United States has an important and equal interest, and that its merits are so plain and great that a candid presentation of the propositions in its support, to the popular understanding, will enlist in its behalf an earnest, intelligent and powerful advocacy on the part of the general public that must silence every prejudice, overcome every hostile interest, and command from a Government, which is but the instrument of its will, the legislation and public aid which are invoked. As the interests represented and urged by the Convention are purely public in their character, its reliance for their recognition and promotion is purely upon the public spirit of the nation, to whose impartial reason it addresses itself.

The main conclusion of the Convention is, that a southern transcontinental railway, from the waters of the Mississippi, via El Paso, to the Pacific Ocean, on or near the 32d parallel of latitude, is imperatively demanded—

1. *As a measure of sound statesmanship*, more effectually providing for that constant intercourse, business and social, by which the great States growing up on the Pacific slope are to be permanently bound in a common interest with our Eastern and Southern communities and the most intimate relations promoted between all sections of our common country—a sound policy, already recognized by the Government in its grant of bonds and lands to the Union and Central and Kansas Pacific roads, and of lands to other trans-continental lines on the 32d, 35th and 47th parallels—a policy thus far, in fact, defeated, because the private capital relied upon and necessary to complete this system of highways could not be obtained on the conditions limited, leaving the responsibility still resting upon the Government to secure the completion of at least one additional trans-continental line.

2. *As a means of national defence*, securing to the Government a line to the Pacific, unobstructed at all seasons of the year, for the prompt transportation of its troops and supplies in the event of war, exposing the ports and countries of the Pacific Coast to insult or attack, and yet sufficiently removed from the border to be fully capable of protection against any hostile force.

3. *As a local military necessity.* The experience of the nation on the Central, Union and Kansas Pacific roads having proven that the rail and telegraph and the facilities thereby provided furnish the only sure means of intercepting and punishing the hostile Indians, unmistakably indicates the adoption of the same method to prevent constant depredations in Western Texas, New Mexico and Arizona, making life and property secure and establishing there the same law and order that prevail along the present Pacific line.

4. *As a measure of practical economy* in the administration of the Government. The experience of the present Pacific roads already has shown that the expense of maintaining a military establishment for the protection of the territory through which it passes from Indian depredations, will be largely reduced, by enabling the Government to transport troops and supplies at one-fifth of the present cost, and by enabling it to dispense with two-thirds of the present force, through facilities afforded for the transportation and movement of troops. It is estimated that the saving under this head alone will be from eight to ten millions of dollars per annum, while, at the same time, the Government will be enabled to provide more efficiently and economically for the care and maintenance of the Indian tribes under its charge.

5. *As a commercial necessity* to the twelve millions of people inhabiting a belt of country from four hundred to seven hundred miles in width, and stretching along the entire South Atlantic Coast, the Gulf of Mexico and Old Mexico to the Pacific Ocean, who, by reason of their geographical position, cannot share directly in the benefits conferred by the present Pacific line.

6. *As a direct saving to the people of the entire country*, by furnishing a competing line between the two oceans for the immense and hourly increasing traffic growing out of the internal trade between the Atlantic and Pacific States, and the foreign trade with the Sandwich Islands, China, Japan, Australia and Western South America, all of which now pays tribute to a single line that enjoys and profits by its monopoly, created but not controlled by the Government, and against whose arbitrary and exclusive policy no adequate protection exists, or can be now furnished, except by the competition of the proposed line

through the Southwestern States and Territories. The present monopoly is fostered by a Government loan of $55,000,000 of six per cent. Government bonds, the annual interest on which, amounting to three millions three hundred thousand dollars, is paid directly out of the Treasury, besides large grants of public lands. The policy of the corporation is dictated solely by considerations of profit to its owners, and its own interest as a private company, entirely failing to answer the supposed object of its creation—that of furnishing an open highway, free, without discrimination, on equal terms to all having occasion to use it, such as the people of this country have a right to demand. The only remaining remedy is to build up a sound, healthy and legitimate competition, subject to the regulating power of Congress, reserved in the legislation granting the public aid, which shall limit the rates and charges of transportation to a moderate, fair and reasonable return upon the basis of the actual cost of the road, and furnish equal facilities to all, without discrimination against any.

7. *As a means of communication* with the rich and productive States of Old Mexico, securing a large and lucrative traffic now either non-existent or diverted to other countries, and by connecting with lines of railroad now projected from the capital of Mexico to its northern border, stimulating and developing the mutual and profitable exchange of products between the two countries.

8. *As an act of duty* on the part of the Government to furnish the necessary means of protection to citizens whose guardianship it assumed, under treaty obligations, in the acquisition of the Mexican territory in which they were resident, and all others who have been induced by the grants of land made to aid the building of railroads, to settle in the Territories which those roads were intended to develop.

9. *As an act of justice* and encouragement to the people of the Southern States, who have reason to complain of the partiality of the Government, which since its organization has expended for public improvements in the Northern States and Territories $175,000,000 of public moneys, while in the Southern States and Territories the public expenditures for similar purposes have been but $19,000,000. Aside from this, the whole system of Southern railways virtually terminates

at the Mississippi river, and is cut off from all direct connection by rail with the Pacific Coast. It is but just that these railways should have equal facilities for extension on their own lines to the western boundary of the Republic, and participate with the parallel lines with which they compete in the great through trans-continental traffic, as well as to be fed and replenished by the rich trade to be developed by the construction of a grand trunk line to the Pacific, on their own line of latitude with Mexico, and through our domestic territories, rich in mineral and agricultural capacities, waiting for population and development.

These are the considerations, in substance, that led the Convention to its conclusion that the construction of the proposed railroad connection between the Valley of the Mississippi and the Pacific Ocean is imperatively demanded. If there were involved no question of Government aid, and no prejudices on that subject, their full and controlling force would be freely and generally admitted.

It is quite certain that if, in this case, the aid of the Government credit, as asked, be denied, the road cannot be built. Two things must concur to attract to such an investment the necessary amount of private capital. First—Each contributor must be satisfied of the *certainty* that the work will be completed; for its ability to pay interest and repay capital depends on its being completely built, as on that depends its value and its ability to earn income. Second—There must be not only a certainty that it will some day be completed, but also that it will be completed within some definite period; because, otherwise, there is no means of calculating its cost, which, including interest on capital not paid by income, grows with every delay in construction.

In a work of such magnitude as this, these conditions cannot be fulfilled upon the basis of the credit of the undertaking itself, nor of that of its individual or corporate promoters. Even if the first could be met, and individual capitalists could be furnished with reasonable assurance that the work would not drop unfinished, the element of time and delay would at once enter and so enlarge the cost of construction, by accumulations of interest to be paid only out of increased capital, as to make the enterprise impracticable.

Nothing less will furnish the required conditions of success than the aid of Government credit, guaranteeing the punctual payment of accruing interest on the capital advanced. This is the form of Government assistance invoked in behalf of this enterprise. No advance of public money is asked for, and it is confidently claimed that, upon the securities and with the guards and restrictions proposed, the Government will never be required, on account of its guarantee, to *advance* a single dollar, much less to *lose one*.

If this can be made to appear, what possible objections, on any public ground, can be urged against the application? It is confidently claimed that it will so appear from a candid and careful consideration of the scheme proposed. The line of road embraced in the project is described in the resolutions of the Convention.

1. That a Southern line to the Pacific Ocean should be built on or near the 32d parallel, from Shreveport, via El Paso to San Diego, where it will make connections with the waters of the Pacific in a safe and excellent harbor, and connect also with the railway lines now building from San Francisco to the southern part of California, thus securing a continuous line to that great city and port.

2. That there should also be constructed extensions from the most eligible points on the Texas and Pacific road to New Orleans, Memphis and Vicksburg, and from a point near the 103d meridian to Vinita, in order to reach the Mississippi river, and to connect with every road and harbor of the Atlantic Coast, and with every railway east of the Rocky Mountain slope.

3. That to insure to the nation the greatest benefits from this line of road, and to prevent its being controlled in the interest of any one party or section of country, there should be established such regulations as will maintain the road from Shreveport to the Pacific as an open highway, and a competing line to all trans-continental railroads, to be used on equal terms by all connecting roads which are now or may hereafter be built. Similar regulations to be applied to the branches receiving similar aid to the Texas and Pacific trunk line.

4. That it should be built at the lowest possible cost, in order that the people shall be protected against undue or oppressive charges,

and shall be secured in its use at the lowest possible rate required to protect the comparatively small capital actually expended on its construction—a result which can be greatly aided by its construction at this time, when material and labor can be secured at prices much below those that have prevailed for many years past—and that Congress shall at all times reserve the power to protect the people against speculation and oppression in the use of this national highway.

5. That the building of the main line should proceed under such regulations as will insure the construction of the road continuously from the point of its present completion in Texas to San Diego, in California, or until it meets an extension of the same line from San Diego.

The line contemplated is that for the construction of which the Texas and Pacific Railway Company has been incorporated and organized under acts of Congress and statutes of the State of Texas, including its consolidations with other companies, and embracing the line of the Atlantic and Pacific Railroad from Vinita to its point of junction near the 103d parallel of longitude. The trunk line extends from Shreveport, in the State of Louisiana, to San Diego, in California. Of this line the division lying between Shreveport and Fort Worth is partly built, and will be completed by the Company itself out of its own means, making 443 miles for which no public aid is required or asked. It also includes certain extensions necessary to connect the trunk line with the general system of railroads lying east of the Mississippi river. St. Louis is provided for by the existing Iron Mountain road to Texarkana and the existing connection by the Pacific road of Missouri via Sedalia, and the Missouri, Kansas and Texas road. The proposed connection with the Atlantic and Pacific will give it an additional and more direct route to the Pacific Coast. The extensions needing public aid for their completion will be to New Orleans, to Vicksburg and to Memphis. To finish the construction of what is needed to perfect connections with these points it is estimated will add no more to the distance to be supplied with Government aid than the portion of the main line between Shreveport and Fort Worth, as to which it has already been stated that it is excluded from the application. The whole distance of road thus to be constructed, and for which the Government aid will be required, is estimated to be about 2,000 miles.

The extent and mode of this aid, as recommended by the Convention, is by a guarantee on the part of the United States of interest, not principal, on a limited amount of five per cent. construction bonds issued by the Company, payable in fifty years, so that the entire liability assumed shall not in any event exceed $2,000 per mile per annum, nor the interest on the actual cost of the line and branches actually constructed, such liability to be secured by a first mortgage upon all the railway property and franchises of the companies and upon the lands granted by the United States; and any deficiency in the earnings of the line and branches to meet the interest maturing on these bonds while the road is in course of construction, to be met by the deposit in the United States Treasury of one-eighth of the whole authorized issue and the sale of the same if it becomes necessary, after applying all net earnings and proceeds of lands, and the sums due for Government transportation, mail and telegraph service, to meet the interest maturing as aforesaid, so that there shall be no outlay by the Government; these bonds to be issued only to the actual amount of cash expended upon the road and branches, and upon the certificate of sworn commissioners, appointed by the Government to supervise the building of the line and its branches, and their redemption at maturity to be assured to purchasers and holders by providing a sinking fund out of the revenues of the road and branches, to be paid by the companies into the treasury of the United States, of such amount as may be sufficient to pay off and discharge the entire bonded obligations of the companies on which the Government has guaranteed the interest.

It will be observed that the maximum of the bonds to be issued under this plan will be $40,000 per mile, and of these $5,000 per mile are to be held by the Government, to be sold only to meet deficiencies in the payment of interest during the progress of the work. It is estimated that an average of $35,000 per mile, or $30,000 for the plain country and $40,000 for the mountain country, will be sufficient;

but no bond is to be issued except as it represents the actual amount of money reasonably expended in construction, under the supervision of Government inspectors, and upon their sworn certificates of the fact. Here is perfect security, so far as human administration can make it, that no fictitious issue of obligation will be made, and every holder of a bond will have the assurance that every dollar of his money advanced has gone into the security which he holds for its repayment.

To indemnify the Government against loss on account of its guarantee, and to secure the payment of the bonds at maturity, the provision made by the plan is deemed adequate beyond all doubt. It consists of a first mortgage on the road and its land grants—a first mortgage that cannot be displaced, except with the unattainable consent of every holder of the bonds, besides that of Congress—the retention by the Government of all sums earned for transportation, and for postal and telegraphic service, the proceeds of the sale of public lands granted in its aid, the net earnings of the road, and $5,000 per mile of bonds to be sold, and proceeds applied to the payment of interest in case of default.

The whole liability of the Government thus to be secured cannot in any event exceed $2,000 per mile per annum. The gross earnings of the line, sufficient to yield that amount of net revenue, need not exceed $5,000 per mile per annum. The actual receipts of the Union and Central Pacific roads amount to much more than double that sum, upward of seventy per cent. of which is from local business, all of which has been created since that line of road was built. The net earnings of that entire line, according to the last published reports, amounted to $6,279 per mile per annum, or sufficient to pay five per cent. coin interest on an indebtedness of more than one hundred thousand dollars per mile.

The natural advantages of the country traversed by the Southern line are as great, if not much greater, than those of the country through which the existing line passes, while the shorter distance, low summits, easy grades and freedom from snow will materially diminish operating expenses. In addition to the resources of our own Southern and Western States and Territories, some of the richest portions of Mexico lie adjacent to the proposed road, with a population of two millions of people, simply waiting its construction to pour in upon it a very large and valuable traffic. The reports of committees of Congress and the records of the Government show conclusively that the construction of the existing line of railroad to the Pacific has, since its completion, saved to the Government annually about $3,000 per mile, and certainly an equal if not a greater saving will be effected by the construction of the Texas and Pacific line. The committee of the last House of Representatives on this subject is authority for the statement that to hold in subjection the numerous savage tribes scattered through the territory to be traversed by the road, and protect the lives and property of its civilized inhabitants, there are now stationed troops aggregating about one-fourth of the entire available force of our army, maintained and subsisted at an expense which cannot fall short of $10,000,000 per annum, and that it is evident that the construction of this road will enable the Government to withdraw three-fourths of the troops now stationed in the country traversed by it, and render the remaining fourth far more efficient than the whole force now employed there, and that the saving so effected, added to the diminished cost of transporting military stores, Indian supplies and the mails, will aggregate every year more than the annual amount of the interest on all the bonds proposed to be issued.

As to the value and importance of the connection to be established by means of the Southwestern Pacific road with Mexico, we have the high testimony of the Hon. J. W. Foster, the United States Minister near that government. In an address before the Chamber of Commerce of the city of New Orleans on the 18th day of November, 1875, reported in the *Republican* newspaper of that city, he refers also to the projects aided by the Mexican government for perfecting that connection. He says:

"While the Southern Pacific Railroad, which would open to the United States the boundless wealth of precious metals hidden in the upper Sierra Madre and the agricultural advantages of the Northern States of Mexico, halts and languishes for want of Government aid, and while the International of Texas, leading to the Rio Grande, has been embarrassed for want of or delay in the legislation of that State, Mexico has given substantial evidence of its desire to aid every feasible railroad project looking toward a connection with the United States, or having a tendency to develop commercial relations with us. At the last session of its Congress a concession was granted to the International Railroad Company of Texas, represented by Hon. Edward L. Plumb, to construct a railroad from its junction with the Rio Grande to the city of Leon, a distance through Mexico of between 600 and 700 miles, where it will connect with the trunk system of railroads of that country; and the government agrees to pay as a subsidy to the Company $15,288 per mile, with a large additional premium if the road is completed before the time fixed in the concession, and admit all its materials free of duty. The Congress at the same session granted a concession to Mr. W. B. Blair and others, of California, to construct a railroad from Guaymas, in the State of Sonora, to the United States boundary, leading in the direction of Tucson, the capital of Arizona Territory. To aid this project the government proposes the magnificent donation of alternate sections of thirty-five square miles of public lands of that State per lineal mile of road, with exemption from taxation and other privileges similar to the former."

Who will say that the policy of Mexico, although exhausted by more than half a century of revolutions, struggling with poverty and staggering under a large domestic and foreign debt, is not the wisest and best it could pursue? If so, certainly it would be wise on the part of our Government and people to meet and imitate it.

The aid rendered by the Government to the companies constructing and operating the present line to the Pacific forms a strong contrast with that asked for in behalf of the Southern line. It amounted to $55,000,000 of the bonds of the Government itself, bearing interest at the rate of six per cent. per annum, the interest on which to be paid primarily out of the public treasury. The railroad companies, by a recent decision of the Supreme Court of the United States, are held not to be bound to repay interest until the maturity of the principal of the bonds, which are payable thirty years after date; they are secured by a *second* mortgage, and the right of the Government to retain *one-half only* of the amount due from the Government for transportation, and to receive but *five per cent.* of the net earnings of the road. And Congress reserved no right to legislate on the subject of the charges of the Company for transportation to individuals until its net earnings should amount to enough to pay 10 per cent. on the cost of the roads, which is practically no control at all.

Aided by this bounty of the Government, the present line enjoys a monopoly of the trans-continental trade. The alternative is presented to perpetuate that monopoly, with all the necessary abuses and oppressions which are inherent in unlimited power moulded by human selfishness, by refusing the aid required to establish a sound and healthy competition, or on the other hand, in the only practicable way, by assisting in the construction of a new and better and cheaper line to emancipate the present and future traffic across the continent, the volume and value of which are increasing beyond all anticipations, and will realize all that even the most enthusiastic have imagined, from the arbitrary tribute exacted by an irresponsible dictator. That its power is built upon a Government subsidy is of itself a sufficient reason why, under the restrictions and limitations proposed for the public security in the scheme now presented, the Government credit should be safely and usefully employed in solving for the continent the great problem of cheap, economical transportation, yielding to capital enough, but exacting from production no more than, under the supervision and guardianship of the Government itself, shall from time to time be found adequate to a healthy equilibrium between the great forces of production and distribution.

The line of said road in behalf of which the present appeal is made is intended to connect the entire Southern system of railroads—terminating at the Mississippi river and reaching through the interior to the Atlantic—with the Pacific Coast. That its construction and completion would put them on an equal footing with the parallel lines to the North, for the trans-continental trade, is quite evident, and that they have a right to expect that equality follows from the character of our Government as equal and impartial in its administration, discriminating neither for nor against any. That it would rapidly develop the sparsely settled country in the Southwest and people the territories between Texas and the Pacific with a tide of emigrants flowing along their accustomed lines of latitude, is equally evident to all who have observed the conditions according to which our borders have advanced toward the West. That it would give new life to the railroad system of the South, by furnishing it its natural and legitimate extension, those most interested will bear unquestionable testimony—a result that of itself would be the sign and consequence of an active and revived industry wherever their lines penetrate. The South would live again, and find a new and better life than ever before, in the busy and diversified industry of a contented, because prospering population. Does not this consideration weigh heavily in the argument for the public aid to this enterprise? We have been waiting long years for the people of the South to forget the calamities of our civil war. Nothing will tend so greatly and so certainly to bury the remembrance of them forever as the rising of that tide of prosperity which is sure to come in upon them, and upon us all, like a flood, when the Government shall stretch out its hands to them, to help and not to hurt, and to lend to them for a time, without cost or loss to itself, that public credit which will be so much strengthened and increased by the general prosperity which it will be used to promote. Such a measure would be the great healing act of Federal legislation, giving its assurance that the people of the Union and their common representatives, in the exercise of the public power and the employment of the common wealth, know no sections in the country, no divisions among the people, but are zealous and anxious to exert all their functions so as equally to promote the growth and prosperity of every part and member.

The Convention submits its proceedings and conclusion with confidence to the judgment of the people of the United States. It asks that they may be scrutinized with care, but judged without prejudice. It feels confident that a thorough knowledge of the facts and an intelligent comprehension of the case, in all its circumstances and consequences, will confirm the soundness of its views. It relies on a plain presentation of their plan to secure the general suffrage in its favor, and asks the co-operation of the people at large, in the promotion of the measure, solely on the ground that its success is demanded by a consideration of their own interests.

On behalf of the Convention,

STANLEY MATHEWS, *President.*

JAMES O. BROADHEAD, Mo.
WILLIAM PRESTON, Ky.
JOHN H. KENNARD, La.
R. W. THOMPSON, Ind.
MORTON McMICHAEL, Pa.
PETER COOPER, New York.
JAS. R. ANDERSON, Va. } *Committee.*
WILLIAM JOHNSON, N. C.
D. FELSENHELD, Cal.
HENRY G. SMITH, Tenn.
A. G. CLAPTON, Texas.
JOSEPH E. JOHNSTON, Ga.
C. K. MARSHALL, Miss.

FIRST DAY.

TUESDAY, NOVEMBER 23d, 1875.

The Convention was called to order in the Temple, corner of Fifth and Market streets, at 11 o'clock A. M., by Col. JAMES O. BROADHEAD, Chairman of the Local Executive Committee.

COL. BROADHEAD: Gentlemen of the Convention, you will please come to order. Rev. Dr. ELIOT will open the Convention with prayer.

PRAYER BY REV. W. G. ELIOT, D. D.

Almighty and most merciful God, our Heavenly Father, without whom we are nothing and can do nothing, let Thy blessing rest upon us while we are here assembled. We have come together in the interest of peace and of National Union. Wilt Thou guide our minds to wisdom of counsel. Wilt Thou fill our hearts with the spirit of fairness, of justice and brotherly kindness. May there be no place here for discord; may no angry word be spoken. May we leave behind us all narrow selfishness and sectional feeling, remembering that we are here as citizens of the same great Republic, to work together for the common good. Oh, God, wilt Thou bind us together more and more closely, not only by the bands of iron, but by the stronger bonds of love. Thou hast taught us in Thy Word that we are members one of another. By sore experience we have learned that when one member suffers, all suffer with it. We can neither suffer nor rejoice alone. Wilt Thou, therefore, teach us to conduct our deliberations in accordance with the great law of Christian brotherhood, not only individually, but as representing different communities and States. May we have grace given us to do as we would be done by. We trust ourselves to Thy guidance. We thank Thee for all Thy mercies. We pray for Thy blessing upon our beloved country which Thou hast so greatly distinguished. May this people become free indeed, by escaping from the bondage of sin, by rising above the wickedness of strife; and to Thy name be the glory and the praise for ever more, through Jesus Christ our Lord.

ADDRESS OF COL. JAMES O. BROADHEAD.

Mr. Broadhead: Gentlemen of the Convention, by the direction of the Executive Committee, of which I am Chairman, it becomes my duty to call this Convention to order, and to explain briefly the causes which have brought us together, and in doing so, I will read first the call for this Convention:

ADDRESS TO THE PEOPLE OF THE UNITED STATES.

The Executive Committee, appointed by a mass meeting of the citizens of St. Louis, to make arrangements for calling a National Convention to consider the subject of the construction of a Pacific Railroad through the States and Territories of the Southwest, and to take such action in its favor as might seem fit, hereby announce that such Convention will be held in St. Louis, on the 23d of November next; and we formally and cordially invite the people of the several States and Territories, through their Governors and Boards of Trade, Chambers of Commerce, Cotton Exchanges, and other commercial or municipal organizations, whose action can be conveniently had, to appoint delegates to attend and participate in its proceedings.

It is made a National Convention, because the enterprise is thoroughly national in its scope and influence. While it will be of vital importance to a vast region of rich territory, three times as large as the thirteen original States of this Republic, and now almost destitute of railroad facilities, the completion of such a work will yield great benefits to every section of the country.

The proposed railroad will have at least seven Eastern terminal points on the Mississippi or the Gulf—these radiating branches meeting at some convenient point in Western Texas, and thence constituting one grand trunk line to the Pacific Ocean. The States of Texas, Louisiana, Arkansas, California and Missouri; also Mississippi, Tennessee, Kentucky and Illinois, with the Territories of New Mexico, Arizona and the Indian Territory, and the Northern States of old Mexico will be directly on the main line or its branches.

The road may be considered as completed to Fort Worth in Northwestern Texas, to which point the exertions of the Company will carry it during the coming year; from this point to San Diego on the Pacific Coast, a distance of 1,457 miles, the work is beyond the reach of individual enterprise.

I may leave out the reasons which are stated by the Committee, because it, perhaps, would make this opening too long, but I will read the concluding portion of the address:

In view of the facts we have mentioned, and the importance of this movement to the people of this whole country, we earnestly invite your co-operation. We hope that delegates may be sent from every part of the country, in order that the will of the people may be ascertained, and such expression given to their wishes as will insure their being carried out by their representatives at Washington.

And now, gentlemen, in answer to the call I have just read, I see before me delegates from twenty-seven States and Territories [applause], consisting of men of science, engineers, farmers, merchants, bankers, planters, manufacturers and statesmen of no mean repute—representatives of the intelligence, culture and patriotism of our common country [applause]—men, in some respects, of antagonistic interests, and of almost every shade of political sentiment, and between some of whom, in years not long passed, there was a gulf which seemed almost impassable; and certainly there is nothing in all the circumstances which surround this assemblage that can give so much of hope for the future, as the fact that men who have differed so widely upon questions that affected the very existence of the American nation, should have come together in fraternal council from the four corners of the republic to consult how best they may advance its prosperity and glory. [Applause.] Gentlemen, we are here in the interest of peace. [Applause.] Peace has her victories, and the crowning glory of our people is that, whilst they are at least the equals of other nations in the achievements of arms, whether in foreign or domestic wars, they are making deeper foot-prints in the paths of progress, and securing more brilliant and lasting triumphs in the arts of peace than any other nation. [Loud applause.] Now, gentlemen, we have met for a practical purpose, and whatever may be the result of the deliberations of this Convention, and whatever effect its action may have upon the interests of individuals or corporations, the movement in which it originated was not brought about by any one who has or was supposed to have a pecuniary interest in its action. It was not a suggestion of the Texas and Pacific Railroad Company, or any one interested in that company or any other railroad company; but the movement was brought about from a conviction on the part of those who originated it that another line of trans-continental railway was needed by the commerce of the country; that it was due especially to the southern half of our confederacy [loud applause]; that it would revive the industries of the whole country, and open new avenues of wealth by which the whole country could be benefited, and to that extent would lighten somewhat the burdens now resting upon the shoulders of the whole nation. It is the duty of the statesman and of the patriot to adopt the best means that present themselves for the accomplishment of the end in view.

There was presented at the last session of Congress a bill amending the charter of the Texas and Pacific Railway and the Atlantic and Pacific Railway, which came near passing into a law, and which presented to our minds the cheapest and most feasible method for securing a Southern Trans-Continental Railway. And I will here remark, that it is well known to persons who have directed their attention to the subject, that the two roads, the Atlantic and Pacific and the Texas and Pacific Railway, are both chartered by acts of Congress, and have both grants of land along the proposed routes of these roads. I will undertake now to give a synopsis of this bill, because it has not previously been fully spread before the country. The provisions of that bill are substantially as follows:

That authority be granted by the Congress of the United States to the Atlantic and Pacific Railroad Company to construct a line of railroad from its present western terminus at Vinita, southwestwardly by the most practicable route, to intersect the line of the Texas and Pacific Railway Company, and the Texas and Pacific Railway Company was also authorized to construct its line from Fort Worth westwardly, so that the connection can be made with the road of the Atlantic and Pacific Railroad Company at some convenient point to be agreed upon, not further north than the 33d parallel of latitude, and not further west than the 103d degree of longitude, and from such point westwardly to the Rio Grande and to San Diego Bay, on the Pacific coast, through Texas, New Mexico, Arizona and California.

The Texas and Pacific Railway was required to be constructed to the point of junction within three years from the passage of the act; and the line of the Atlantic and Pacific Railroad, from its eastern terminus to the point of junction, and the main trunk line from the junction to San Diego Bay, within six years from the passage of the act; and the right of the Atlantic and Pacific Railroad shall be held to have lapsed in regard to its present line whenever that company shall file with the Secretary of the Interior a survey and location of its line to the point of intersection. The Texas and Pacific Railway was required to commence the work of construction within six months from the passage of the act, and to do so much work each year until it should be completed. And it was further provided that the line from Shreveport to New Orleans should be constructed and put in operation within three years.

It was further provided that whenever the Texas and Pacific Company, or the Atlantic and Pacific Company, or the New Orleans, Baton Rouge and Vicksburg Company shall file a certificate, signed by the president and engineer, that ten or more consecutive miles of any portion of said lines have been constructed and are ready for service, the President of the United States shall require such Commissioner or Commissioners as may be appointed by him for that purpose to examine the same and report to him; and if it shall appear that ten or more miles of road and telegraph line have been constructed and equipped as required by law, the Secretary of the Treasury shall indorse, for and in the name of the United States, a guaranty of interest on bonds to be issued by each company. The guaranty is to be on bonds issued on road actually constructed and equipped, and is to be at the rate of five per cent. per annum in gold, and payable on the first days of April and October of each year. The bonds are to be secured by a first mortgage lien on the constructed road, with its equipments, franchises, earnings and property of every kind, including all lands granted by the United States to aid in its construction; and in the mortgage, provision is also made for a sinking fund, to be paid into the Treasury of the United States, of one per cent. in gold coin on the whole amount of bonds issued, to extend for a certain period named, and thereafter of two per cent. until the bonds are all redeemed, or until a sufficient fund is raised to redeem them at maturity. The bonds to be executed are to be deposited with the Secretary of the Treasury to the extent of $40,000 per mile of road constructed and equipped, to run for forty years, with coupons for the half-yearly interest. One-half the road shall be considered as located in the plain or open country, one-half in the rough or mountainous country; and the Secretary of the Treasury shall only deliver to the companies for road constructed in the plain or open country the bonds at the rate of $30,000 per mile, and for the rough or mountainous country bonds at the rate of $40,000 per mile of constructed road.

The acceptance of the provisions of the act by either company should constitute a first lien upon the road and telegraph, the rolling-stock, shops, fixtures and property of every kind, including the franchises and all lands granted by the United States in aid thereof, and the companies are to prepare and file a mortgage to that effect.

And it is further provided by the act, that in order to provide more specifically for the interest on these bonds, and a sinking fund to redeem the bonds at maturity, there shall be set apart and paid into the treasury of the United States ten days before the maturity of the interest coupons:

1. The entire cash proceeds of the sales of lands granted by Congress to aid in the construction of the road.

2. The whole amount that shall be earned and be due from the Government for transportation of troops and supplies, and for its postal and telegraph service.

3. A sufficient amount from the earnings of the road to make each interest payment, and also to provide for a sinking fund after ten

years from the passage of the act, equal to one per cent. for fifteen years, and two per cent. thereafter of the amount of bonds issued and outstanding. These amounts to be invested by the Secretary of the Treasury in taking up those bonds at par, or to be invested in United States bonds at their market value, until the amount equals the amount of bonds issued; and, as further security, out of every $40,000 of bonds authorized to be issued by the company, $5,000 shall be reserved by the Government to secure the payment of the interest, which will be $12\frac{1}{2}$ per cent. on the amount of bonds issued per mile.

These bonds, as before stated, are to be registered and placed in the office of the Secretary of the Treasury.

It is provided that there shall be no discrimination against any connecting road, but on all business exchanged with another road the same rate per mile for passengers and per ton per mile for freight shall be charged as shall be charged for similar business on its own line, or on any other route.

It is also provided that Congress shall at all times have the right to regulate the rates for transportation of freight and passengers, and for postal and telegraphic service, and may exercise a general supervision and control over the road, so far as may be necessary to secure the interests of the Government.

With these restrictions it is utterly impossible for the Government to lose anything, or even to be liable to pay out a dollar. The bonds are only issued upon road actually constructed and in operation, and it is not possible that a road running through such a country as this does would not yield enough to pay the interest on its bonds. The security, however, is beyond question ample; and for immediate payment we have the proceeds of the sale of lands, the postal, telegraphic and mail service and the earnings of the road.

It will be perceived from this synopsis of the bill before the last Congress, which embraces the main proposition for the consideration of this Convention, and which embodies the offer made by the Texas and Pacific Railway Company and the Atlantic and Pacific Railway Company, that the Government is asked to guarantee the interest on the first mortgage construction bonds of the companies, to be issued at an average of $35,000 per mile of completed road; $5,000 of the bonds to be reserved to secure the Government in case the net earnings of the road, the cost of mail, postal and telegraph service, and the sale of lands, do not equal the interest on the bonds guaranteed and delivered to the company.

The annual interest charge, leaving out the $5,000 per mile reserved, will be $1,750 per mile per annum. Will the Texas and Pacific Railroad yield $1,750 per mile? That company has now completed and in operation about 300 miles of railroad in the State of Texas, and is free from debt. It yielded, as I am credibly informed, during the last month $168,000 gross, over $100,000 net earnings, which is at the rate of $333.33⅓ per mile per month, or $4,000 per mile per annum net earnings.

The Union and Central Pacific Railroads earned during the last year $6,481 net per mile, upwards of 70 per cent. of which was from local traffic. With those who are at all acquainted with the country through which the routes of the two roads pass, there can be no doubt that the local traffic of the Texas and Pacific road would largely exceed that of the Union Pacific and Central Pacific within a very short time after the completion of the road. The Union and Central Pacific have been subsidized to an extent of $55,000,000 in United States six per cent. bonds, and the payment by the Government of the interest on those bonds to the amount of $3,300,000 per annum, practically amounts to an additional subsidy of that amount per annum, if, as is claimed by the company, and as has been decided by one of our courts, they are not bound to repay the interest to the Government until the maturity of the bonds at the end of thirty years from their issue, making the whole amount of subsidy $154,000,000.

Can private enterprise compete with such a monopoly, fostered, as it is, by Government subsidies?

The last annual report of the President of the Union Pacific Railroad from Omaha to Ogden shows a net income of $6,733,391, ending June 30, 1875—an increase over the preceding year of $1,576,420; and the President says, further, that "the traffic of the road may be increased until the earnings shall reach $20,000,000 per year, without any call for expenditures demanding an increase of the bonded debt of the company; that the road has a capacity for doing over double its present volume of business without an expenditure which may not be met by its increasing revenues." What is the use of talking about cheap transportation when such a gigantic monopoly, created and perpetuated by the Government, has the whole carrying trade across the continent? [Applause.] It is idle for private capital to undertake to compete with it.

The intersection of the two roads at the crossing of the 32d parallel and 103d meridian would be at a point near the southeast corner of the Territory of New Mexico, and on almost a direct line between Vinita, the present terminus of the Atlantic and Pacific Railroad, and the town of El Paso on the Rio Grande. It would be about 600 miles from its present terminus; 200 miles more would bring it to Fort Bliss, on the Rio Grande.

It is considered, however, that the best line for the Atlantic & Pacific Railroad would be to cross the Canadian river at old Fort Arbuckle, and the Red river at the mouth of Big Washita, thence along the Washita, on the divide east of that river, to the most northerly bend of the Brazos, and down the Brazos to a connection with the Texas & Pacific Railway, just south of the Double Fork of that stream. Such a road would give St. Louis a connection with San Diego at a distance of 2,029 miles, and to San Francisco 2,391 miles.

Two hundred and ninety-nine miles of the Texas & Pacific Railway have been examined and received by Commissioners appointed by the Government, and from Fort Worth westward the route of this road, on the 32d parallel, has been surveyed with great care, and the elevations and grades ascertained. The divide of the continent in the Sierra Nevada range is 4,893 feet on grades not exceeding 66 feet to the mile, and the total length of grades between 80 and 105 feet will not exceed 45 miles. The highest elevation on the whole road is 5,027 feet at the Hueca Pass, in Hueca Mountains, just east of El Paso. The highest elevation on the Union Pacific is 8,235 feet, and on the Central Pacific, at the crossing of Sierra Nevada Mountains, 7,042 feet. These greatest elevations, occurring so far south as the 32d parallel, insure the road from obstructions by snow at all seasons of the year.

General Pope, who in 1853 belonged to the Board of Topographical Engineers, and made a survey of this route from Fulton to El Paso during that year, under the direction of the War Department, says:

"The vast deserts between the valley of the Rio Grande and the frontiers of the Western States, contract to their least width along the belt of country between the 32d and 34th parallels of latitude; the average distance over these vast deserts is reduced by less than one-half along a route where the extremes of heat and cold are absolutely unknown."

After most of the surveys made in 1853 and 1854 under the direction of the War Department, and after the Gadsden purchase, by which we acquired a portion of what is now Arizona, Lieutenant J. G. Park, of the Board of Topographical Engineers, made a minute survey of a route for a railroad from the valley of the Rio Grande, near El Paso, to the Pacific Coast. He says, in his report made to the War Department in 1857:

"The route by the 32d parallel possesses decided advantages for the construction of a railroad from the Mississippi to the Pacific Ocean, because—

" 1. It is the shortest by making it to San Diego.

" 2. The climate is peculiarly favorable, there being no obstacles to parties working throughout the year, and no snows to embarrass the track.

" 3. The elevations to be overcome are the least."

Now, Lieut. Park (who made, with the assistance of Engineer Campbell, under him at the time, perhaps the most minute survey of any of those parties appointed by the United States from 1853 to 1857 to make surveys of routes across the continent, beginning with the 32d parallel and ending with the 49th) says:

"The most remarkable feature of this route is the extended elevated plain lying between the Rio Grande on the east, and the San Pedro, a tributary of the Gila, on the west. The greatest elevation by the survey of 1854 was about 5,000 feet, and by additional data obtained during the spring of 1855, this has been reduced. So that this table-land affords a route of transit from the waters of the Atlantic to those of the Pacific at an elevation not exceeding 4,600 feet, the lowest yet determined between the parallels 32 and 49."

To complete this route the line will extend beyond the Pimas villages, down the left bank of the Gila river to the crossing of the Colorado at Fort Yuma. It is upon this table-land that we find the remains of an early civilization, which show that they must at one time have supported a large population.

Subsequent surveys have served to confirm the report of Lieut. Park.

But I shall not dwell upon the topographical advantages of this route; that it is the shortest from ocean to ocean there is no doubt, and the distance from New York to San Diego is estimated to be 300 miles shorter than the present route from that city to San Francisco.

But it is in a commercial point of view that this route is preferable to all others. On its construction a rich and permanent market awaits the producers, manufacturers and traders of the whole country. If we take Omaha as a starting-point on the present route across the continent, after leaving the valley of the Platte river there is no farming land on the line of that road for nearly 2,000 miles, until you have crossed the Sierra Nevadas and reach the plains of California, except it be the valley of the Salt Lake.

On the Southern route, if we take Shreveport as a starting-point, the road will pass through the Empire State of the Southwest [applause]—as rich in agricultural resources as any portion of the continent—until it strikes the Staked Plains; then, after crossing these plains and the Guadalupe and Hueca Mountains, it reaches the fertile valley of the Rio Grande; thence across the table-lands of Southern Arizona to the head-waters of the Gila river, and down that stream to the crossing of the Colorado. A large portion of that route is capable of sustaining a dense population, while on either side, through the Territories of New Mexico and Arizona, the mountains are filled with the precious ores. On this road the commerce of the Northern States of the Republic of Mexico will find an outlet to the markets of the world and secure to us an immense trade, the greater portion of which is now diverted into other channels.

While the construction of this road will immediately benefit the States of Texas, Louisiana, Arkansas, Mississippi and Tennessee, and more remotely, but not less surely, the whole country, by opening new avenues of trade and developing the agricultural and mineral resources of the great Southwest, and adding untold millions to the wealth of the nation, it gives what the whole country is equally interested in—a competing line of transportation. [Applause.] Competition is said to be the life of trade, and I may say that it is the very soul of cheap transportation. [Loud applause.]

It was stated in a California paper that just after the defeat of the bill under consideration which was before the last Congress, the Union Pacific and Central Pacific Roads increased the freight per carload from San Francisco to Omaha as follows: On first-class freight, from $650 to $1,200; on second-class freight, from $400 to $1,000; on third-class freight, from $380 to $800; on fourth-class freight, from $360 to $600.

If this be true, and we know it may be true, for there is no competing line to prevent it, we can see what an enormous tax upon the commerce and industries of the country may be imposed by this gigantic monopoly. It is, in fact, a tax upon the commerce of the world, because no man can form any idea of how much of the productions and manufactures of more than 200,000,000 of people will pass over this trans-continental highway.

I have obtained from reliable sources the export and import tonnage between San Francisco and China and Japan from 1870 to the 1st of October, 1875, and I find that in 1874 it was nearly double that of 1870.

The Chicago Board of Trade was invited to send delegates to this Convention. They declined upon the same ground taken by the New York papers, that the times were too hard for the Government to undertake any new obligations of this kind. [Derisive laughter.] When these two very economical cities, New York and Chicago [renewed laughter], shall be less favored than they are now by the Union and Central Pacific Railroad monopolies, they will perhaps be more favorable to a competing line.

The Union and Central Pacific Railroad Companies and all their friend are opposed to this Convention, and they have made vigorous efforts to defeat its objects. The *Alta California*, the organ of the Central Pacific Railroad Company, of the date of October 26th, contains the following:

THE OLD STATESMAN ON THE WAR PATH.

Ex-Senator Wm. M. Gwin leaves San Francisco this morning in the director's special car, overland for Richmond, Charleston and the principal centers of the South, and afterward Washington, to call around him, for consultation, his old-time confreres in Congress, and to destroy and banish the unpatriotic heresy of an inflation paper money currency. The well-wishers of the Nation will hail with pleasure this crusade of California's great old Democratic law-giver in behalf of a sound metallic basis for business and commercial prosperity. It seems like an inspiration to see this celebrated man forsaking the comforts of a luxurious home and a devoted family, going eastward to wage a war against an irredeemable paper currency, and to warn his countrymen of the danger to their best interest and to implore them to rescue the national credit from impending danger. He goes East, we are informed, at the invitation of Gov. Stanford, and accompanies the railroad party of Charles Crocker and family. When the fight comes on between the Southern Pacific and Texas Pacific, the old ex-Senator will be a valuable friend in the court of his Southern friends to speak well of the claims of Mr. Crocker and his associates for the control of the western end of the new trans-continental route. The railroad men will be securing a valuable ally and aiding a national cause at the same time.

Now, how many speeches Senator Gwin has made on the currency question at the South I have not heard, and what this "celebrated man who has forsaken the comforts of a luxurious home and a devoted family" has accomplished towards defeating the object of a Southern Pacific Railway [laughter], or securing to the Central Pacific the control of the western end of it, is for the delegates from the Southern States to answer. [Applause.] I am informed that he has been through the South, but has not accomplished anything. [Loud applause.]

The question of constitutional power on the part of Congress has been raised as an objection to the passage of this bill or any other of a similar character. It is, perhaps, never too late to raise a question of constitutional power. It is like a plea to the jurisdiction—always in order. But since Mr. Calhoun declared that the Mississippi river was an inland sea, in order that the power of Congress might be invoked to improve it, our wisest and purest statesmen have found it necessary, upon one pretext or other, to depart somewhat from this strict rule of interpretation, and to conclude that the promotion of the general welfare, the regulation of commerce between the States, and military necessity, will require and justify the exercise of such powers.

The subsidy granted to our distinguished fellow-citizen, James B. Eads, for opening the mouth of the Mississippi, that that stream may run unvexed to the sea, came under that provision which gives Congress power to regulate commerce, and the grants to the Union Pacific and the Central Pacific are the works of military necessity.

Quartermaster Meigs, in his report to the Secretary of War on the 31st of January, 1873, estimates that the saving cost to the Government in the transportation of freight for the Government, moved on the line of the Union Pacific Railroad, would have been $6,507,282 85, or what is equivalent to a saving to the Government of 66 per cent. in the cost of transportation.

The Military Committee of the House of Representatives, in their report of May 25, 1868, on General Sherman's letter to the Secretary of War, recommending Government aid to extend the Union Pacific Railroad, Eastern Division, as a "military necessity" and a measure of public economy, say that the cost of Government transportation for 1861, on the Union Pacific Railroad, Eastern Division, was $511,908 24; that if the same supplies had been wagoned, the mails carried by stage, and the troops marched, the cost would have been $1,358,291, showing a saving to the Government of $846,382 80 on that single line of transportation.

A committee of the last Congress, reporting on the subject of this very bill under consideration, states that it costs the Government annually $10,000,000 to maintain an available force sufficient to protect the lives and property of the white inhabitants of the country traversed by this line of road. Can any one doubt but that the building of this road will in a great measure settle our difficulties throughout that whole region of country? The facility with which troops and munitions of war can be carried from point to point, and the settlement of the country along the line of the road, will give security against Indian depredations along the frontiers that we never had before.

I may say in this connection, in regard to Gen. Sherman, gentlemen, as I have had occasion to mention his name, that I have just received a letter from him, which I will read, as it is short. He says:
"I thank you for the courtesy of an invitation to take a seat in the Convention to be held to-day at the Temple at 11 o'clock A. M., in the interest of the Southern Pacific Railroad, and feeling a deep interest in the subject, I will endeavor to be present." [Loud applause, which was continued on the discovery that Gen. Sherman was already seated on the platform. On learning this fact, Col. Broadhead continued]: I knew, gentlemen, he would be here if he said so [laughter and applause], as he is fully in accord with you.

We maintain that all works necessary to the public defence and to the improvement of internal commerce should be constructed by the national arm, and if the Government can get some one else to do the work cheaper, and at the same time retain a control over it for the public good, it becomes a duty to do so, and that is just the case before us to-day. The construction of this road is a work of public necessity; it will cost the Government nothing but the loan of its credit. It is called for by the highest considerations of public policy; it is the shortest, cheapest and safest route across the continent; it is the highway of the world's commerce; it is demanded in the interest of cheap transportation by the whole country; it is demanded especially as an act of justice to the people of the southern half of the Confederacy, and in the same proportion as it revives her paralyzed industries will it add to the national wealth. [Loud applause.]

It is, gentlemen, the highway across the continent; it is the road to India; it is the track of Columbus; and along this highway will meet, after its construction, people of all nationalities and of all languages belonging to the civilized world, and we may hope that the predominant influence of our own race will be felt, and thus the light of Christian civilization, which is marching westward with the star of empire, and has already reached the shores of Asia, will continue its westward march until, having reached the seats of the earliest civilization, it shall have encircled the globe. [Loud applause.]

I trust the action of this Convention will be earnest and harmonious, and if our efforts are successful we will have the consolation of knowing that we have added much to the sum of human happiness and contributed largely to the prosperity and glory of our common country. [Loud applause.]

Now, gentlemen, in further organization of this Convention, I move that Gen. J. R. Anderson, of Richmond, Va., act as temporary Chairman of this Convention.

The question was put and the motion was carried.

Col. Broadhead: Gen. Anderson will now please come forward and take the Chair.

Gen. Anderson came upon the platform amid loud applause, and on being introduced to the Convention by Col. Broadhead, spoke as follows:

ADDRESS OF GEN. ANDERSON.

Gentlemen of the Convention:—I thank you very cordially for the honor you have done me in calling me to the Chair. Since we have heard from Col. Broadhead the able and lucid explanation of the objects of this Convention, I would deem it out of place for me to detain you a moment longer from hearing the interesting speeches which we know will succeed the organization of this body. [Applause.] I must, however, gentlemen of the Convention, congratulate you upon the many evidences we have of the harmony which is about to prevail in the proceedings of this Convention. [Applause.] It is a great work that we have to do. The building of a highway across the continent upon the line proposed is a measure not only of vast importance to the whole tier of Southern States, but of vast importance to the growth and prosperity of the whole Union. [Loud applause.] Of vast importance, did I say? Why, the day is rapidly coming when the building of this road will be a necessity to the interests of the country.

Gentlemen of the Convention, upon the main question which I fancy will claim our attention, the agreement upon the form of an application for Governmental aid to this work, I believe little if any diversity of opinion exists, and as to the details, I rely upon the spirit of patriotism, the spirit of fairness and practical good sense of the members of this body, and look for harmonious action. [Loud applause.]

I now, gentlemen of the Convention, call the Convention to order and announce the body ready to proceed in further organization.

TEMPORARY ORGANIZATION.

Mr. Palmer, of South Carolina: Mr. Chairman, for the purpose of further proceeding with the organization of this Convention, I move, sir, that a committee of one from each State be appointed by the respective delegations to act as a Committee on Organization.

Mr. Slayback, of St. Louis: I move to include the Territories, and to add that that committee also act upon credentials.

Several Delegates: No, no.

Mr. Slayback: Then I will add that the Territories be included.

Mr. Palmer: I accept it as far as I am concerned as the mover of the resolution.

Mr. E. N. Hill, of Arkansas: Before that motion is put I desire to say that I do not think we have effected a temporary organization as yet. I think before the Committee on Organization is appointed we should have a temporary secretary also. In order to complete this organization I move, sir, that a temporary secretary be elected.

Mr. Filley, of St. Louis: Mr. Chairman, the Chairman of the Executive Committee was authorized by the Executive Committee to report temporary officers, including a secretary and assistant secretary.

Mr. Hill, of Arkansas: He has not done so, or I should not have taken the floor.

Mr. Broadhead: I beg pardon of the Convention for the omission. If the gentleman will withdraw his motion for a few moments I will announce the temporary secretaries.

Mr. Hill: I withdraw it.

Mr. Broadhead: I now move that Messrs. D. H. McAdam and L. L. Walbridge be appointed as temporary secretaries.

The question was put and the motion carried.

Mr. Palmer: I now renew my motion for the appointment of a Committee on Permanent Organization.

Mr. Filley, of St. Louis: Before this motion is put, it strikes me it is necessary to appoint a Committee on Credentials, and if the gentleman will temporarily withdraw his motion, I will make a motion to appoint a committee of one from each State and each Territory on credentials, which I believe is the first business in order.

Mr. Palmer: I will give way for the time being.

Mr. Jones: I think it is entirely out of order to appoint any committees until the Convention is fully organized.

Mr. Filley, of St. Louis: I now renew my motion, Mr. Chairman, to appoint one delegate from each State and Territory as a Committee on Credentials.

THE CHAIRMAN: How shall this committee be appointed?

MR. FILLEY: By the Chair.

SEVERAL DELEGATES: No, no.

MR. FILLEY: By each delegation.

THE CHAIRMAN: What is the motion?

MR. FILLEY: My motion is that a Committee on Credentials be appointed in the usual way.

THE CHAIRMAN: The motion is that a Committee on Credentials be appointed by each delegation; that one member from each delegation form that committee.

The question was put and the motion was carried.

A DELEGATE: I name Mr. Bell for that committee.

MR. HODGE, of Kentucky: Let the Secretary call the roll of States, and then the chairmen of the different State delegations will respond with the name of the delegate they wish to propose for that committee.

The roll of States was then called, which resulted in the announcement of the following named gentlemen by the chairmen of the different delegations as members of the Committee on Credentials:

ALABAMA—JOSEPH HODGSON,
ARKANSAS—B. J. BROWN,
CALIFORNIA—WALLACE LEACH,
GEORGIA—P. M. B. YOUNG,
ILLINOIS—GEORGE W. PARKER,
INDIANA—S. C. WILSON,
IOWA—W. J. K. BOYD,
KANSAS—C. K. HOLLIDAY,
KENTUCKY—THOMAS L. JONES,
LOUISIANA—J. S. HARRIS,
MICHIGAN—J. D HAYES,
MINNESOTA—W. S. DAVIDSON,
MISSISSIPPI—JOHN R. HICKS,
MISSOURI—D. P. ROWLAND,
NEBRASKA—JUDGE CONVERSE,
NEW JERSEY—JACOB W. CRANE,
NEW YORK—W. P. BROWN,
NORTH CAROLINA—W. P. JOHNSTON,
OHIO—W. S. STREATOR,
PENNSYLVANIA—J. S. GRAHAM,
SO. CAROLINA—WM. F. McMASTERS,
TENNESSEE—N. E. ALLOWAY,
TEXAS—SAMUEL EVANS.
VIRGINIA—LLOYD J. BEALL,
WISCONSIN—G. H. LARKIN,
NEW MEXICO—S. P. ELKINS,
DISTRICT OF COLUMBIA—SAMUEL S. SMOOT.

MR. BROADHEAD, of St. Louis: I will now state to the members of the committee just appointed, that they can meet in the room at the rear of this hall, and I will further state that the Secretary of our Executive Committee has a full list of all the delegates as far as they have reported, with their credentials, and if they will meet at the place designated, they can transact their business in a few moments.

The Committee on Credentials then retired.

WELCOMING ADDRESS BY MAYOR BRITTON.

The Chairman: Gentlemen of the Convention, allow me to introduce to you Col. James H. Britton, Mayor of the city of St. Louis, who will now address you. [Applause.]

Mayor Britton then addressed the Convention as follows:

Gentlemen of the Convention:—On behalf of our city government and the whole body of our people, I welcome you to the city of St. Louis, and assure you that we appreciate fully the honor of your presence, and regard with the profoundest interest the object of your deliberations. This influential Convention, representative of all quarters of the Union, has assembled to consider a question of true national importance, but in which this city and State, together with the other cities and States of the Valley of the Mississippi, are peculiarly and vitally interested. It was not, however, in a sectional or selfish spirit that the city of St. Louis secured the assembling of this Convention here. We have no ambitions apart from the body of the Union, apart from the general prosperity of the whole country; for whatever confidence we have—and it is both deep and strong—in the future of this city and State, it is based only on the progress and possibilities of the wonderful country God has given us for a common heritage. Like all the people of the United States, we are animated by the restless energies of American civilization; we are builders and workers, and impatient to develop the industries of our people and the boundless natural resources that surround us. In all our plans and labors, however, we have felt one great and pressing need; together with all the people of the South and West, we feel the lack of one great element of growth, of one powerful implement of progress. Our own development is linked in with the development of the continent, and neither is fully possible until this need is supplied. What is this imperative necessity that restrains, like a band of iron, the expanding energies of a great people, and that passes beyond the reach of private enterprise to accomplish? Gentlemen, it is expressed in the call for this Convention, and it will constitute the object of your deliberations. It is the construction of a trans-continental railroad, connecting us with the ports and commerce of the Pacific, and at the same time so located as to develop the interior of the continent. It must, above all things, traverse those wide and fruitful regions of the interior of the continent where settlement can follow it, planting cities and villages, and farms, where now are the wastes of unoccupied nature, and opening the doors for industrious millions to till the soil, work the mines and gather in the riches that have awaited for centuries the incoming of the Saxon race.

The citizens of St. Louis are not envious of the Northern railroad now existing; we have no criticisms to make on this route or its usefulness; we only know that it is of little or no benefit to us—that it cannot aid in the development of the interior because it passes through a region where settlement and agriculture are well nigh impossible. We are not disposed to criticise the past; we have to do with the future only. We know that the need of the hour is a railroad through the arable lands and genial climate of the Southwest, and we know this was the route originally recommended by the Government engineers. We know that this was the need when the National Railroad Convention of 1849 assembled in this city, and in which many of the gentlemen now present participated, and we know that it is practically unsupplied this day. We know, also, that this need is not only felt by the people of this city and State, but by every State—by the whole population of this great valley of the Mississippi—and if our action is as united as our wants and interests, it cannot fail of success. It cannot fail, because our want is the want of the whole country; for, until the vast regions of the interior are developed and filled with population, the destiny of the United States is unachieved.

In view of these facts, we hail the assembling of this Convention here with enthusiasm and satisfaction, hoping most earnestly that its influence and harmonious action will result finally in the accomplishment of the great enterprise proposed. [Applause.] We cannot believe that the National Government will ignore the voice of a body like this, enforced as it will be by every consideration of patriotic hope and pride. We cannot believe that the influence of corporations inimical to this enterprise, nor the suggestions of selfish and sectional interests, can prevent a full understanding of the merits of the proposition by our whole people, nor defeat a just consideration by Congress of a project that concerns the welfare and development of the whole country.

Gentlemen of the Convention, our citizens welcome you cordially to St. Louis, and tender you their warmest hospitality. We regard this Convention as a historical episode, opening a new era of national development. We are proud of its occurrence here, and, confident of the result of its deliberations, a feeling of unusual satisfaction and pleasure adds emphasis to the hospitable spirit with which St. Louis always receives her visitors from other States. [Loud applause.]

Mr. Converse, of Nebraska: I now renew the motion to appoint a Committee on Permanent Organization.

The question was put and the motion was carried.

INVITATION TO GEN. JOSEPH E. JOHNSTON.

Mr. Broadhead, of St. Louis: I would suggest, Mr. Chairman, as Gen. Joseph E. Johnston is present in the Convention, that he be requested to take a seat upon the platform. [Loud applause.]

Gen. Johnston then came upon the platform and was welcomed by Gen. Sherman, the two shaking hands amid tumultuous applause.

COMMITTEE ON PERMANENT ORGANIZATION.

The Chairman: The Secretary will now call the roll of the States and Territories, in order that the Chairman of each delegation may announce the names of the delegates for the Committee on Permanent Organization.

The roll of States was called, and the following names were announced as the Committee on Permanent Organization:

Alabama—GEO. B. CLITHERALL,
Arkansas—EZRA N. HILL,
California—J. W. A. WRIGHT,
Georgia—L. N. WHITTLE,
Illinois—WM. H. BARLOW,
Indiana—R. J. BRIGHT,
Iowa—JOHN E. BALDWIN,
Kansas—H. CALDWELL,
Kentucky—L. S. TRIMBLE,
Louisiana—WM. S. HAVEN,
Michigan—J. D. HAYES,
Minnesota—ALEX. RAMSEY,
Mississippi—ALEX. WARNER,
Missouri—E. H. NORTON,
Nebraska—J. M. EDDY,
New Mexico—G. A. HAYWARD,
New Jersey—GEORGE PETERS,
New York—W. SANFORD,
North Carolina—WM. JOHNSON,
Ohio—S. M. COVINGTON,
Pennsylvania—K. J. MOREHEAD,
South Carolina—WM. WALLACE,
Tennessee—THOMAS H. REEVES,
Texas—J. Q. CHENOWETH,
Virginia—FITZHUGH LEE.

Mr. Leonard, of Louisiana: I move that Gen. G. T. Beauregard, of Louisiana, be invited to take a seat upon the platform. [Applause.]

FREE USE OF THE WESTERN UNION TELEGRAPH.

The Chairman: I hold in my hand a communication from the Superintendent of the Western Union Telegraph Company, which I will request the Secretary to read to the Convention.

The Secretary read as follows:

St. Louis, November 23, 1875.

To the President of the Southern Pacific Railroad Convention:

Dear Sir:—I have the honor to tender the free use of the wires of the Western Union Telegraph Company for the family and social messages of the members of your Convention, and for the telegrams of your officers on the business of the Convention.

Respectfully,

R. C. Clowry, *Sup't.*

A Delegate: I move that the communication be received with the thanks of the Convention.

The question was put and the motion was carried.

INVITATION TO GEN. G. T. BEAUREGARD.

Mr. Leonard, of Louisiana: I call for the motion that Gen. Beauregard be invited to a seat upon the platform.

The Chairman: A motion was made that Gen. Beauregard be invited to a seat upon the platform.

The question was put and the motion was carried.

The Chairman: Gen. Beauregard will please take his seat upon the platform.

MOTION FOR A RECESS.

Mr. Filley, of St. Louis: I move, Mr. Chairman, in order to give time to the committees already appointed to prepare their reports, that the Convention take a recess for one hour, at which time the committees will undoubtedly be prepared to report.

Several Delegates: No, no.

Gen. Lee, of Virginia: Tell us where the Committee on Permanent Organization is to meet.

The Chairman: The Chair is desired to ask that the members, on rising and addressing the Chair, announce their names. I am also requested to state that the Committee on Permanent Organization will meet forthwith at the Southern Hotel, Parlor No. 5.

Mr. Barlow: I offer the following resolution, and desire to have it referred to the Committee on Permanent Organization.

At this point Gen. Beauregard came forward and took his seat upon the platform amid applause.

INVITATION TO JEFFERSON DAVIS.

Mr. Trimble, of Kentucky: I move, Mr. President, that the Hon. Jefferson Davis be requested to take a seat upon the platform.

Several Delegates: No, no.

Mr. Garner, of Tennessee: Mr. President, a word in the interest of peace, harmony, patriotism and union. I rejoiced to see Gen. Sherman and Gen. Johnston walk up and shake hands, and now I trust that any Commanding General on either side in the late war will be requested to take a seat upon the platform. I care not on which side he was engaged; I take them all in my heart, and I would be rejoiced to see them all come forward upon the platform, whether from the North, the South, the East or the West. I therefore move that the Commanding Generals on each side—I do not know their names, but all who are here—be requested to take seats upon the platform. I know that we should be glad to see them all come forward, not only the Hon. Jefferson Davis and Fitzhugh Lee, but also the Generals from the North, whoever they may be.

A Delegate: Mr. Chairman, I think this whole thing is begging the question. If a motion of this sort were to prevail, there wouldn't be room enough on the platform to accommodate all the Generals here present. [Laughter and applause.]

Mr. Broadhead, of St. Louis: I move, for the purpose of enabling the Committee on Permanent Organization to have time to deliberate, that this Convention now take a recess of one hour.

A Delegate: I think it very necessary that we have a Committee on Resolutions.

Mr. Trimble, of Kentucky: Mr. Chairman, I think I am entitled to the floor, and I wish to say a few words in reference to the motion to invite the Hon. Jefferson Davis upon the platform. I differed with Mr. Davis upon the questions of the past, but I see distinguished men from all parts of the country have been invited to seats upon the platform, and I know of no one in the whole country who has done more within the last few months to arouse an interest from one end of the country to the other for the great cause which we are here assembled to promote to-day — the opening of the mouth of the Mississippi River, and connecting us by railroad with the Pacific Ocean and the world. I therefore advocate this motion with no personal feeling for Mr. Davis, or political feeling, but as an act of justice, and I hope that this Convention will banish all feeling, all sectional feeling, whether East, West, North or South, and invite every man who is interested in this cause, as we know Mr. Davis to be, as well as in the opening of this river, to join with us in our deliberations. I have nothing personal in the matter. I have done my duty, and I submit the question to the Convention.

MR. DAVIS: Mr. Chairman —

THE CHAIRMAN: The question is, shall Mr. Davis be invited to a seat upon the platform?

The question was put and the motion was carried. There were, however, several voices in the negative.

MR. JEFFERSON DAVIS: Mr. President, I intended to say to the Convention before this motion was put, that for personal considerations I could not accept the kindness you have shown. I am Chairman of the Mississippi delegation; my functions are to be performed off the platform, and I have no wish to take a place upon it; but pitying the poor contemptible spirit manifested by those who cried "no," I will tell them that if they had allowed me I should have declined the honor if it had been freely offered. [Applause.]

RESOLUTION.

MR. BURWELL: I offer the following resolution:

Resolved, That the Committee on Permanent Organization report to the Convention a rule to govern in casting the vote whenever a scaled vote be called for.

RECESS.

MR. BROADHEAD: I insist on my motion that the Convention now take a recess for one hour.

INVITATION TO VISIT THE NEW MERCHANTS' EXCHANGE.

MR. STANARD, of St. Louis: Before that motion is put, Mr. Chairman, I wish to say that it was hoped by the merchants of St. Louis that we would be able to entertain this Convention in the New Merchants' Exchange that is about being finished, but circumstances over which the Executive Committee had no control preclude this possibility. We have a new Exchange that we are proud of, and I am requested by the President and Directors of the Merchants' Exchange to present their compliments to this Convention, and ask that when this Convention take a recess that they will in a body visit the

Merchants' Exchange, which is about completed. It will take but a few moments; the Exchange is only two or three squares from here, and we should be delighted to have you pass through it and examine it.

A DELEGATE: I move, Mr. Chairman, that the invitation be accepted with the thanks of the Convention.

The question was put and the motion was carried.

MR. BROADHEAD: I now renew my motion for a recess for one hour.

The question was put and the motion was carried, and thereupon the Convention took a recess for one hour.

AFTERNOON SESSION.

The Convention re-assembled at 2 o'clock P. M.

THE CHAIRMAN: The report from the Committee on Credentials will now be in order.

REPORT OF THE COMMITTEE ON CREDENTIALS.

HON. THOMAS L. JONES, of Kentucky: I am instructed by the Committee on Credentials, as their Chairman, to report the names received by them as delegates to this Convention. We find that twenty-five States are here represented, with the neighboring Territories, and with delegates from various Boards of Trade, cities, etc. I am requested to say, when the list is read by the Secretary, if it is not entirely correct, the chairman of each delegation from each State is requested to correct it.

COMMUNICATIONS.

MR. BROADHEAD, of St. Louis: Before the list is read, I ask leave to submit a communication received from the Governor of Maine.

To Gen. E. C. Pike:

You are hereby delegated as a representative of the State of Maine in the National Railroad Convention, to be held in St. Louis, Missouri, on the 23d inst. Very respectfully yours,

WILSON DINGLEY, *Governor.*

[Applause.]

Also a letter from Gen. Pike, which is dated Eastport, Maine, November 18, 1875, and addressed to the Chairman of the Committee of the National Railroad Convention, at St. Louis:

Sir:—I enclose herewith a commission from Gov. Dingley to represent the State of Maine at your meeting. I have to regret exceedingly my inability to be present. I am with you in spirit, and shall hope for definite action in the interest of the Southern road.

Very respectfully,
E. C. PIKE.

[Applause.]

This has been received since the appointment of the Committee on Credentials, and I therefore felt it my duty to announce it.

LIST OF DELEGATES.

The Secretary then began the reading of the list of delegates reported by the Committee on Credentials, as follows:

ALABAMA.

CLARK, F. G.................Mobile.	PILLONS, H................
CLITHERALL, GEO. B........... "	PRICE, T. H...............
HODGSON, JOSEPH............. "	

ARIZONA.

BOYLE, M. G....................	CURTIS, C. C.............Tucson.

ARKANSAS.

BROWN, B. J.............Van Buren.	KRAMER, F...............Little Rock.
COUSTON, C. H................	McDOWELL, J. W.........Jacksonport.
CURRY, A. P.............Little Rock	PETTIGREW, J. R.........Fayetteville.
DOSWELL, FRANKLIN......Fayetteville.	PIERCE, C. W...........Fort Smith.
EAKIN, JNO. R.............Little Rock.	TREZEVANT, J. T., JR.....Little Rock.
HARRELL, JNO. M.........Fayetteville.	TREZEVANT, J. T., SR..... " "
HILL, E. N..............Little Rock.	VALIANT, GEO. W..........
HILL, TYRA..................Camden.	WICDER, M. S............Little Rock.
HOUDLETTE, W. S.............	WOOTEN, JAS. H..........

CALIFORNIA.

FELSENHELD, DAVID......San Diego.	STEARNS, JOHN........Santa Barbara.
GRAHAM, GEO. C.............	WILSON, L. B.............
LEACH, WALLACE............	WRIGHT, J. W. A...........

DISTRICT OF COLUMBIA.

SMOOT, SAM'L D...Washington.

GEORGIA.

ADAIR, GEO. W..................Atlanta.
ALSTON, R. A..............................
ANDERSON, EDWARD........Savannah.
ANDERSON, E. C...............   "
ARNOLD, R. W...............   "
BARRETT, JAMES..............Augusta.
BARRETT, W. H........................   "
BASSEY, N. J..................Columbus.
BLUN H........................Savannah.
BARTRUM, P. T....................Macon.
BROWN, W. H...............................
BROWN, J. N...............................
BURRUS, CHARLES...........Columbus.
CLARKE, J M..................Augusta.
COHEN, J. J........................Rome.
CURTIS, N. N..................Columbus.
DOUGLASS, J. A..............Savannah.
ELLIS, W. D.....................Atlanta.
FITTEN, J. A....................   "
FINLEY. W. F..............Gainesville.
FONTAINE, FRANCIS.........Columbus.
GRANTLAND, S...................Griffin.
HARRIS, J. W..............Carter-ville.
HAMMOCK, C. C..................Atlanta.
HICKMAN, H. H.................Augusta.
HOGE, E. F......................Atlanta.
HOOD, E. C....................Columbus.
HOWELL, E. P...................Atlanta.
HOWELL, W. H..................   "
HUNTER, JAMES..............Savannah.
JACKSON, HENRY...............Atlanta.
JEMISON, SAM'L H..............Macon.
JOHNSON, D. T..................Griffin.
JOHNSTON, JOS. E............Savannah.
JOHNSON, J. L.....................Rome.
JOHNSTON, WM. B..........................
LOFTON, W. A..............................
MATHEWSON, J. O.............Augusta.
McGUIRE, JOHN T...............Atlanta.
McGUIRE, T. J...................   "
MURPHY, S. G.................Columbus.
NUTTING, C. A............................
OBEAR, GEO. S...................Macon.
ROSS C. L........................   "
SAUSSY, J. R..............................
TATUM, R. H..............................
THOMPSON, W. T..........................
TIFT, NELSON.............................
TRAMMELL, W. T...............Griffin.
TURPIN, GEO. B...................Macon.
WHITTLE, L. N...................   "
WRIGHT, H G..............................
YOUNG, P. M. B...........................
YOUNG, R. M..................LaGrange.

ILLINOIS.

ARMOUR, G....................Chicago.
BAILEY, J. M..................Freeport.
BARLOW, W. H................Effingham.
BEECHER, C. A..............East St. Louis.
BLACKSTONE, J. P.............Chicago.
BLADES, T....................Watseka.
BUCK, E. B..................Charleston.
CABLE, P. L................Rock Island.
CARTER, J. D..................Chicago.
CARTER, T. J................Springfield.
CHAMBERS, THOS. G......................
FLAGG, W. C.....................Moro.
GILLESPIE, JOSEPH.......................
GLENN, A. A...............Mt. Sterling.
HALLIDAY, W. P..........................
HARDIN, C....................Monmouth.
HUTCHINS J. S...............Belvidere.
JOHNSON, JAMES.........................
LAIRD, J. P.....................Alton.
LINNAGER, D. J..........................
MILLER, R................................
OBERLY, JOHN H..................Cairo.
PARKER, GEO. W............Charlestown.
REDDING, H. G..................Ottawa.
SCHNELL, J....................Clinton.
SHIRLEY, W. C...........................
TAYLOR, S. S....................Cairo.
WALCOTT, G....................Quincy.
WALKER, J. M..................Chicago.
WILCOX, J...............................
WINTER, HENRY..........................

INDIANA.

ALWARD, E. S............................
ANDREWS, L. N...........................
BEACH, JOHN S.............Terre Haute.
BEESON, W. H. H............Vincennes.
BENNETT, E......................Brazil.
BIRD, O.................................
BRACE, O. B.................Vincennes.
BRIGHT, R. J...............Indianapolis.
BROWN, JESSE J..........................
BUNDY, MARTIN L........................
BYRAM, N. L................Indianapolis.
CARPENTER, WILLARD.......Evansville.
CLAYPOOL, E. F............Indianapolis.
DURHAM, GEO. F........Crawfordsville.
DURHAM, W. H...........   "
ENGLE, GEO. B. Jr........Indianapolis.
FINK, RUDOLPH..............New Albany.
FULLERLOVE, T. J..............Albany.
HANNA B W................Terre Haute.
HOAGLAND, PLINEY,........Fort Wayne.
HOWARD, WM..................Madison.
HURLEY, M. M..................Albany.

INDIANA—Continued.

IVES, J. O.....................Indianapolis.
KIRK, JOHN.........................Madison
KNOWLTON, G B. ....
MCCAIN, T. H. B.............Crawfordsville.
McCONNELL GEO. W................ ....
McKINNEY, JOHN............Indianapolis.
McKEEN, R. W................Terre Haute.
MORGAN, W. H ....Crawfordsville.
MILLIGAN, JOSEPH.......................
MITCHELL, ROB'T........................
PIERCE, W. S....... ......Indianapolis.
ROACHE, A. L................ "
ROBINSON, H. H...........................
RUSH, FRED P............Indianapolis.
SEXTON, LEONIDAS.......................
SHERMAN, M. G...........Michigan City.
SMITH, J. M................Crawfordsville.
STILZ, J. GEO.............Indianapolis.
TAYLOR, H. M..............New Albany.
THOMPSON R. W........ .Terre Haute.
VOORHEES, D. W............ "   "
WILSON, L. B.............Crawfordsville.
WILSON, S. C..............................
WRIGHT, GEO. B. ....Indianapolis.

IOWA.

ANDERSON, A. C................ .....Siancy.
BALDWIN, J. T. ....Council Bluffs.
BALLINGALL, P. G............Ottumwa.
BOYLES, J. K................Centreville.
CLARKSON, J. S..............Des Moines
GRINNELL B....... ....Grinnell.
HAMMOND, J. W...... ....
HANCOCK, T. H ....Davenport.
HATTON, T....................Burlington.
HOWARD J. W.............Prairie City.
MERRELL, S....... ....Des Moines.
PRICE, H......................Davenport.
WILLIAMSON J. A..........Des Moines.
WILSON, J. F ....Fairfield.

KENTUCKY.

AIR, WM. N.....................Newport.
BULLOCK, E. I..................Columbus.
BARBOUR, JNO. M............Louisville.
BELKNAP. W. R .... "
BERRY, ALBERT S. ....Newport.
BOYLE, JOHN..................Louisville.
BOWMAN, J. B....... ....Lexington.
BRADLEY, JAMES ....Louisville.
BRADSHAW W F ....Paducah.
BREED E. C..................Louisville.
BULTELL, CUTHBAL........ "
BURNETT, HENRY. ....Paducah.
CALDWELL, ISAAC........ ....Louisville
CARPENTER. M. T............Shelbyville.
CHILTON, R. H.................Louisville.
CRUTCHE, JAMES............New Castle.
CASEY J. B ....Covington.
CONKLIN W L.................Litchfield.
DESHMAN, JOHN... ......Barboursville.
DITTO, A H.................New Castle.
DULANEY, W. H..............Louisville.
DUPONT B..................... ..
FOX. F. T .... "
GIBSON, WILBUR............ ....
GREENE, JAS. O..............Louisville.
HALL, W. C..................... "
HAMILTON, W B........... .. '
HARTWELL, S. A............... "
HAYS, GREEN.................. "
HINES, F H.............Bowling Green.
HAYS, THOS H...............Louisville.
HAWSER WM A............... "
HARLAN J. M................ "
HODGE, GEO. B ....Newport.
HITE. W. C....................Louisville.
JEFFERSON, T. L............. "
JONES, GEORGE W.....................
JONES. T. L......... ....Newport.
KING, JOHN O. A..........................
KEARNY. JNO. WATTS........Louisville.
LATROBE, H. B................ '
LEWIS, J. FLOYD... ....Newport.
LONG, CHAS. R................Louisville.
LONG JNO. L................... "
LOOK, SAM'L J................. "
MARTIN, JNO ....Paducah.
MILLS. R. E..................Louisville.
MILLER, JNO. A.................Paducah
MORRIS, GEO. W. ....Louisville.
MORTON, A. M................Shelbyville.
NEIL, JAS L..................Harrodsburg.
NEWCOMB, VICTOR...........Louisville.
O'BANNON, JAS................Eminence.
PRESTON, WM................Lexington.
PETERS, ARTHUR............Louisville.
RICE, J. M........................Louisa.
SAYNE, E. D ....Lexington.
SCOTT, HORACE..............Louisville
SCHMITT, F. P.................. "
SCHWARTZ, THEO............ "
SELBY. BEN..................Eminence.
SMITH, MILTON...............Louisville.
SWEENEY, ...Owensboro.
SMITH, Z. T....................Eminence.
STANDFORD, E. D............Louisville.
STUCKEY, HARRY............ "
TAYLOR, W. T.................. "
THOMPSON, GEO. C............Paducah.
TRIMBLE, L. S............. .... "
VEIHOFF, H., JR..............Louisville.
WILGUS. J. B................Lexington.
WILSON, E. B ....Louisville.
WINSTON, A. S...............Lexington.
WOOLFOLK, R. H............Louisville.

KANSAS.

CALDWELL, A..............Leavenworth.
CRAWFORD. GEO. A........Fort Scott.
DENTON, HENRY..............Atchison.
DOWNS, W. F. ....
ELLIOTT, L. R.............Manhattan.
GILLESPIE, GEO. W..........Atchison.
GOODLANDER, C. W..........Fort Scott.
HALLIDAY, C. K................Topeka.
HARRIS, A. A..................Fort Scott.
INSLEY, M. H.............Leavenworth.
McDONALD, B. P.............Fort Scott.
McFORD, JAS. S............... " "

MORLEY, CHAS..............Fort Scott.
MORRIS, R. B..................Atchison.
PRICE JNO. M.................. "
RICHARDS, JOHN F........Leavenworth.
RIPPEY, W. D..................Mapleton.
SEARLE, R. H. C................Topeka.
SMITH, JACOB.................... "
SMITH, L. F ....
SMITH T....................Leavenworth.
TWONER, W. F.............Independence.
WEBSTER, J. M..............Lawrence.

LOUISIANA.

BARRETT, W. B ....New Orleans.
BEAUREGARD, G. T........ "   "
BELL, DR......................................
BOARMAN, A..................Shreveport.
CUMMINGS, P. W. H.......... "
EGAN, W. B.................... "
FLANDERS, B. F.........................
HAVEN, W. S.................Shreveport
HARRIS, J. S...................Vidalia.
HEARSAY, H. J ....New Orleans.
HORAN, J. J ....Shreveport.
JOYCE, W. M................................
KENNARD, J. H............New Orleans.

KENNEDY, HUGH....................
LEONARD, A. H......................
LOONEY, R. F................Shreveport.
NASH, WM. F.........................
NEWMAN, W. H......................
PEGRAM, J. W.......................
RANLETT, E. L............New Orleans.
SEGAR A. B ....
SIMMS. B. B.................New Orleans.
SMITH, GEO. L......................
STOUTMEYER, J. N.........New Orleans.
WALLINGTON, W. M..................
WYLIE, W. D.................Shreveport.

MARYLAND.

PRESBERY, GEO. G..

MICHIGAN.

BOWERS, W. R............Grand Haven.
HAYES, J. D...................Detroit.
MAY, F. H..................................

STONE, WM................Grand Haven.
STORRS, C. L................ "   "

MINNESOTA.

DAVIDSON, WM. F..............St. Paul.
MARSHALL, W. R.............. "

RAMSEY, ALEXANDER........St. Paul.

MISSISSIPPI.

ARTHUR, ALEX. H........................
DAVIS, JEFFERSON..........Vicksburg.
FURLONG, CHAS. E........ "
HARDY, GEO T................ "
HARRIS, N H.................. "
HICKS, JOHN R............. "
HUNTINGTON, C. B.....................
KRUM, B. L.................................

MARSHALL, C. K............Vicksburg.
MARTIN, W. T..................Natchez.
RICHARDSON, E D...................
SULLIVAN, JAS. H....................
WALWORTH E. F...................
WARNER, ALEXANDER................
YOUNG, UPTON M............Vicksburg.

MISSOURI.

ALLEN, THOS..................St. Louis.
ARTHUR, W R................. "
ARMSTRONG, D. H............. "
AKERS, THOS. P.............. "
ALLISON, WM. R.............. "

ATCHINSON, W. P ....
AHRENS, H. J. E........................
AIKEN, A. R.............................
ANDERSON, W. W............Louisiana.
ALLEN, T. R...................Allenton.

MISSOURI—Continued.

ASHBROOK, L. M..............St. Louis.	FILLEY, GILES F..............St. Louis.
ASHBROOK, L. L.............. "	GILKESON, J. M................ "
ATTAYWAY. H..................Laclede.	GIBSON, CHARLES............ "
BROADHEAD, JAMES O.......St. Louis.	GARRISON, A. B................ "
BAIN, GEO...................... "	GILL, J C......................Le Roy.
BARRY, J. G.................... "	GREGORY, JAMES A...........St. Louis.
BOFINGER. J. N................ "	GLENN, U. E................................
BRITTON, J. H................ "	GUITAR, O......................Columbia.
BONNER, B. R.................. "	GIBSON, WILBER ....
BROWN, B. GRATZ............. "	GRISWOLD W. D. ....St. Louis.
BARTHOLOW, T. J............. "	HARRISON, EDWIN............ "
BROWN, JOSEPH............... "	HENDERSON, JOHN B......... "
BENT, SILAS................... "	HUTCHINS, STILSON........... "
BRUERE, T....................St. Charles.	HAYS, SAMUEL .... "
BISHOP, E. N...............................	HUDSON, N. C................... "
BARRY, W C....................Warsaw.	HOUSER, D M.................. "
BUSH, J. L.................................	HOWARD, W. P................ "
BOYD, J. H	HALE, J. P.....................Carrollton.
BETHUNE, J. H................Charleston.	HALL, W. A...................Huntsville.
BECKER, V...................St. Charles.	HALL, W. P...................St Joseph.
BLAND, R. P..:..................Lebanon.	HAMILTON, W.................St. Louis.
BROWN, R. H..................Kirksville.	HARDING, H. H............ .. Carthage.
COLLIER, M. DWIGHT.........St. Louis	HOOPER, N R..................Lebanon.
CABELL, E C.................... "	HOCKADAY, JOHN H............Fulton.
COLE, NATHAN................ "	HARRISON, B. B................Lebanon.
CLEMENTS, J T..................Macon	HOSKINSON, J..................Kingston.
COLEMAN, N. J.................St. Louis.	HARRISON, W. P....... ......Hannibal.
CARR, WALTER C............. "	HAVENS, H. E............................
CAHOON, B. B............Fredericktown.	HYDE, J. B.....................Princeton.
CARTER, WM................Farmington.	HEARD JOHN T..................Sedalia.
CAFFE, D. A. H.................Carthage.	HENRY, JOHN W..................Macon.
CHOUTEAU, CHAS. P..........St. Louis.	HESS, C. P...................... "
CASE, A........................Lebanon.	IVEY, J........................Lebanon.
COFFMAN, D. M..............Webster Co.	ITTNER, ANTHONY............St. Louis.
CRAIG, JAMES................St. Joseph.	JONES, F. A.....................Macon.
CARPENTER DAVIS.............. "	JOHNSTON, G. B..............St. Charles.
DAENZER CARL................St Louis.	JAMESON, R. W........Webster County.
DYER, D. P.................... "	JOHNSON, W. P................Osceola.
DAVIS, L. H....................Jackson.	JOHNSON, W. S.........................
DAVIS, L. P................................	JONES, GEO. W.........................
DAVIS, FULTON..............Lexington.	JAYNES, A. D....................Sedalia.
DAWSON L................Jefferson City.	KLINGER, G. A..............St. Charles.
DEAL, H J ....Charleston.	KELLY, W. C.............................
DAWSON, A. M............................	KENNEDY, D. C..........................
DALTON, W F...............Webster Co.	KNAPP, GEO....................St. Louis.
DAENZER, H. P...........................	KATTE, WALTER................ "
DICKEY, SAMUEL............Webster Co.	LAFLIN, S. H.................... "
ELLIOTT, J. S.................Boonville.	LIPMAN, M. J................... "
EDWARDS A. H...............St. Charles	LACKLAND, H. C.............St. Charles.
ELIOT, W. G....................St. Louis.	LAWRENCE, JUDGE.....................
ENO, GUSTAVUS...........................	LINESDY, J. W...........................
EVANS, J. S...............................	LAMAN, J. G....................Lebanon.
FLAD, HENRY..................St. Louis.	LAWSON, FRANK.........................
FOSTER, EMORY S............. "	LEMLEY, J G............................
FILLEY, CHAUNCEY I........ "	LA DUE, JOSHUA................Clinton.
FILLER, J. M.................Mt. Vernon.	McDEARMON, F. F..........St. Charles.
FARRAR, L. B...............Webster Co.	MOORE, J. T...........Laclede County.
FROST, D. M...................St. Louis.	MEYER, J. P....................St. Louis.
FLOOD, JOHN A..................Fulton.	MOORE, F. W...........Webster County.

MISSOURI—Continued.

MCELHANEY, R. L.................
MOORE, J. T......................
MITCHELL, TOBIAS................
MALCOMB, D. W...................
MUDD, HENRY T...............St. Louis.
MAUDE, JOHN B.............. "
MACADAM, D. H............... "
MOULTON, J. B................ "
MACHENS, H. E.............St. Charles.
MCAFEE, BENJ. F............Springfield.
NORTON, E. H................Platte City.
NEWTON JOB......................
O'BRIEN, J. L...............Boonville.
ONSTATT, J. H...............Springfield.
O'NEIL, J...................St Louis.
OVERSTOLZ, HENRY........... "
PHIPPS, ALEX...............Moberly.
PARAMORE, J. W.............St. Louis.
PARKS, R. H................St. Charles.
PARKER, THOMAS..................
PHELPS, JOHN S.............Springfield.
POWELL, W. J....................
PHELAN, M. H............... St. Louis.
ROBINSON, W. P..............Sedalia.
ROWLAND, D. P.............. St. Louis.
RELF, W. S..................Potosi.
RUSSELL, W. H. H...........St. Louis.
ROWE, S. B.......................
RICHARDSON, S. A............Gallatin.
ROZIER, F. C............... Ste Genevieve.
RUSH, J. L.................Webster County.
RICKEY, JOS. K..............Fulton.
SCUDDER, W. H..............St. Louis.
SHRYOCK, L. R............... "
SLOSS J. L.................. "
STANARD, E. O............... "
SAMUEL, WEB. M.............. "
SCHURZ, CARL................ "
SHARP, F. C................. "
SPECK, CHARLES.............. "
STURGEON, I. H.............. "
SELLS, MILES................ "
SLAYBACK, A. W.............. "

SCHULTZ, CHAUNCY F.........St Louis.
SENTER, W. M................ "
SHAW, J. S..................St. Charles.
SUTPEN, F. A................Louisiana.
SHIELDS, W..................St. Louis.
SEAY, E. A..................Rolla.
STORTS, C. H................ "
STANLEY THEODORE....Pleasant Hill.
SWITZLER, W. F..............Columbia.
STEPHENS, J. L..............Boonville.
SMITH, WM..............Webster County.
SMITH, W. F.....................
SPAUNHORST, H. J............St. Louis.
ST. GEM, GUSTAVUS.....Ste. Genevieve.
TAGGARD, T. G...............Benton.
TAYLOR, M. F................Charleston.
TURPIN, R. L....................
TALMAGE, A. A...............St. Louis.
TANSEY, R. P................ "
TODD, ALBERT................ "
TAYLOR, DAN'L G............. "
TRACY, J. L................. "
TIBBS, JOHN S...............Macon.
VAN HORN, R. T..............Kansas City.
VAN FRANK, P. R.........Cape Girardeau.
VAUGH, J. H.....................
WILLIAMS, W. F..............Macon.
WRIGHT P. M.....................
WILSON, H. G................Allenton.
WALLACE, C..................Lebanon.
WILKINS, W. T...............St. Louis.
WILKERSON, J. M............. "
WALLINGTON, W. M................
WADDELL, JOHN W............Lexington.
WILLIAMS, S. G..................
WARMOUTH, J. S..............Rolla.
WETMORE, H. A...................
WILLIAMS, JOHN B............Fulton.
WATERHOUSE, SYLVESTER..St. Louis.
WORDEN, J. D................Moberly.
WILLIAMS, A. J..............Macon.
YEATMAN, JAMES E...........St. Louis.
YOUNG, J. T.................Moberly.

NEW JERSEY.

BEASLEY, MERCER, JR..............
BUCHANAN, JAMES..................
CRANE, JACOB W...............Newark.
GREEN, EDWARD T..................
HARRISON, JOHN D.............Newark.
KILBURN, ISAAC B............ "

NAAR, JOS. L....................
PETERS, GEORGE..............Newark.
RUSHING, JAMES F................
STEWART, JOHN H.................
VROOM, G. D. W..................

NEVADA.

BOYLE, WM. G....................
CLARKSON, J. S..................

SCOTT, WILL J...................
TURNER, GEORGE..................

NEBRASKA.

CONVERSE, J. N..............Lincoln.
EDDY, J. M.................. "
FURNASS, R. W..............Brownsville.

LETT, H. C......................
WHEELER, D. H..............Plattsmouth.

NORTH CAROLINA.

GRAINGER, J B.................... | JOHNSON, WILLIAM....................

NEW MEXICO.

ELKINS S. B................Santa Fe
ELLIOTT, R. S....................
ECKLES. S H.....................
ERFURT A C......................
FRANZ, E D......................

HACKNEY. A. B...........Silver City.
HAYES, A. H................ "
HAYES, MARTIN B........Grant County.
HAYWARD, G. A......................

NEW YORK.

ANDERSON, J. J....................
COOPER, PETER...........New York.
FRANCIS, JAMES............. "
GROOM, WALLACE........... "
GRISWOLD, JOHN D................
HILDRETH, D. M..........New York.

HUNTINGTON, CHAS. E......New York.
MARQUAND, H. G............ "
OPDYKE, CHAS. W........... "
SANFORD, WATSON.......... "
SELIGMAN, DeWITT J........ "

OHIO.

ANDREWS, C. H..........Youngstown.
AMES, GEO, D. ....
BARKER, J..................Sandusky.
BACKUS, A. L..................Toledo.
BONNELL, H.............Youngstown.
BROWN, H. W................Cincinnati.
BISSELL, H. B....................
BRADLEY, CHARLES................
BUCKEYLER, J. L.................
BUTLER, C. P. L..................
BROOK, D. W.....................
BERGIN, THOMAS..................
BISHOP, R. M...............Cincinnati.
CORNELL, A. B............Youngstown.
COVINGTON, S. F...........Cincinnati.
DAVIS, S. S.................. "
DANIEL, G..................Sandusky.
DICKINSON, W. S..........Cincinnati.
DODGE, O. J.....................
DEVENNEY, L.............. Cincinnati.
ELY, GEO. H.....................
GAITHER, A.................Cincinnati.
GLENN, J. M................ "
GLENN, S................... "
GRAY, D. S......................
HALL, J. S................Cincinnati.
HUDSON, J. H..............Sandusky.
HOLLOWAY, C. M............Cincinnati.
HEITMAN, J. D...............Columbus.
HOWARD, N. M.................Toledo.

INGALLS, M. G..............Cincinnati.
JONES, J. P..................Toledo.
JONES, G. W...............Cincinnati.
JOHNSON, G. W C............ "
KLIPPART, J. H..................
KECK, J. S.................Cincinnati.
LEHMER, J. D..............Cincinnati.
LOSS, J. H.................. "
MATHEWS, STANLEY........ "
MATHER, S. L....................
MARX, G......................Toledo.
MITHOFF, ...
MINOR, J R................Sandusky.
NEUBENT, S. G................Toledo.
OSBORN, W. M.............Youngstown.
OTIS, C. A......................
PFAFF, C. T. ....
SHOEMAKER, M................Toledo.
SPECK, C. B.............Youngstown.
SEEMAN, G................Cincinnati.
STREATER, W. S..................
SESSIONS, F. C..................
STUDEE, J H....................
THOMAS, C. W.............Cincinnati.
THOMAS, SAMUEL..................
WALBRIDGE, U. S.............Toledo.
WALES, C. T................ "
WAGONER, C................. "
WILHELM, O. A...............Wooster.
WISE, J. S.................Cincinnati.

PENNSYLVANIA.

ALLEN, G. N.....................
BAER, G. F......................
BENNETT, J. F...................
BRUNOT, F. R...............Pittsburg.
BUZBY, G. L.....................
BOAS, E. P......................

BEAUER, T......................
BUCK, S. W.....................
BRICKELL, D. E..................
BIGHAM, T. J..............Pittsburg.
CHALFANT, J. W............ "
COLEMAN, G D...................

PENNSYLVANIA—Continued.

CHASE, W. G................................
CROSSAN, J. McD...............Pittsburg.
DRACO, J. D....................................
DRAVO, JOHN F................Pittsburg.
ECKERT, H. S................................
ERRETT, R....................................
FOX, D. M......................................
FRITZ, D. J....................................
FRALEY, F......................................
FOLLOWOOD, W..........................
GALBRATH, W. A....................Erie.
GRAY, R. C.........................Pittsburg.
GRISCOM, C. A..............Philadelphia.
GRAHAM, J. L....................Pittsburg.
HAYWOOD, B................................
HITNER, D. O................................
HOFFMAN, C. J..............................
HUTCHINSON, J. N......................
HOOPES, E....................................
JONES, F. B....................................
JACOBS, ABRAHAM.....................
JEFFRIES C. T................................
KAUFMAN, C. S..............................
KAUFMAN, W. M............................
KUHN, G H....................................
KING, A..
KILLAN, J. N..................................
KENNEDY, B. C.............................
KOUNTZ, W. J...................Pittsburg.
KIROBB, J. K..................................
McMICHAEL, M..............Philadelphia.
McCARTHY, W. C................Pittsburg.
McCORMICK, H............................

McPHERSON, E............................
MARTIN, W. W..............................
MOREHEAD, J. K..............Pittsburg.
MORRILL, D. J..............................
MULHALL, J. P..............................
MOORE, W. D................................
NOBLE, O...............................Erie.
NOYES, A. C..................................
PARDEE, A....................................
RAULE, H...............................Erie.
REMAK, G....................................
REEVES, S. G................................
SCHALL, M....................................
SNOWDEN, A L..............Philadelphia.
STEEL, J. I....................................
SMALL, D. E..................................
STANTON, M. H............................
SHAFER, P. W................................
SWANK, J. M................................
STOCKDALE, J. T..........................
SEMPLE, W....................................
SAWYER, B. C..................Pittsburg.
SCHOONMAKER, J. N............ "
TOWER, C............................. "
WETHERELL, J. P..........................
WESTERMAN, J............................
WILLIAMS, E. H............................
WOOD, J..
WRIGHT, W. W..............................
WRIGHT, J. A................................
WELSH, H D................................
WEBB, G..
ZIMMERMAN, A. H......................

SOUTH CAROLINA.

DAVANT, J. C....................Beaufort.
EARLE, W. E....................Greenville.
McMASTER, F. W................Columbia.
PALMER, JOHN B.............. "

WALLACE, W....................Columbia.
SCOTT, R. K.......................... "
SEIBLE, E. W........................ "

TENNESSEE.

ALLOWAY, N. E................Nashville.
BAXTER, W. M..............Chattanooga.
CALDWELL, R. P................Trenton.
CLAIBORNE, THOS............Nashville.
CLAPP, J. W......................Memphis.
COLE, EDWIN W..............Nashville.
CRUSEMAN, J. P..........................
DAVIS, F. S.......................Memphis.
DOAK, H. M....................Clarksville.
EDMUNDSON, R. B............Memphis.
FLEMING, JOHN M............Knoxville.
GARNER, JOHN E.............Springfield.
GLOVER, J. L................................
GRACEY, F. P................................
HEISS, HENRY..................Nashville.

HENRY, GUSTAVUS A....................
JOHNSON, C. M................Nashville.
LATHAM, T. J....................Memphis.
LOWE, S. B....................................
McGHEE, CHAS. M............Memphis.
PATON, A. A........................ "
REITER, G. W................................
REEVES, T. H....................Jonesboro.
SATTERWHITE, J. A..........Nashville.
SAUNDERS, ROLFE............Knoxville.
SMITH, HENRY G..............Memphis.
SPENCE, D. H C..............Murfresboro.
THOMPSON, JACOB............Memphis.
TOPP, ROBERTSON.............. "
WOOLF, ADAM..................Nashville.

TEXAS.

ANDERSON, MOSES..
ADAMS, S. J...................Dallas.
ANDREWS, N. B...............Galveston.
ALEXANDER, J. P............Ft. Worth.
BAKER, W. R..................Houston.
BARZIZA, D. V.................. "
BRAGG, BRAXTON............Galveston.
BAGLAND, E. B...............Longview.
BABCOCK, W...................Paris.
BALL, A J....................Weatherford.
BOWER, E. G....................
BARKLEY, J. E................Dallas.
BARRY, JOSEPH.................
BLASINGAME, W..............Sherman.
BROWN, J. G..................Longview.
BROOCKS, J. H..................
BROWN, R. W..................Longview.
BINKLEY, C. C.............Grayson County.
BRILEY, H. T................Longview.
BLEDSOE, JOE.............Grayson County.
BERLINA, B.....................
BEES, A H......................
BROWN, JOS. H...................
BLANCHARD, W. B.............El Paso.
BURROUGHS, L. K.............Austin.
CAUDIS, L....................El Paso.
CHENOWITH, J. Q........Farris County.
COCKRELL, J. V...............Sherman.
CRAWFORD, W. L.............Jefferson.
CLOPTON, A. C.................. "
CLARK, W. J.....................Dallas.
CARROLL, W. G...............Longview.
CABELL, W. L..................Dallas.
CHAPMAN, R. A...............Sherman.
CLARKE, J. H................Clarksville.
COCKRELL, F...................Sherman.
COOK, F. J..................... "
CULBERSON, D. B...............Jefferson.
CAMPBELL, T. J................ "
CROWDUS, J. W..................Dallas.
COMUS, J. M...................Longview.
CONNER, W. C....................
CHAPMAN, A......................
CALDWELL, J. T................Dallas.
CLARK, M, C...................Dennison.
DURHAM, M. L................Longview.
DAHONEY, E L...................Paris.
DELANEY, W S................Columbus.
DUNCAN, J. M.................Longview.
DEXTER, GEO. J..................
ELLIS, L A......................
EVANS, SAMUEL..................
ESTES, B F...................Texarkana.
EVARTS, JUDGE................Ft. Worth.
ELLIS, C. E..................Dallas.
EPPERMAN, B. H..............Jefferson.
EROY, H S....................Dallas.
EDWARDS, L. E..................
FITZHUGH, L. H...............Austin.

FRASER, A. B.................Ft. Worth.
FORT, W. A...................Waco.
FOREMAN, J...................Plano.
FRY, S. J.......................
FIELD, THOMAS................Dallas.
FOULKES, J. S...............Bryan City.
FRANCIS, C. C............Rusk Cherokee.
GIBBS, B.....................Dallas.
GROVE, D. E..................... "
GOOD, J. J..................... "
GAINES, B. R................Clarksville.
GRAHAM, G. A..............Farris County.
GOODJOHN, Z. H..................
GRACE, C. D..................Bonham.
GRIBBLE, R. D...................
GRUBER, E. H.................Dallas.
HARRISON, W. M..............Jefferson.
HAGUE, J. P....................
HUGHES, W. E................Dallas.
HYATT, H. C..................Jefferson.
HOLLAND, W. C................Dallas.
HANCOCK, J...................Austin.
HAYS, B. F...................Bonham.
HAYS, J. B...................El Paso.
HOLMES, W. C................Sherman.
HUTCHINS, W. J..............Houston.
HARRISON, T..................Waco.
IVEY, A E.................Farris County.
JAMES, J.....................San Antonio.
JONES, J. M..................Longview.
LEE, R. J....................Clarksville.
LANE, W. P...................Marshall.
LATIMER, A. K...............Clarksville.
LANG, W. W...................Marlin.
LYDAY, W. H..................Bonham.
McKAY, A.....................Marshall.
MARTIN, J. M.................Sherman.
MILLS, J. S...............Grimes County.
MOBREY, H. P.................Marshall.
McALPINE, W. K..............Galveston.
McALPINE, D..............Grimes County.
McKINNEY, S. A...............Denton.
MAXEY, S. B..................Paris.
MILLS, R. Q..................Corsicana.
MAGOFFIN, JOSEPH............El Paso.
MONTROSE, H. L..............Texarkana.
McCOY, J.....................Dallas.
MOORE, JOHN M..........Corpus Christi.
OSPENHAUSER, C.............Pilot Point.
OBENCHAIN, A. T.............Dallas.
PADDOCK, R. R...............Ft. Worth.
PENNMAN, J..................Jefferson.
PEAKE, C. M.................Ft. Worth.
PEAK, JUNE.....................
REED, L. C.....................
RANDLE, W....................Bonham.
RUSSELL, A. H................Marshall.
RAGLAND, E. W...............Longview.
ROSS, C. L.....................

TEXAS—Continued.

SCHLEICHER, G.	Cuero.
SEANDS, F. W.	
SORLEY, J	Galveston.
STEWART, BENJ. F.	Longview.
SWAIN, W. J.	Clarksville.
SEVEY, R. B.	
STEGALL, A. H.	Dallas.
SEXTON, F. R	Marshall.
SCOTT, W. J	
SHANNON, W. R.	Weatherford.
STRIBBLING, C. K.	Ft. Griffin.
SCHULTER, F. A	Jefferson.
STEMMON, J. W	Dallas.
SWISLER, JOSEPH M	Austin.
SCRUGGS, J. B.	Dallas.
SWINDELLS, J. H.	"
SUMMER, F. W.	
SCOTT, WM J	Denison.
SCOTT, M. P	Dallas.
SHORE, W. J.	"
SIMPSON, J. B	"
THOMPSON, R. V.	Dallas.
TAYLOR, E. W.	Jefferson.
TERRILL, J C.	Ft. Worth.
THROCKMORTON, J. W.	McKinney.
TEMPLETON, J D,	Ft. Worth.
THURMAN, J. H.	
TAYS, J. W.	
THOMAS, W. G.	Austin.
WALKER, J. G.	Dallas
WINN, W. H	
WOODWARD, J. D.	Denison.
WITHERSPOON, J. D	Longview.
WELBURN, W. L.	"
WORK, J. A.	
WALKER, I. G.	
WEST, J. C.	Waco.
WAGLEY, W. C.	Houston.
WRIGHT, G. M.	Paris.
WRIGHT, J. T.	Dallas.
ZIMPLEMAN, G. B	Austin

VIRGINIA.

ANDERSON, J. R	Richmond.
BEALL, J. LLOYD	"
BURWELL, W. P.	"
CABELL, H. C.	"
COHRAN, J. L	Charlottesville.
CONRAD, HOLMES	Winchester.
DANIEL, S. M	Richmond.
ELLIS, CHARLES.	"
FIELD, J. G	Culpepper Court House.
HUNTER R. W.	Winchester.
HUBBARD, E. W.	Alexandria.
IMBODEN, J. D.	Richmond.
KENT, LINDEN	Alexandria.
LEE, FITZHUGH	Richmond.
STEARNS, FRANKLIN.	"

WISCONSIN.

COBB, GEO. W.	LARKIN, CHAS. H.

Pending the reading of the foregoing list, a delegate moved that the further reading of the names of delegates be dispensed with, and the Secretary state the number of delegates to which each State was entitled, as reported by the Committee on Credentials.

The question was put and the motion was carried.

COMMUNICATIONS.

The Chairman: A letter has been received and handed to the Chair, from George H. Morgan, of Kingsboro, Tennessee. It is a long letter, and will not be read unless called for.

The President: I have also a communication from Charles C. Rozier, Mayor of Ste. Genevieve, Missouri, appointing Gustavus St. Gem, of that city, to represent him on this floor.

I have also a communication from Jno. N. Dyer, Librarian of the Mercantile Library, which the Secretary will read.

The Secretary read as follows:

MERCANTILE LIBRARY,
ST. LOUIS, November 23, 1875.

Col. James O. Broadhead, Chairman of the Executive Committee, Southern Railroad Convention:

DEAR SIR:—The delegates to the Southern Railroad Convention are respectfully invited to visit the rooms of the St. Louis Mercantile Library Association during their sojourn in the city. They will find the reading-room supplied with the daily newspapers from all sections of the country.

Very respectfully,

JNO. N. DYER, *Librarian.*

MR. TREZEVANT, of Arkansas: I move that the Secretaries be allowed until to-morrow morning to prepare a corrected list of delegates, and they be further instructed to furnish to the chairmen of the delegations a list of the names reported by the committee, and that we now proceed, as the report has been adopted, to the permanent organization of the Convention.

MR. SLAYBACK, of St. Louis: I claim that the gentleman is out of order. The Committee on Permanent Organization has not reported; it has not had time; besides, to-night the delegates will require tokens of admission to the banquet, and as soon as possible it will be arranged to give them that recognition as well as other civilities, which we hope they will enjoy.

MR. TREZEVANT: The gentleman, perhaps, misunderstands the object of my motion, which is, that instead of waiting for the count now being made as to the names of the delegates, that the Secretaries be allowed till to-morrow morning to make the announcement, so that if the Committee on Permanent Organization is prepared to report they can now proceed to do so.

THE CHAIRMAN: It is moved that the chairman of each delegation be requested to furnish the Secretary a list of the delegation. Is that correct?

MR. TREZEVANT: No, sir; that has been done, and the committee have made their report; that report has been accepted. The Committee on Credentials has made its report, and that has been accepted by the Convention, so that now the composition of the Convention is determined. Now, I wish to dispense with the further consumption of time, so far as that work is concerned, in order that we may proceed to the organization of the Convention, as it is getting late. My motion, therefore, is this: That the Secretaries be allowed till to-morrow morning to make a report to the Convention of the number of delegates present from each State, and that they be requested to furnish to the chairman of the delegation from each State a list of those accredited under the resolution of the Convention, and that we now proceed to the permanent organization and business of the Convention.

Mr. Jones, of Kentucky: The Secretary of the Committee on Credentials is already in possession of the names of the delegates to this Convention from the different States and Territories, and if there is any want of accuracy in them they will be corrected. The States and Territories may be called, and the numbers ascertained at once of the different States and Territories which are entitled to badges as members of the Convention. They have already been furnished from most of the States and Territories.

The Chairman: The Chair decides that time will be allowed to the Secretary, unless objection is made.

Mr. Covington, of Ohio: Mr. Chairman, I desire to present the report of the Committee on Permanent Organization.

The Chairman: The report will be read.

The report was read as follows:

President—Stanley Mathews, of Ohio.
First Vice-President—William Preston, of Kentucky.
Secretary—John M. Harrell, of Arkansas.
Official Reporter—L. L. Walbridge, of Missouri.
Sergeant-at-Arms—J. E. D. Couzins, of Missouri.

The Chairman: Gentlemen of the Convention, you have heard the names of the officers proposed by the Committee on Permanent Organization; if no objection is made, the question will be put upon the election of all the officers named in that report.

The question was put and the report was agreed to.

Mr. Soussey, of Georgia: In all conventions which I have had the honor of attending, the votes have been according to the votes in Congress, and it seems to me if the Convention is going to change that rule and only have one vote from each State, it is possible we are infringing on a time-honored principle; I therefore move an amendment to that report, that in the votes to be taken in this Convention, the votes shall be cast by the chairman of each delegation, according to the number of representatives in Congress, of Senators and Representatives.

MR. HARRISON, of Texas: I would move to lay that motion on the table.

THE CHAIRMAN: The Chair is of the opinion that will carry the whole report with it.

MR. HARRISON: Then I will withdraw the motion.

THE PRESIDENT: The question now is on the adoption of the amendment.

The question was put and the amendment was rejected.

THE PRESIDENT: The question now recurs on the adoption of the report of the committee as far as the scaling of the vote is concerned.

The question was put and the report was agreed to.

THE CHAIRMAN: The committee further report that this Convention adopt the rules governing the House of Representatives in the Congress of the United States; are you ready for the question?

The question was put and that portion of the report was adopted.

THE CHAIRMAN: Judge Stanley Mathews, permanent Chairman, just elected by the Convention, will please come upon the platform and take his seat.

Mr. Mathews then came forward and took his seat as presiding officer of the Convention.

THE CHAIRMAN: Gentlemen, I have the honor to present to you your permanent President, Judge Stanley Mathews. [Loud applause.]

ADDRESS OF PRESIDENT MATHEWS.

GENTLEMEN OF THE CONVENTION:—The surprise with which I heard the nomination and received the notice of my election as permanent Chairman of this Convention is so great that it deprives me of the power of making an adequate acknowledgment. It is with very profound gratitude that I receive this compliment. It is with the greatest possible distrust in my fitness and ability to discharge rightly its duties, that I accept it. I am sure, gentlemen, that you will credit me with sincerity when I say that I regard it as the proudest honor of my life. [Loud applause.] For I recognize, gentlemen, in this Convention a body whose assembled weight and respectability, and title to consideration by the whole American population, surpasses that of any in which I ever had the honor to participate. The names of men the most honored and influential in every State and quarter of the Union are enrolled in the list of membership, and I am sure that the well-considered and unanimous voice of this Convention, in favor of the great project which has assembled it, will not only be heard but felt in the success of the measure which it presents. [Applause.] I represent, gentlemen, in part, a city that has evidenced in this matter its faith by its works. It has been, and is now, in the process of investing ten millions of dollars of its own money in a full belief in the success and prosperity of the Southern system of railroads. [Applause.] This day, through the States of Kentucky and Tennessee, its engineers and employees are busy making a great highway, in which it is the sole corporator, to tap at Chattanooga the whole network of Southern railroads which is to find its natural outlet and its great success in the extension now proposed to the Pacific Ocean. Of course, gentlemen, there are differences of opinion there, as there always will be everywhere in regard to the expediency and policy of every business enterprise; but on various occasions and at different times the people of Cincinnati, in every mode in which they could express themselves, have reiterated their determination to see that enterprise accomplished, and unless this matter that is now in our charge is carried forward to a successful result, their investment will not prove what it ought to be.

But, gentlemen, I should be ashamed to advocate the construction of the Southwestern Railway to the Pacific Ocean, and particularly to invite and request the co-operation and aid of the General Government in its behalf, solely on the ground that my own city was pecuniarily interested in that extension. It is not upon that ground, though that is my apology and excuse for my presence here. There is a larger interest; there is a broader interest, a deeper interest than that which attaches to any locality, and that is the interest of the whole. [Loud applause.] It is because I recognize in this enterprise the features of its nationality; because I believe that it will not only prove advantageous to my section, and not only prove advantageous to the localities through which it will be actually constructed, but that it will shower and spread its blessings upon every part of the United States, that I believe it ought to command the sympathy and support and votes of all. [Loud applause.]

As a mere Government enterprise, I believe, gentlemen, that it ought to be undertaken. If it were right and fit and proper under any circumstances for the Government of the United States, in its own name and by its own agencies, and with its own money, to construct a great national highway merely in aid of its military arm, I think that the circumstances of the case would justify it in a necessary expenditure of money here. [Applause.]

It is a well-established fact, as I find made the subject of a report of a committee on that subject to the last House of Representatives, that the interest on the reasonable cost of this entire enterprise does not amount to more than would be saved in the transportation of materials and supplies, and the furnishing of troops that are now stationed along the route on which that road would pass. [Applause.]

Then, gentlemen, if the Government itself, as a measure of its own, would be justified in being at the sole cost of this structure, there certainly is no harm in its co-operating and helping to the extent to which it will be asked. Upon principle, gentlemen, as a general rule, I think we would all agree that Government subsidies ought not to be granted; *prima facie* they ought to be withheld; a strong case ought to be made to show an exception, but there is no rule in government, in law, in politics or in society which does not admit and require exceptions. And it is because I believe that subsidies ought rarely to be granted that I advocate the aid that is required for the successful construction of this Texas and Pacific Railway; because I believe the facts which are presented constitute it a just and reasonable exception to the operation of such a rule. [Applause.]

I believe another sufficient reason, gentlemen, is one that has been adverted to in the very able presentation of the subject by the chairman of the local committee, Col. Broadhead, this morning—that it is required by a sound and healthy competition.

Now, I am in favor—as I suppose and believe, gentlemen, that you all are—of building up, not tearing down; and if the object simply was to create a competition, to establish a rivalry to the existing Pacific Railroad, that of itself would not be a sufficient reason for our action. And another reason would be that the Government ought not to enter into competition with itself; having already advanced largely to the Union Pacific and the Central Pacific, that it ought not to undertake the construction of a competing line of railroad without a sufficient excuse. It has no interest as a Government in building an opposition to itself. But, gentlemen, the circumstances of the case as shown, point out the absolute necessity, to the existence of that sound and healthy rivalry which is required for the purpose of promoting the best interests which are sought to be obtained by an inter-railway communication between the two oceans, that this, the last and longest deferred, ought to have been the first in construction. [Applause.] For these reasons, gentlemen, and for many others which time does not permit detail of, I am frank to say that I am cordially in sympathy with the object which has called us together. I have no right to speak for any one else, but I believe the people among whom I was born and raised, and where it was my proud lot to have cast my destiny, are also largely in the same sympathy and state of mind. I believe that the city of Cincinnati, asking no special favors in regard to this matter, earnestly desires, for the sake of the whole country, that it may soon have the welcome news that the iron horse is lapping its parched tongue in the waves of the Pacific Ocean [applause]; for wherever there is a railroad that bears wealth and trade and commerce from one section to the other, Cincinnati will find some way to tap it. [Applause.]

Gentlemen, I crave your pardon for intruding upon you at this time any of these remarks; I knew not what else to say in answer and response to the call which I received to occupy this Chair. I return my grateful thanks, and trust that you will lend me your aid and co-operation in the effort to bring to a successful and harmonious conclusion the proceedings and deliberations which are now to take place. I am very much obliged to you, and will now announce to you that the Convention is ready to proceed with its further business.

At the conclusion of Mr. Mathews' speech there were loud cries for Gen. Preston, of Kentucky.

Gen. Preston, on taking the chair as Vice-President, amidst great applause, addressed the Convention as follows:

GENTLEMEN OF THE CONVENTION:—I feel it due to acknowledge the honor you have done me by making me the Vice-President of the body assembled here to-day. I came from my home after a long retirement, induced to do so by the magnitude of the object which convokes you all, and to meet many faces that I have greeted with pleasure, because they are marked by momentous events of my life. I feel happy to say that you are here combined for a noble purpose, and to bring all that energy and power I know to belong to the gentlemen of the North who inaugurated and fostered this enterprise, with that sincerity, candor and honesty that have marked my associates of the South. [Applause.] It is only by that combination that we can succeed. We may indulge in platitudes on the subject of the necessity of progress, but we must know that the great routes which now so fortunately connect the waters of the Atlantic with the Pacific Ocean, leave the South untouched. It is in that spirit that discerning and enterprising men have seen that all that territory has to be opened to commerce, and that our object is confined not by the jurisdictional lines of the United States, but stretches beyond our frontier, in order that the full tide of wealth and commerce may pour northward through this valley of the Mississippi. [Applause.]

You talk about a trunk line, and you make it on the rough diagram which we have before us, at the point indicated by the cars. Where does that trunk line lie? And if, in the desultory remarks I make, I do not touch upon ground already occupied by the very able address of the Chairman of the Convention, and also by the Chairman of the local committee that invited us here, I will offer only an impression or two in acknowledgment of your call in regard to the purposes for which we are assembled.

When we turn to that map, we see that even there, by some of those singular and mysterious laws, such as the chemist witnesses in the angles of crystallization—which, proceeding with a regularity that is inscrutable to human wisdom, yet propagate themselves in certain lines—that the Southern statesmen and soldiers have never failed, as they pass towards Mexico, but have swept down all barriers, and have enlarged this empire by their energy and enterprise until we gained vast territories and narrowed the frontiers of Mexico. [Applause.]

In the vicissitudes of my life I have passed, from day to day, on foot from Shreveport over that line westward to our frontier on the Rio Grande, and walked from day to day through the valleys of Mexico to the central city of that empire. I have stood at San Luis Potosi in the solitude of my march, which only lent, I think, more interest to my meditation. As I came near the great mines of the Real del Monte, near San Luis Potosi—the object of Gen. Taylor when he pushed his armies southward towards Buena Vista—when I saw the mineral wealth that laid there untouched and under the clumsy management of Mexican machinery and Mexican direction, and thought of the power behind me, of the American mind, of the American invention, of the American patience and the American talent for organization, I did believe as faithfully as Benton, when he pointed westward for the East, that through this very point would spring a railway to Mexico that would bring us the trade of sixty millions a year and ten millions of people. [Applause.] And that is the power, sir, that the South holds in this Convention. [Great applause.] It is her heritage from God. And that we come to offer, with all our aid, at the feet of this Convention, to swell the stream of your commerce and civilization, which is the true treasure of the country, not only to St. Louis, but Memphis, New Orleans, Vicksburg, and even remote Kentucky and Virginia, assembled here to-day, and to let that fertilizing stream of wealth and commerce with augmented volume flow northwardly in its rightful direction, like the gulf stream, which, breaking by some mysterious law through the Isthmus of America, yet sweeps with its warm waters through icy northern seas, giving life and comfort to commerce, clothing with verdure mighty England, and diffusing wealth to the civilized world. [Applause.]

Let us, then, make the iron river, more certain in its delivery than the treacherous waves of ocean. There is none of the wealth of man that passes to the bottom of the deep in railway transportation. It has none of the accidents that belong to maritime commerce. The railway is a power controlled and regulated by man, and perfectly under the command of commerce as the steed that knows his rider. We can by our energy make that road; and here, representing and associated with men whose names are historic—whose whole lives have shown that they have been true to their promises; men from those States most immediately affected by this vast enterprise—we come forward in response to the call of gentlemen of the most enterprising minds of the North, to say, "Count on us. Our hearts want peace. We know no qualification of our word when it is given. [Applause.] We change no opinions. We are simple and poor, but industrious. We pay our portion of the taxes with a crop that constitutes seven-tenths of all of your export—seven times more than all the protected manufactures of the North. The cotton-fields of the South, though disturbed, are yet plentifully producing the most gold-buying product of America." [Applause.]

We are now trying to pay your taxes; to bear the burden of the debt, and stand by the Government with the fidelity that has always marked the Southern character; and I here, in the face of these gentlemen assembled, say to gentlemen more familiar with Northern organizations and Northern enterprises, that we come with sincere hearts to aid in the great work of conducting this magnificent enterprise to successful completion. [Applause.]

If this combination were a clique or a ring, or a committee assembled at Washington, I would not be in it. [Applause.] But it is here in the presence of representative men from thirty States that I join with the Chairman in saying that I feel happy to hear the assurances he gave from the great State of Ohio, that our neighbor would take the lead in this just and great enterprise, until hereafter, when men look around and see what we men were doing in this generation, whatever our faults may have been, or whatever our faults may be, they will see that we are yet true to our country, and that through our delegations in Congress, and our Senators, when you look for the most steadfast friends of the great Texas and Pacific Railroad, you may still count on the Southern States. [Applause.]

I feel that I am trespassing too much on your indulgence [cries, " Go on !"] in acknowledgment for which I have nothing more to say, except that with my delegation I shall be here to co-operate in harmonious action towards the great common end, so that when the after-ages shall ask what we have done, we can point to the Southern Railroad—for it is Southern—and say, " We, men of the South, under many sorrows and disasters, at least have left this as a generous legacy to the glorious commerce of America." [Loud applause.]

Mr. Imboden, of Virginia: I rise for the purpose of submitting a resolution, probably one as great in importance as any to be considered. I move, sir, that a committee consisting of two from each State be appointed by each State and Territory, to be designated by the delegations from the States and Territories, as a business committee on resolutions. I indicate two from each State and Territory, sir, because the essential business of this Convention will have to be considered by that committee, and the larger the committee, the greater weight and force its recommendations will have in this body. I feel satisfied, sir, from the spirit that has been manifested here, that if a discreet selection is made—and I have no doubt it will be done—by each delegation, that the report of that committee will carry such weight when it comes to this body that we shall be saved much time in its consideration, and it will be accepted as the voice of the body.

Mr. E. N. Hill: Before the motion is put I desire to state that I have an additional report from the Committee on Permanent Organization.

The President: The report will be read in advance of the motion.

Mr. Hill: I present the names of the Vice-Presidents and Assistant Secretaries.

Mr. Smoot, of the District of Columbia: Will the gentleman please turn his face this way and lift up his voice? [Laughter.]

Mr. Hill: I have had some little difficulty in getting the names, as they were generally put down in pencil and very hurriedly. If the delegates find any name is wrong I will correct it as soon as the correction is made known to me.

Mr. Hill then read the report as follows:

ALABAMA—Francis B. Clark, Eli S. Shorter, Thomas H. Spence, Joseph Hodgson, Vice-Presidents; H. Pillons, Secretary.

ARIZONA—Wm. G. Boyle, Vice-President and Assistant Secretary.

ARKANSAS—John R. Eakin, Tyree F. Hill, J. T. Trezevant, Sr., Vice-Presidents; M. S. Wieder, Assistant Secretary.

CALIFORNIA—J. W. A. Wright, Vice-President; Assistant Secretary, no appointment.

CONNECTICUT—E. B. Goodsell, Vice-President and Assistant Secretary.

GEORGIA—W. B. Johnson, J. O. Matthewson, Vice-Presidents; C. C. Hammond, Assistant Secretary.

ILLINOIS—Joseph Gillespie, T. J. Carter, W. T. Holliday, C. A. Beecher, Vice-Presidents; David J. Lonergan, Assistant Secretary.

INDIANA—E. S. Alward, Leonidas Sexton, Vice-Presidents; E. F. Claypool, Assistant Secretary.

IOWA—J. A. Williamson, J. W. Hammond, Vice-Presidents; J. W. Hammond, Assistant Secretary.

KANSAS—A. Caldwell, Lem. T. Smith, G. A. Crawford, C. K. Halliday, B. P. McDonald, Vice-Presidents; R. B. Morris, Assistant Secretary.

KENTUCKY—Ex-Gov. Beriah Magoffin, J. W. Kearney, George B. Hodge, Vice-Presidents; B. Smith, Assistant Secretary.

LOUISIANA—Gen. P. T. G. Beauregard, G. L. Smith, Alex. Boarman, J. H. Kennard, J. J. Horan, Vice-Presidents; E. S. Ranlett, Assistant Secretary.

MICHIGAN—J. B. Hays, Gen. F. H. May, Vice-Presidents; H. R. Boyle, Assistant Secretary.

MINNESOTA—W. R. Marshall, Vice-President; W. F. Davidson, Assistant Secretary.

MISSISSIPPI—N. H. Harris, Chas. E. Furlong, W. T. Martin, Alex. Warner, E. D. Richardson, Vice-Presidents; J. H. Sullivan, Assistant Secretary.

MISSOURI—J. O. Broadhead, W. P. Hall, R. T. Van Horn, W. F. Switzler, B. F. McAfee, Vice-Presidents; D. H. MacAdam, Assistant Secretary.

NEBRASKA—J. N. Converse, H. C. Lett, J. M. Eddy, Vice-Presidents; D. H. Wheeler, Assistant Secretary.

NEVADA—George Turner, Vice-President and Assistant Secretary.

NEW YORK—W. P. Groom, J. J. Anderson, H. G. Marquand, D. M. Hildreth, D. P. Seligman, Vice-Presidents; Assistant Secretary, no appointment.

NEW JERSEY—I. D. Harrison, J. F. Rusling, J. D. W. Vroom, Vice-Presidents; James Buchanan, Assistant Secretary.

NEW MEXICO—M. S. Otero, G. A. Hayward, A. C. Erfort, Vice-Presidents; S. M. Eckles, Assistant Secretary.

NORTH CAROLINA—William Johnson, Columbus Mills, M. P. Pegram, Robert Bridges, E. C. Eades, Vice-Presidents; Assistant Secretary, no appointment.

OHIO—Guido Marx, C. W. Otis, G. W. Jones, Vice-Presidents; A. W. Francisco, Assistant Secretary.

PENNSYLVANIA—D. J. Morrell, C. M. McCarthy, A. L. Snowden, J. T. Wetherell, T. Beaver, Vice-Presidents; B. F. Jones, Assistant Secretary.

SOUTH CAROLINA—Ex-Gov. Rufus K. Scott, J. B. Palmer, William Wallace, F. W. McMasters, Vice-Presidents; E. W. Teefle, Assistant Secretary.

TENNESSEE—E. W. Cole, Thomas Claiborn, J. M. Fleming, H. G. Smith, J. W. Clapp, Vice-Presidents; H. M. Doak, Assistant Secretary.

TEXAS—T. B. Sexton, H. B. Andrews, S. J. Edwards, Vice-Presidents; B. B. Paddock, Assistant Secretary.

VIRGINIA—E. W. Hubbard, Franklin Stearns, J. L. Cochran, Vice-Presidents; Chas. Ellis, Assistant Secretary.

WISCONSIN—Geo. W. Cobb, Vice-President and Assistant Secretary.

WYOMING—Silas Reed, Vice-President and Assistant Secretary.

DISTRICT OF COLUMBIA—S. S. Smoot, Vice-President and Assistant Secretary.

Mr. HILL: The resolution under which this was presented was that each State should submit the names of not more than five Vice-Presidents and one Assistant Secretary.

Mr. LARKIN: I believe Wisconsin is represented in this Convention, but I see no names on the list from that State. If in order, I move that my colleague, George W. Cobb, be put upon that list.

Mr. SMOOT, of the District of Columbia: Mr. Chairman, the committee has neglected to report any Vice-President from the place where we have to go to get our legislation, namely, Washington City. I was a member of the committee, and handed my name to the honorable Secretary at the meeting at the Southern Hotel, and I represent the place where all the legislation is to come from to carry out the measure we propose, and I don't propose to be omitted. [Laughter.]

THE PRESIDENT: I would suggest that any omission will be supplied by the delegations sending their names to the Secretary of the Convention.

MR. SMOOT: Then I would like to give my name to the Secretary of the Convention. I will do so for fear he may forget it. Samuel S. Smoot—S-m-oo-t, Smoot. [Laughter and applause.]

MR. IMBODEN, of Virginia: I would like to inquire what has become of my motion?

THE PRESIDENT: The Chair thinks it is proper that the report of the committee should be first disposed of before any motions are acted upon. The report has now been read; what shall be done with it?

A DELEGATE: I move that it be adopted, and that any omissions in the names of Vice-Presidents from different States be corrected by the Secretary.

THE PRESIDENT: It is moved and seconded that the report of the Committee on Permanent Organization be adopted.

The question was put and the motion was carried.

COMMITTEE ON RESOLUTIONS.

THE PRESIDENT: The motion of the gentleman from Virginia, Mr. Imboden, is now in order, which is that the Convention proceed to appoint a Committee on Resolutions, consisting of two from each delegation of the States and Territories, to be designated by them respectively.

MR. SMITH, of Tennessee: I move to amend that resolution by providing that all resolutions offered to this Convention shall be referred to the Committee on Resolutions without debate.

MR. IMBODEN, of Virginia: That is a substantive proposition, and, with all respect to the gentleman, I think it should be adopted separately from the one I offered.

THE PRESIDENT: The question is on the adoption of the motion of the gentleman from Virginia, to appoint a Business Committee on Resolutions in the mode designated.

The question was put and the motion was agreed to.

THE PRESIDENT: It is now moved that all resolutions offered to the Convention by individual members be referred without debate to that committee.

MR. MACADAM, of St. Louis: I move, sir, to strike out the words "without debate." I take it that it is one of the purposes for which we are here assembled—to discuss propositions which are presented.

A DELEGATE: I move to lay the amendment on the table.

ANOTHER DELEGATE: The words "without debate" is the best thing in it.

THE PRESIDENT: It is moved and seconded that all resolutions offered by individual members be referred to the Committee on Resolutions without debate; it is also moved to amend that by striking out the words "without debate." The question will be on the amendment.

The question was put and the motion to strike out the words "without debate" was lost.

THE PRESIDENT: The question is now upon the original motion to refer all resolutions to the committee without debate.

The question was put and the motion was carried.

THE PRESIDENT: The first business in order after the adoption of this motion is to execute it, and that is to appoint the committee. For that purpose the Secretary of the Convention will call the roll of States and Territories; the delegations, as they are called, will respond by naming two persons to act on that committee.

The Secretary then proceeded to call the roll, and the following were announced as the Committee on Resolutions:

ALABAMA—F. B. Clark, Thomas H. Price.
ARIZONA—W. G. Boyle.
ARKANSAS—James R. Pettigrew, Frank T. Doswell.
CALIFORNIA—J. W. A. Wright, D. Felsenheld.
GEORGIA—Ed. C. Anderson, Geo. W. Adair.
ILLINOIS—J. M. Bailey, E. B. Buck.
INDIANA—Richard W. Thompson, M. L. Bundy.
IOWA—J. A. Williams, J. T. Baldwin.

KANSAS—L. T. Smith, Geo. A. Crawford.
KENTUCKY—E. D. Stanford, J. B. Bowman.
LOUISIANA—H. J. Hearsay, J. W. Stoutemeyer.
MICHIGAN—W. R. Bowes, F. H. May.
MINNESOTA—W. R. Marshall, Wm. F. Davidson.
MISSISSIPPI—E. D. Richardson, Upton M. Young.
MISSOURI—J. O. Broadhead, R. T. Van Horn.
NEBRASKA—J. T. Converse, J. M. Eddy.
NEVADA—George Turner.
NEW JERSEY—John H. Stewart, Ed. T. Green.
NEW MEXICO—R. S. Elliott, M. S. Otero.
NEW YORK—John J. Anderson, H. G. Marquand.
NORTH CAROLINA—C. Mills, William Johnson.
OHIO—W. S. Streater, Jas. H. Laws.
SOUTH CAROLINA—William Wallace, J. B. Blimmer.
TENNESSEE—Jacob Palmer, Charles McGee.
TEXAS—T. J. Campbell, J. G. Walker.
VIRGINIA—H. C. Cabell, R. W. Hunter.
WISCONSIN—C. H. Larkin, Geo. W. Cobb.

THE PRESIDENT: The Business Committee on Resolutions, as ordered by the resolution to that effect, is now constituted. If proper, they can withdraw for the purpose of preparing their report.

ADJOURNMENT.

MR. ANDERSON, of Virginia: I move, when this Convention adjourn, it adjourn to meet to-morrow morning at 11 o'clock.

MR. SMOOT, of Washington, D. C.: I move to amend the motion of my honorable friend by making it 10 o'clock instead of 11.

MR. ANDERSON: I will accept the amendment.

MR. WRIGHT, of California: As chairman of the California delegation, the delegation of that State requested me to present a series of resolutions, that they might be referred to the Committee on Resolutions already appointed, and, although the resolutions are to be referred without debate, as these resolutions are brief, they request that they be read before they are referred.

THE PRESIDENT: The resolutions will be read as soon as the motion for adjournment has been acted upon. The question now is on the motion of the gentleman from Virginia, that when this Convention adjourn, it adjourn until to-morrow morning at 10 o'clock.

The question was put and the motion was carried.

RESOLUTIONS OF CALIFORNIA DELEGATION.

Mr. Wright: As chairman of the delegation of California, I am requested to read the resolutions. Mr. Chairman and members of the Convention, these resolutions are presented by a delegation from a State, sir, which you all know is as much interested in the speedy construction of this Pacific Railroad as any of the different States of the Union, and for these reasons I beg leave to read these resolutions before they are referred to the Committee on Resolutions.

Whereas, The demands of our people are steadily increasing for cheap transportation and greater facilities for the same between the older States of this Union and the Pacific Coast; and

Whereas, Permanent competition, protected by judicious legislation, is our surest method of securing cheap transportation; and

Whereas, In the absence of efficient routes of transportation by water, the construction of a second railroad across our continent becomes our only means to secure the much needed competition with the lines of the Union and Central Pacific as well as with that branch of the Central Pacific known as the Southern Pacific of California, or with existing lines running westward; and

Whereas, The Texas and Pacific Railroad Company, which proposes to construct their lines of rail and telegraph through to the Pacific Coast at San Diego, offers the most feasible and least expensive plan to our Government and people for the establishment of this most desirable enterprise; and

Whereas, It is impossible for any private corporation with its unaided capital to accomplish a task so herculean, especially when its efforts are at every step combated before the people as well as in our Legislatures and in Congress by a powerful monopoly, built up by injudicious gifts of the people's land, and which now seeks to control forever the transportation interests of our Pacific States; and

Whereas, The construction of this additional railroad to the waters of the Pacific, if established and maintained as a competing line, will not only relieve from unjust exactions and discriminations our commercial, manufacturing and agricultural interests, but will develop vast regions of agricultural and mineral wealth and fill them with an industrious and thrifty people; and

Whereas, Many representative bodies of our industrial classes, noted for their conservative and determined opposition to the lavish and unrestricted subsidies granted in the past to various railroad corporations, and also many Boards of Trade and State Legislatures, have by resolution requested Congress to grant to that truly national enterprise, the Texas and Pacific Railroad, the moderate aid now asked, provided that such aid is surrounded by the safeguards necessary to protect the Government from fraud and the people from wrong; therefore,

Resolved, That the National Transportation Convention, composed of delegates from States and Territories and assembled at St. Louis, this November 23d, 1875, do most respectfully and earnestly petition Congress that at as early a period as possible during its approaching session it will consider and grant the earnest wishes of our people, expressed in many forms, for properly guarded National aid to secure a speedy construction of the Texas and Pacific Railroad to its western terminus at San Diego.

Resolved, That we heartily recommend that each State Legislature be earnestly requested to instruct, and the people to petition their members of Congress to pass, at an early day, the bill which was reported to them last winter by a special committee, and known as the Texas and Pacific Railroad Bill, seeing to it that the United States Government shall ever exercise such control of that road as will maintain it for all time as a competing road across the continent, and that all unjust discriminations against any railroad which connects with it, at any point east or west, shall be prevented, in order that the equal rights of all cities and localities to its benefits may be inviolably maintained.

MR. WRIGHT: Of course, Mr. Chairman, I have no time to make any extended remarks, but I will mention one point in this connection. The name of the Southern Pacific Railroad is designated there, and I wish to say that the delegation from California are anxious for this Convention to understand one point, that whereas you gentlemen here on this side of the Rocky Mountains, when you speak of the Southern Pacific, refer to that road which is on our most southern territory; the people of California, when they refer to the Southern Pacific Railroad, have reference to a branch road of the Central Pacific; and in order that there may be no misunderstanding, I desire that this Convention may understand that when we refer to the Southern Pacific Railroad we do not refer to the Southern Pacific Railroad which is called by that name on the other side of the Rocky Mountains, otherwise citizens of California might claim that this Convention was in favor of the Central Pacific or its branches. [Applause.]

THE PRESIDENT: The resolutions will be referred to the Committee on Resolutions.

A REQUEST FROM THE COMMITTEE OF ARRANGEMENTS.

MR. FILLEY, of St. Louis: The Committee of Arrangements are anxious that the chairman of each State delegation shall name to the Committee of Arrangements, who will meet in the committee-room back of the platform, the number of delegates in attendance, that they may be supplied with tickets to the banquet and badges and tickets to the excursion. The delegates from St. Louis who are subscribers are entitled to tickets, which will be supplied at the post office. The delegates from the State of Missouri will be supplied in the committee-room. Now, if the chairmen of these delegations will report at the committee-room, they will be supplied with banquet tickets and excursion tickets and badges for their entire delegations. [Applause.]

INVITATION TO THE EXPOSITION OF AUTHORS, FOR THE BENEFIT OF THE WOMEN'S CHRISTIAN HOME.

THE PRESIDENT: Gentlemen, I have received the following communication which I desire to read:

ST. LOUIS, November 23, 1875.

To the President of the Southern Pacific Railroad Convention:

SIR:—I beg to lay before the Convention the accompanying note from the ladies who are giving a magnificent entertainment at the Rink for the purpose of erecting a suitable building for the Women's Christian Home. Believing that there can be but one view, and that in favor of the work which was conceived and is being carried out by the ladies of this city, I submit this communication.

Very respectfully,

ERASTUS WELLS.

The invitation is as follows:

Hon. Erastus Wells:

DEAR SIR:—

Knowing so well in the past your ready heart and helping hand, allow me through you to tender to the members of the Railroad Convention an invitation to be present in a body at the Rink, after the adjournment of the Convention. The ladies feel assured that not only will those gentlemen enjoy the reward of a good deed done in behalf of a noble charity, but they will there find evidence of what the brain and ingenuity of ladies of a sister State may accomplish, and may realize to some extent the results to follow from their own grand enterprise, calculated to bind us more and more together with hooks of steel. Very respectfully,

MISS PINK HAMILTON.

THE PRESIDENT: It was suggested by Col. Broadhead that the Committee on Resolutions meet at five o'clock this afternoon at the Southern Hotel, where an appropriate room will be provided.

ADDITIONAL RESOLUTIONS.

MR. SMITH, of Tennessee: A Convention was held a few days ago at Memphis which purported, to a large extent, to represent the States of the South in respect of the matter of the Southern Pacific Railway. I hold in my hand the resolutions which that Convention adopted, with a request that they should be submitted to this Convention assembled here to-day. They are short and are proper to be heard and understood, we think, by all the members of the Convention, rather than to be referred without reading to the Committee on Resolutions. I will read them:

The National Government furnished the means necessary to construct the railways connecting the country of the Pacific with the northern portion of the Union, which railways, while useful and beneficial to the whole Union, are peculiarly and in a large degree exclusively beneficial to the States of the North, and have a tendency, existing alone, to the prejudice of the interests of the States of the South.

The people of the North were unable, without Governmental aid, to construct the Northern railways; much less are the Southern people now, or so far as the distant future can be foreseen will they be able, without Governmental aid, to construct a railway with the necessary connections, which shall link their destinies and interests with the country on the Pacific Coast, as well as with the whole country of the Union.

We have heretofore borne and will continue to bear cheerfully, according to the measure of our ability, the burden upon the common revenue of the debt created to construct the railways of the North.

In view of these considerations, and of others not now necessary to state, the people of the South appeal to their fellow-countrymen of the North and to the Government of the Union, to bestow upon them such favor and substantial aid as will enable them to construct a railroad, with suitable connections, which shall unite them on the one side with the great country of the West, and on the other with the rich and prosperous and powerful country of the North.

And the more readily do we make this appeal, fully assured that the aid may be bestowed in such manner as will not increase the debt of the Government, while it will aid greatly to restore and augment the prosperity and happiness of the people of the South. Therefore,

Resolved, That we ask the Congress of the United States to grant the credit of the National Government to aid and accomplish the construction of the Texas and Pacific Railroad from its eastern terminus at Shreveport, in Louisiana, to the coast of the Pacific at San Diego or other suitable place on that coast; and also to aid and accomplish the construction of such railways as will connect the eastern terminus with the cities of Memphis, of Vicksburg and of New Orleans, with such conditions and provisions as will effectually secure to the lines of roads leading to these cities from the eastern terminus of the Texas and Pacific Railway, and along the whole line of that railway, absolute equality as between themselves, and as to all other railway connections and intersections, in the advantages and facilities for the transportation of freight and passengers, and for all other uses to which the Texas and Pacific Railway can be applied; and with such provisions and conditions as will compel the construction of the road continuously from the point of its present completion in Texas to the western terminus on the Pacific Coast.

Resolved, That the President of this Convention appoint a committee of ten persons, who shall be charged with the duty and power to take such measures as may hereafter be proper to prosecute the objects of the foregoing resolution.

Resolved, That the omission of St. Louis in the foregoing resolution is not to be understood or construed as the expression of any opposition or hostility to that city, it being the desire to ask Congress to give its aid to a southern road on the 32d parallel of latitude, which we understand to be the Southern Texas Pacific Railroad, for which we have assembled in convention here in the city of Memphis.

THE PRESIDENT: The resolutions will be referred under the order of the Convention.

MR. HALLIDAY, of Kansas: I desire to offer the following, and wish to have it referred to the Committee on Resolutions, as a branch to the main line proposed by the resolutions just offered and previously offered. I will read:

Resolved, That the Congress of the United States shall be and the same are hereby memorialized to grant at the same time and in the same act of Congress, and as an essential, component part of said act, the same amount of aid per mile upon the same terms and conditions as that provided for the main line of the Texas Pacific Railroad, for the construction of a branch railroad of the same grade and character, from the point on the Atchison, Topeka and Santa Fe Railroad where said railroad crosses the western boundary of the State of Texas, and makes its southwestwardly direction and intersection of said main line at the point where said main line crosses the Rio Grande river, or at some eligible point on said main line eastward of said river.

THE PRESIDENT: The gentleman will hand his resolutions to the Secretary and they will be referred under the order of the Convention.

MR. PALMER, of South Carolina: I desire to offer the following:

Resolved, That the basis of the action of this Convention is declared to be that the road in the interest of which it is held shall be required to extend the same facilities and give the same rates in freight and passengers to all connecting railroads, whether terminating at Southern or Northern cities.

THE PRESIDENT: The resolution will be referred to the Committee on Resolutions under the rule.

EXPLANATION.

MR. SLAYBACK, of St. Louis: In order that there may be no misunderstanding, I wish to state that the delegates from Missouri, by calling at the room in the rear of the platform, can get their badges and tickets.

MR. SMOOT: As a courtesy to the ladies of St. Louis who have extended an invitation to this body to visit an entertainment by them for benevolent purposes, I move that the invitation be accepted, and that as many gentlemen of this Convention, either individually or in a body, who can attend, will attend. I move that a vote of thanks be extended to the ladies of St. Louis. [Applause.]

The question was put and the motion was carried.

The Convention thereupon adjourned until to-morrow morning at 10 o'clock.

SECOND DAY.

WEDNESDAY, NOVEMBER 24th, 1875.

The Convention met pursuant to adjournment.

THE PRESIDENT: The first business in order will be the reading of the Journal of yesterday.

READING OF JOURNAL DISPENSED WITH.

MR. E. N. HILL, of Arkansas: I move that the reading of the Journal be dispensed with.

The question was put and the motion was carried.

COMMUNICATION.

THE PRESIDENT: I have received a telegram from Mr. Frank Ogden, Graham, Texas, which I will take the liberty to read at this time:

GRAHAM, TEXAS, November 23, 1875.

To the President of the Railroad Convention:

Your Convention can, if it will, exert the influence to complete the Texas Pacific Railway, which national necessities demand and local requirements urge. Thousands of emigrants are coming in—an evidence that the Government will no longer waive, but hasten to execute, the trust.

Respectfully, FRANK OGDEN.

LETTER OF GEN. SIMPSON.

The following letter from Gen. John H. Simpson, of the United States Engineer Corps, in answer to an invitation to be present at the Convention, was read by the Secretary, and was ordered to be published in the proceedings of the Convention:

ENGINEER OFFICE, UNITED STATES ARMY,
ST. LOUIS, MO., November 23, 1875.

Chauncey I. Filley, Esq., Chairman Committee of Arrangements, etc.:

DEAR SIR:—I feel honored by your invitation to join the excursion in compliment to the delegates to the National Railroad Convention convened in this city; but, in consequence of other engagements, will have reluctantly to decline.

The great Southern Atlantic and Pacific Railroad I have always regarded as essential to the country's continued prosperity, winter as well as summer; and as the Union Pacific and branches, in its Northern location, does not fulfill both conditions, and, besides, does not immediately promote the interests of the Southern States and of Mexico, I consider the Southern Pacific Railroad as well worthy of the most serious and immediate attention of the Government and of Congress, and I hope the Convention will not fail to excite in both such an interest as will insure the commencing and building of the road in the shortest possible time.

Very respectfully, your obedient servant,

J. H. SIMPSON, *Colonel of Engineers, U. S. A.*

REGULAR ORDER OF BUSINESS.

THE PRESIDENT: The Convention is now ready to proceed with business. I will inquire if the Committee on Resolutions are ready to report?

ADDITIONAL DELEGATES.

CHAIRMAN OF INDIANA DELEGATION: Mr. Chairman, I have a communication setting out the appointment of two additional delegates from the State of Indiana.

MAYOR'S OFFICE,
TERRE HAUTE, IND., November 22, 1875.

To the Hon. James O. Broadhead, St. Louis:

I have this day appointed Hon. Julius W. Hanna as a delegate to the National Railway Convention to be held in your place, the 23d inst., *vice* Albert Bell, Esq., who is absent East, and unable to attend.

Very respectfully, your obedient servant,

U. B. EDMUNDS.

— 80 —

THE PRESIDENT: I have also the appointment of the Hon. Daniel Voorhies, of Indiana, by the Governor of that State.

CREDENTIALS.

MR. LEACH, of California: I ask leave, Mr. President, to present the credentials of John B. Stearns, of California. I ask to have his name entered as a delegate from California. He did not arrive yesterday.

THE PRESIDENT: The credentials of John B. Stearns, of Santa Barbara, California, with a commission issued by the Governor of that State, are presented; if there is no objection, his name will be enrolled as a member of the Convention.

ADDITIONAL DELEGATES.

The following additional delegates, who had not arrived on Tuesday, were enrolled:

MISSOURI—Hon. N. C. Hudson, R. L. Turpin, George W. Jones and W. Gibson.

KENTUCKY—J. A. Miller, B. S. Stewart, Henry Burnett, George C. Thompson and Col. Bradshaw.

NEW MEXICO—Martin B. Hayes.

KANSAS—L. R. Elliott.

ILLINOIS—Messrs. Bissell and Moberly.

TEXAS—W. G. Thomas, John M. Swishler, J. K. Burroughs, L. G. Edwards, J. E. Moore, C. C. Francis, H. L. Montrose, Joseph Magoffin, L. B. Hayes, J. P. Hagar, W. B. Blanchard, Will. J. Scott.

VIEWS OF COL. THOMAS A. SCOTT.

THE PRESIDENT: Gentlemen, I have received a communication from Col. Scott, President of the Texas and Pacific Railway Company, expressive of the policy of that Company, and his views in respect to the proper means to be taken to secure its accomplishment; by your leave I will read it.

SEVERAL DELEGATES: Leave, leave.

The President then read as follows:

St. Louis, November 23, 1875.

To the Hon. Stanley Mathews, President of the National Convention to consider the subject of the construction of a Pacific Railroad through the States and Territories of the Southwest:

My Dear Sir:—It gives me pleasure, in accordance with the invitation extended, to present, as briefly as the subject will admit, a few facts in regard to the Texas and Pacific Railway, in connection with the construction of a through line between the States and Territories of the South and Southwest and the Pacific Ocean. It is only necessary, I think, to state briefly the national character of this enterprise, and the urgent need for it, to enlist the cordial and earnest interest of this Convention and the country at large in its completion.

The present line to the Pacific, it is well known, follows generally the route of the forty-second parallel of north latitude as far as Great Salt Lake; and the entire country is now dependent upon that road for railway facilities to and from the Pacific coast. The mere presentation of this fact is sufficient in itself to show the necessity for the construction of another line. A territory over 700 miles wide, stretching along the entire South Atlantic coast and the Gulf of Mexico, and containing twelve millions of people, is without any direct communication with the waters of the Pacific, and its inhabitants are compelled to. make a long and expensive detour to reach the eastern terminus of the present line. To meet this want three other companies have been organized, at different times, to construct through lines across the continent. The one in which St. Louis was specially interested, and which seemed at one time to have secured the aid necessary for its prompt construction, was the thirty-fifth parallel, or the Atlantic and Pacific road; and we all remember the strong feeling manifested in favor of that enterprise by the people of San Francisco, and the determination evinced a few years since to make that line a success.

The same difficulty existed then as now, viz: the impossibility of negotiating securities, at any reasonable price, to an amount necessary to furnish the funds for constructing so long a road; and after maturely considering the subject, and discussing it very thoroughly and carefully, the friends of that enterprise believed that their true interest was to unite that line, by an extension from its present terminus at Vinita, to connect with the Texas and Pacific road—a line chartered on the thirty-second parallel, and by its geographical position having strong claims especially to the support of the southern and southwestern sections of our country. The kindly feeling which has always existed between St. Louis and the South no doubt helped to bring about this determination, but, at the same time, it was seen that provisions in the charter of the Texas and Pacific road, by which all connecting lines were placed upon an equal footing, would give St. Louis, through the Iron Mountain road to Texarkana, and the Atlantic and Pacific road, greater advantages than she would have derived from the construction of the thirty-fifth parallel line. This being the case, and it being quite as much to the advantage of the Texas and Pacific road that it should have direct communication with so important a city as St. Louis, and thus reach the country east and north of it, the scheme received the cordial assent of our company, and was presented in this shape before the last Congress. Its advantages to St. Louis have been fully discussed through its press, and I believe there is but one feeling upon the subject, and that is a cordial endorsement of the policy proposed, and a universal recognition of the advantages to be obtained by saving the construction of over 1,500 miles of railway, restoring to the Government over 30,000,000 of acres of land now donated for railway purposes, and concentrating upon one line the business which otherwise would be divided between two.

The Texas and Pacific now reaches from Shreveport and Texarkana, via Dallas, to near Fort Worth, and is intended to extend, via El Paso, through New Mexico and Arizona to San Diego on the Pacific Ocean; and as railway lines are now building from San Francisco to the southern part of the State, it will also have direct rail connection to San Francisco. The Atlantic and Pacific, by running southwest from Vinita, will strike this line east of the 104th meridian, and from that point west there will be but one trunk line to the Pacific. In this manner, and with the extensions hereafter referred to, the whole belt of country between St. Louis on the north and New Orleans and Galveston on the south, including every southern port on the Atlantic Coast, will be provided with its own highway to the Pacific, open at all times of the year, and crossing the mountains at an elevation not exceeding 5,000 feet, as against 8,000 on the northern line. This road will be unobstructed by snow, has an extremely favorable alignment, and presents to the Southern people the same advantages which are now enjoyed more especially by the people north of the Ohio river. As the country to be thus served by its construction embraces more than one-half of the entire territory of the United States, it demonstrates clearly the national character of the enterprise, which is also based—

1. Upon the advantages to the Government itself in the direct management and large economies of its military, Indian, postal and territorial departments.

2. Upon the advantages to the people of the country of a competing line between the two oceans.

3. Upon its beneficial effect especially upon all the lines of railway in the South.

4. Upon the advantages accruing to the leading industries of the whole country, by the demand for labor and material of all kinds, consequent upon the construction of the line ; and,

5. Upon the increased revenue of the Government from its sales of lands brought into market by the road, and the great additional values that will be created as a basis for taxation for the Government.

1. The records of the Government show clearly the enormous expenditure now required to ineffectually protect the regions through which this road will run. There are at this time over twelve regiments of infantry and cavalry stationed in Texas, New Mexico and Arizona, whose utmost efforts cannot make large portions of that territory safe for persons and property. A reasonable estimate of the cost of maintaining each regiment per year is one million to one million and a half of dollars, so that the Government now expends annually perhaps about fifteen millions of dollars in trying to do the work which the construction of a single line of railway has effectually done along the Central and Union Pacific roads, that territory being now protected by less than two regiments. The charges for transportation are so onerous in the southern territory, and the cost of subsisting troops so enormous, that this outlay cannot be largely reduced except by the Government securing the advantages of railway communication. Experience has shown conclusively that when Indian parties, on their return from forays upon the settlements, can be intercepted through the medium of telegraphic communication and steam travel, their raids soon come to an end; and in the country now occupied by the Kansas, the Union and the Central Pacific roads —that was formerly devastated by Indian hostilities—there is absolute safety for both persons and property. With the Southern line completed, the Government would require the services of not exceeding one-fifth the number of troops now employed, and could thus save from ten to twelve millions of dollars per year, and in addition secure a much better service, that would render this vast region perfectly safe and be the means of providing for the development of new sources of great wealth and value to the nation. The official records

of the War and Navy Departments show, as appears by the reports of their Secretaries to the Congress that passed the bill under which the present Pacific road was built, that the cost of transportation at that time was $7,357,781 per annum—an expense now reduced, through the removal of the causes which necessitated it, to about half a million of dollars yearly.

2. The feeling of the country has been strongly enlisted for some years past in the problems connected with cheap transportation, and, incidentally, with the development of large tracts of country now closed to settlement by reason of the difficulty of conveying the products of the soil to market. In the States east of the Mississippi, water channels furnish one of the solutions to this question; but west of the Mississippi, where the great rivers are absent that furnish such important commercial highways, there is no resource but to build railways to develop the country, open it for settlement, and carry its mineral and agricultural products to market. In addition to this local business, the great trans-continental traffic between the far east and our own country and Europe, which is simply in its infancy, is pressing upon the attention of our country, and the single line now existing between the two oceans will, undoubtedly, soon fail to provide the necessary facilities for its accommodation. Not only this, but as long as this traffic is confined to a single line the competition which develops trade in other sections of the country is entirely wanting, and many branches of business which would increase rapidly, if furnished with anything like the advantages given to commerce east of the Mississippi river, are either entirely dormant or in a very depressed condition, owing to the burdens levied upon them. The Union, the Central and the Kansas Pacific roads have, as is well known, already developed an enormous mineral wealth throughout Colorado, the Salt Lake Valley, Nevada, and other regions on their routes, which has not only enriched those Territories, but also aided materially in the exchanges of our whole country. Reliable records show that the mineral regions of New Mexico and Arizona, to say nothing of Old Mexico, are certainly as rich, if not far richer, than the country lying on the now constructed line.

This territory is largely closed to development by reason of Indian depredations, and cannot be successfully opened except with such advantages for transportation as will enable the materials needed in the mining and reduction of the precious metals to be carried at reasonable cost, and with such protection for life and property as can only come through the building of this road. Certainly the State of

California will not object to the rich harvest which she must reap from the development of this territory, as her geographical position will enable her to control a liberal portion of the traffic thereby created.

It is believed that, without in any manner interfering with the legitimate business of the present line between Omaha and San Francisco, such a share of the hereafter increasing through traffic will be enjoyed by the contemplated Southern road, and such a large local business be developed, as will in an equal period of time, as fast as completed, insure quite satisfactory returns, and a traffic equal in quantity to that now transacted upon the Northern lines. With proper development all branches of traffic must rapidly increase, so that, although the Pacific roads may hereafter carry at a less price, they will, by carrying a larger traffic at a smaller profit, reap proper returns, and at the same time greatly reduce the expense to the producer and consumer. In this connection, it must be remembered that under the proposed bill the Government retains so direct a supervision of freight and passenger rates upon the Southern line, that under no circumstances can unreasonable or unjust charges be levied upon traffic, through a combination with competing roads or otherwise, or a monopoly be in any manner created.

3. In commenting upon the direct advantages to the Government, and the people of the whole country, it is also well to bear in mind the beneficial effects which this road cannot fail to have directly upon the entire Southern system of railways, and indirectly upon all the railway property of the country. Many of the Southern roads, it is well known, have been in a languishing condition since the war; they have had no special advantages to stimulate the revival of their traffic, and from the general prostration of the industries of their people, have been in trouble and embarrassment. There is no doubt that, with the opening of a direct line through to the Pacific Ocean, a large and entirely new traffic must pass over these lines, and in that way promptly aid in restoring their former prosperity. Not only this, but the section of country which a Southern Pacific road will develop will be one suitable in climate and production to the citizens of our Southern States, as well as of other countries, and consequently will invite emigration to a large extent, and in this manner bring in a new element to develop further wealth and increase the capital of the country.

Simple justice would seem to require that the Government should extend, if it properly can, the same aid towards furnishing facilities to the South which has been extended so lavishly to the North.

There is certainly nothing unreasonable in this view of the case when we remember that only $17,000,000 have been expended, since the organization of the Government, in aid of Southern improvements, while during the same period of time over $190,000,000 have been granted to the Northern States and Territories.

4. But the North, at this time, has an especial interest in the construction of this line. In the North are situated most of the rolling-mills, the car shops, and other manufactories which must furnish in great part the material to be used upon this road There is now, and has been for two years past, great distress prevailing through all our mining and manufacturing regions, consequent upon the greatly diminished demand for their productions. It is believed that it is not beyond the province of the Government in some measure to relieve this distress if it can do so by promoting, in some proper manner, an enterprise which is national in its character, the aid asked for which is so trifling in comparison with the assistance rendered by Great Britain, Russia, France, and other foreign countries to similar enterprises, and the completion of which would result in such great economies in the administration of the Government itself. The mining of the ore, the making of the pig, and the working up of so many tons of rails, all of which must be made of American iron or steel; the building of engines and freight and passenger cars needed to operate the line; the bridge and other materials necessary for the road, and the grading of the same, will require an army of laborers, whose earnings and the money expended for materials will enter into the channels of trade, stimulate the industries of the North and of the whole country, and go far towards inaugurating a return of our former prosperity.

There are also many additional reasons why this line should be built. The border States of Old Mexico, and ultimately its other States, will furnish to the road a very valuable traffic connected with the development and production of the vast mineral wealth well known to exist in Chihuahua, Sonora, and the other States which lie contiguous to our southern boundary. The same Indian devastations which have crippled Arizona and New Mexico have effectually stopped the satisfactory and profitable development of these mineral resources, and have made it impossible to work the many important mines, except at great peril to life. The population which will be immediately benefited by this line, in these and the adjoining States of Mexico, numbers over one million of people; and the relations between that country and our own are of such a character as to render it important to both Governments that there should be facilities for prompt communication, and, if necessary, rapid transportation of troops and supplies. If the facilities necessary to develop this country are not furnished by American enterprise, its trade will no doubt soon drift away from us into the control of other countries.

The plan which it is proposed to present to the Government has received very careful consideration, and, it is believed, is in such form that no loss can result from guarantee of the interest only upon the bonds needed to construct the line. The objections that have been so strongly urged to the action taken in the case of the Union and Central Pacific roads, are entirely obviated by the plan proposed. There the Government issued its own bonds, and then consented that they should be made a secondary lien to the bonds issued by the company, and their land grants were not reserved as a means of securing the Government. In the present case the company issues its own bonds, and as they will go into the hands of outside purchasers, with the guarantee of the Government upon them that the interest shall be paid (the company making ample provision through sinking fund, to be paid into the Treasury of the United States, to redeem the principal), there can, of course, be no interference with the mortgage securing the same, which, it is to be noted, is a first lien upon all the road, equipment, franchises and other property of the company, including the lands granted by the United States to aid the construction of the line. The utmost liability, then, which the Government might have to meet, if the line never earned a dollar, nor sold an acre of land, would be the interest at five per cent. upon the bonds ; and an examination of the earnings of the road already constructed between the two oceans, will, I think, remove any fear that may be entertained as to the ability of the Texas and Pacific road to meet the light payment that will be required of it.

It is proposed that the utmost limit of the bonds to be secured by a first mortgage upon the road, its franchises and lands granted by the Government, shall be $40,000 per mile, but that not exceeding $35,000 per mile on the average shall be used for construction, and not a dollar of these bonds shall be issued, except it be absolutely required to construct and equip the road, so that if less than $35,000 per mile be sufficient, only the amount of bonds required will be used. Should, however, the limit of $35,000 per mile be reached, the entire liability would be but $1,750 per mile per annum. The net earnings of the present Pacific line are from $6,000 to $8,000 per mile per annum ; it runs through a country by no means so rich in agricultural and mineral resources, and is subject to interruptions by snow and obstacles, which increase the cost of operation; so that if that line can earn a sum over all working expenses that would more than pay the interest on $100,000 per mile of bonds bearing six per cent. interest, there is no reason why the proposed line should not earn, beyond a possibility of a doubt, the interest on $35,000 per mile, at five per cent., should that amount be issued. It is also proposed that there shall be deposited with the Secretary of the Treasury $5,000 per mile of the $40,000 of bonds, so that in case, during construction, while the line is in an uncompleted condition, its earnings and the proceeds from land sales are not adequate to the interest as it matures on outstanding bonds, these reserved bonds can be sold by the Secretary at the expense of the company to place the treasury in funds to meet all liabilities of the Government. I do not see how a fairer proposition can be made to the Government, or one safer in every respect.

It will be remembered that under the original charter of the Texas and Pacific road, it is in the most explicit terms provided that it shall be an open highway to all connecting lines, without any discrimination whatever, so that each section of the country, and each road coming in connection with it, shall have equal advantages for the traffic passing to and from the trunk line to the Pacific and intermediate points.

This is especially to be borne in mind for the reason that efforts have been made to create a different impression, and to prejudice the enterprise by statements that the line would be run in the special interest of one or more Eastern roads, and therefore it was incumbent upon the others to oppose it. I desire to state explicitly and emphatically that neither the Pennsylvania Railroad nor any other railway company has any interest in the Texas and Pacific road; that it is entirely free from all alliances; that it is and will be run simply in its own interest, and that every line connecting with it can depend in the most unqualified way on receiving equally fair treatment at its hands; that it will not be used, so far as I have any connection with it or influence upon its management, to advance the interests of one road in preference to another; but that it shall be kept as it was chartered to be—an open highway between the waters of the Atlantic and Pacific—in order to secure to the roads of the Mississippi Valley and all others the advantages of this trunk line to the Pacific. It has been deemed essential that certain extensions should be made from it to form connections with the different systems of railways now reaching the Atlantic coast. Galveston and Houston being already provided for by the present roads from Dallas, Mineola and Longview, the connections referred to embrace a line to New Orleans, which, as one of the great commercial ports of the South, has a vital interest in a direct connection with this line; an extension to Vicksburg, so as to connect directly with the system of roads through Mississippi, Alabama, Georgia, North and South Carolina, Tennessee, Kentucky and Virginia; and an extension to Memphis, which will give that city a direct line, and excellent connections thence through the whole of Tennessee, Kentucky, Virginia, and the States lying east thereof. And in order that these important extensions may be provided for without increasing to any great extent the responsibility of the Government, it is proposed that there shall be no guarantee of the interest on bonds for 443 miles of the Texas and Pacific line now constructed and in course of construction east of Fort Worth, but that the aid heretofore asked for that portion of the road shall be used to complete the important connections to the cities named, the Texas and Pacific Company finding individual capital to finish the division referred to. St. Louis is provided for by the existing Iron Mountain road to Texarkana, and the existing connection by the Pacific road of Missouri, via Sedalia, and the Missouri, Kansas and Texas road; the proposed connection already referred to with the Atlantic and Pacific will give her an additional and even more direct route to the Pacific coast, and, as before noted, the same practical advantages which she would have had if the 35th parallel line had, as originally contemplated, been extended direct to San Francisco.

It is now almost impossible to negotiate railway bonds, either in this country or Europe, unless they are those of well-known and dividend-paying corporations, and it would be many years before a line of the magnitude of the Texas and Pacific road could place its securities, except at a very great sacrifice. One heavy item in the capital account of all companies so situated is the discount to which they inevitably have to submit in the negotiation of their bonds; these being sold at rates from 10 to 25 per cent. or more below par, the company perhaps receives on an average but three-fourths of the principal of the bonds, and yet has to pay interest upon the face value of the same, and meet the principal in full at maturity. This, of course, requires that a heavier charge shall be levied upon the community using the line, and thus traffic, that might be carried at low rates of transportation, is compelled to pay high prices, and the advantages of the road not only circumscribed, but an onerous burden placed upon the producer and consumer. This would more especially be the case in a line over 1,600 miles in length, where, unless the securities could be promptly negotiated, the interest would rapidly accumulate, and make a very heavy permanent charge upon capital. Under the ordinary arrangements made for the sale of bonds, it would be found impracticable to build more than about 100 to 200 miles of road per annum, so that before the entire line could be completed, ten years' interest would have accrued upon a portion of the securities used in its construction; while on the other hand, if the Government should lend its credit to this enterprise in the moderate form proposed, the entire line could be completed within four years, and a great saving be thus made to the company and to the public who would use the road.

The Convention will no doubt recognize the importance of harmonious and united action upon the question before them. It is, of course, natural that each special locality should highly estimate its own advantages, should honestly be convinced that it has special claims to consideration, and that it would possess facilities which should secure to it a direct connection with the main trunk road. The danger is, however, that in discussing the merits and advantages possessed by different cities and localities, attention may be drawn from the vital point, which is to secure the construction of the trunk line itself; and that those who are opposed to the road will be quick to seize upon any pretext for delaying its completion, or creating discord among its friends. There are, of course, interests which are inimical to the construction of any competing line, and there is no doubt that strong efforts will be made to prevent the Government from extending any proper aid to this great work. I believe, however, that if its friends are zealous in the support of the measure, and will concentrate their strength upon it, and not allow themselves to be entangled in outside issues, Congress will see that the enterprise is one of a national character, and demanded by so many considerations of sound economy and policy, that they will, under proper safeguards and restrictions, grant the aid desired, and enable the Southern road to the Pacific to become an accomplished fact.

In framing the bill which was laid before Congress last winter, every precaution was taken to insure a rigidly honest and economical disbursement of funds in the construction of the line. To that end sworn commissioners were to be appointed by the Government, whose certificate should be necessary, to the effect that the amount called for had been actually expended in cash upon the road, before any bonds bearing the guarantee of interest by the Government could be received by the company. I desire distinctly to state, what I am sure is the feeling of all friends of the bill, that no objection will be made to the most rigid supervision which may be suggested, but that, on the contrary, it is the desire of the friends of the measure, which it is proposed to submit to Congress, that it shall be placed upon so fair and honorable a basis that any gentleman who supports it can do so with entire confidence that the affairs of the company will be administered in the most thorough manner and under the closest governmental supervision. I trust that in the deliberations which are about to take place the importance of the end in view will be borne in mind, and that, if necessary, such concessions will be made as will enlist the hearty and united support of the gentlemen now present from all sections of the country, and that will at a very early day secure favorable action from Congress. The measure rests on a broad basis. Its advantages are confined to no section, but must benefit the whole people, and you can, therefore, confidently appeal to all sections of our common country. The new territory to be developed belongs to all, the commercial advantages will be shared by all, and in granting the aid asked for just claims are recognized, and the bond of union strengthened between the North and the South, between the great States now stretching along the Atlantic seaboard and the prosperous communities that are rapidly developing on the shores of the Pacific.

In submitting the foregoing statement, I desire to assure you and the great Convention over which you have the honor to preside that the interest paramount with me is to see this national highway constructed for the benefit of present and future generations. I am confident it can be done in a form that will preserve it as an open highway to all on the general basis herein submitted, and all the practical results anticipated by the country be fully realized.

If any better plan can be devised I shall take great pleasure in supporting it, whether connected with it officially or not.

Very respectfully,

THOMAS A. SCOTT,
President Texas and Pacific Railway Co.

A DELEGATE: I desire, sir, to submit a resolution to the Convention in regard to the clear and satisfactory communication which we have just heard from the distinguished President of the Texas and Pacific Railroad, and I will send it up to be read.

The Secretary read as follows:

Resolved, That the communication received from Mr. Thomas A. Scott, President of the Texas and Pacific Railway, be received and entered on the minutes and made a part of the proceedings of the Convention, and that the thanks of the Convention be extended to him for his satisfactory presentation of the necessity for, and the advantage to the Government and the people of the country resulting from a great Southern trans-continental railroad to the Pacific, on the 32d parallel; that the Convention also desire to recognize the eminent services of Mr. Scott in connection with the construction of a Southern line to the Pacific, and to express the high appreciation entertained by them, North and South, of the fidelity and ability with which he has at all times discharged the duties entrusted to him. [Applause.]

The resolution was unanimously adopted.

ADDITIONAL DELEGATES.

MR. BROADHEAD: I ask leave to report an additional list of delegates sent in this morning.

THE PRESIDENT: The following list of delegates is reported this morning: J. D. Woodward, Denison, Texas; M. C. Clark, Denison, Texas; Martin B. Hays, Grant County, New Mexico; George Walcott, Quincy, Illinois; William J. Scott, Denison, Texas; J. S. Clarkson, Nevada. If there is no objection, these names will be entered.

RESOLUTION OF THANKS.

MR. BARLOW, of Illinois: I desire to offer the following, which, with your permission, I will read:

Resolved, That this Convention tenders to the generous citizens of St. Louis its heartfelt thanks for the distinguished courtesy, kindness and munificence with which we have been treated, and the affairs of this Convention have been conducted, and we certainly hope that when the great Southern Pacific Railroad is completed they may derive material prosperity therefrom commensurate with the energy they have displayed in forwarding this great enterprise. [Applause.]

MR. SLAYBACK: Mr. President, that resolution ought to be referred to the Committee on Resolutions.

THE PRESIDENT: I think that resolution does not belong to that class.

A Delegate: I move to amend by striking out "Southern Pacific" and inserting "Texas Pacific."

The President: The question is on the amendment.

The question was put and the amendment was agreed to.

The President: The question now is on the adoption of the resolution as amended.

The question was put and the resolution was adopted.

COMMUNICATION FROM CITIZENS OF EL PASO.

The President: There has been handed to me a communication addressed "To the National Railroad Convention convened in the city of St. Louis, Missouri, to consider the location and building of and advocate the interests of the Texas and Pacific Railroad," and a report made on that subject by a large assemblage of citizens of El Paso, and signed by Allen Blacker, Chairman, and Jos. Wilkin Tays, Secretary. If the Convention so order, without reading it, it will be made a part of the proceedings, and entered upon the Journal.

There was no objection.

The communication was as follows:

To the National Railroad Convention convened in the city of St. Louis, Missouri, to consider the location and building of and advocate the interests of the Texas and Pacific Railroad:

Gentlemen:—When the call of your Executive Committee reached the valley of the El Paso, the leading citizens, composed of merchants, planters, miners, freighters and traders, determined to respond to it in a manner worthy the great object to be accomplished. Two meetings have already been held on this side of the river, and one has been called on the other, in the State of Chihuahua. The meetings held on this, the American side of the river, have been largely attended, both by our own citizens and by those of the Republic of Mexico. A spirit of enthusiasm pervades all classes. The new-born hope of a great railroad passing across desert and mountain into this rich and fruitful valley, has dawned upon American and Mexican alike. We have been requested, as their committee, to present the feelings of the people, and the great advantages which this locality has as a railroad point. We accept the trust, premising, however, that it is done without libraries or a bureau of statistics from which to collect facts and figures. We shall aim no higher than to present generalities and specialties as briefly as possible.

From the very inception of a Southern Pacific road, El Paso was selected as one of the landmarks. Every charter granted by the State of Texas stipulated El Paso as a point that must be touched. We are confident that should this be deviated from, our State would withhold, or at least modify, the liberal subsidies heretofore granted. It has universally been conceded by railroad men in the United States, and particularly in the Southern States of the Union, that El Paso would be a point on any Southern Pacific road built. The principal points first selected on a great railroad, before local and speculative interests set in to complicate and mystify, are almost certain to prevail. It was so with Omaha, on the Northern road, and it will be found to be so with El Paso on the Southern road.

One of the great objects of a Southern Pacific road is to get below the snow-line, so that communication may be uninterrupted throughout the year. An almost formidable barrier to such a road is the Guadalupe and Sacramento Mountains, and others, lying between the Rio Pecos and the Rio Grande. Major Hurd, an experienced engineer, formerly attached to the Northern road, but latterly chief engineer of the Texas and Pacific in the field, spent the winter of 1872 in these mountains searching for a practicable route. He determined that a good passage existed just south of the celebrated "Guadalupe Pass;" that no practicable route could be found in these mountains below the 34th or 35th parallel; and that this latter route has its objections on account of the severity of the winters. We think that it can be regarded as settled by all the surveys that no passage through these mountains below the snow-line can be found, except those heretofore selected for the 32d parallel road. In this view, this is not only the natural route, but should be adopted as the National, for this ocean-to-ocean road.

Another object in building on the 32d parallel is to tap the trade of Northern Mexico at El Paso. We must bear in mind that there is a rival in the International Railroad seeking this trade, and for every mile the Texas and Pacific is carried north of El Paso, two miles in latitude will be given to the International; it is so much easier going south than north.

Another reason for building on the 32d parallel is to give a fair distribution of railroad facilities to the South, making this a Southern, in contradistinction to the Northern and Central Pacific roads. If the road is located north of the 32d parallel, it is necessary to be done so much further north, that both from its position and connections it loses its Southern characteristics and becomes a Northern road. The South, in such an event, would justly feel that the balance of railroad power was against her.

We propose now to point out and meet the objections that are made to building the road by El Paso. It is urged that for 1,000 miles there are neither population nor products to warrant the building the road on the 32d parallel of latitude. As to population, it is true it is sparse; but with the teeming population that is now flowing into Texas, her plains, now covered with cattle, will soon be corn and cotton fields, and their herds will seek pasturage on places lying waste and desolate.

The valleys of the upper Brazos and Colorado, with deep soil and well covered with timber; the plains of the Rio Pecos, with thousands of acres of the richest land well situated for irrigation; the valley of the Rio Grande, whose fertility, products and capability of sustaining a large population are well known; the valleys of the Rio Mimbres and the Rio Gila, with their tributaries, just now being developed, are all calling to the homeless of the world to come, possess and enjoy the finest climate on the continent. All considered, the question of population would be settled so soon as the road was built to carry them to the various localities.

Then, as to production, it is evident, from what we have said about population and climate, that the agricultural yield of this country will be very great, not only in the cereals, but in vegetables, including the El Paso onion, the sugar-beet, and fruits of the best quality, including grapes rich in wine. Besides all these, the Rio Gila promises to be one of the finest cotton-growing regions in the country.

But this road passes through a country rich in natural productions, which, when known and developed, will add largely to the revenues of the road. Building material is of vast importance throughout the South. On the Rio Pecos, at Delaware creek, there is the finest quality of sandstone; in the Guadalupe and Hueca mountains there is superior granite; and on the plains north of El Paso there are hills, covering hundreds of square miles, of fine granulated gypsum that requires only to be calcined to make the finest finishing material on the continent. Then there is the kaolin deposit on the Pecos, the silver, lead and bismuth of the Chinata mountains, and the coal of the Chinchas mountains. The salt lakes of El Paso, from which about 1,000 tons annually are carried into the State of Chihuahua on ox-carts, forms no inconsiderable item.

Passing on to New Mexico and Arizona, there is the silver and gold of Silver City and Rinos Altos, the copper of Gila, which, for want of fuel, must be sent for reduction to St. Louis. The recent developments in Arizona show that further developments are likely to astonish the world.

Concluding, we state that we are willing to rest our superior claims alone on the trade from the northern States of Old Mexico. Northern Mexico is tapped at El Paso; an extensive trade may be at once established in semi-tropical fruits, sugar, coffee, and many other productions of the country. The mineral wealth of Northern Mexico is unbounded; many of the oldest and richest mines are unworked for want of proper machinery to exhaust the water. What a field for American enterprise and capital is here, and what a source of revenue to a railroad built on the 32d parallel and touching at El Paso, the key to the trade of Northern Mexico. We are confident that the wise men who shall meet in St. Louis on the 23d day of next November will be able to grapple with the great questions of the hour, and point out the best modes for an early development of this and like sections. We cheerfully submit our claims to them.

With great respect, &c.,

ALLEN BLACKER, *Chairman.*
JAS. WILKIN TAYS, *Secretary.*

ADDITIONAL DELEGATES.

Mr. SEXTON, of Texas: I ask leave to present additional delegates from Texas, reported this morning.

Leave was granted.

THE PRESIDENT: The following names I am authorized to state have been enrolled since the report of the Committee on Credentials, yesterday morning, as additional delegates: Missouri, R. L. Turpin, Mayor of Carrollton, George W. Jones, and Wilbur Gibson; from Kentucky, John A. Miller, Paducah; from Texas, Benj. F. Stewart, W. G. Thomas, of Austin; L. G. Burrows, L. E. Edwards, John M. Moore, Corpus Christi; D. C. C. Franks, Cherokee; H. L. Montrose, Texarkana; Joseph McGoffin, El Paso; J. B. Hays, El Paso.

THE PRESIDENT: If there is no objection, these names will be inserted.

COURTESIES TO THE PRESS.

Mr. Tatum: I have a resolution extending the courtesy of the Convention to the members of the press and inviting them to seats on the floor.

Resolved, That the usual courtesy be extended to the members of the press of this city, and that they be invited to take seats on the floor.

The question was put and the resolution was agreed to.

RESOURCES OF GRANT COUNTY, NEW MEXICO.

Mr. R. S. Elliott: I have the honor, representing a citizen of New Mexico, temporarily, to present a communication addressed to the President of the National Convention, being a report of a committee appointed to make known the resources of Grant county, New Mexico, and inasmuch as I know from personal observation that not only is there no exaggeration in this paper, but that it really falls far short of the truth, I beg leave to submit it with the hope that it may be published in the proceedings of this Convention.

The President: If there is no objection, that course will be taken.

The communication is as follows:

To the President of the National Railroad Convention to be held in St. Louis, Missouri, November 23, 1875:

Sir:—In obedience to instructions of a mass meeting of the citizens of Grant county, convened at Silver City, New Mexico, October 28, for the purpose of making known the resources of the county, and what may be expected of her in the way of freight for a railroad, we have the honor to report:

Grant county, New Mexico, is in what is termed the warm temperate belt, and lies between the 31st and 34th parallel of north latitude, and its western boundary is marked by the 32d degree of longitude west from Washington, which corresponds to 100 degrees, 2 minutes and 29.25 seconds west from Greenwich, and extends from east to west about 150 miles. Her soil in the valleys is a rich alluvium of river deposits, highly charged with mineral salts, and containing sufficient sand to make easy cultivation. Her climate is mild in winter, and frost never impedes the plow. Her agricultural resources are only equalled by Southern California. On the Gila river corn has yielded 75 bushels per acre, oats two crops per annum, 75 bushels each crop, barley 80 bushels per acre, and wheat 64 bushels. Vegetables grow exceedingly well and to an enormous size: squashes 125 pounds, cabbage 45 pounds, beets 20 to 40 pounds, onions from the seed, $2\frac{1}{2}$ pounds each, and other vegetables yield accordingly, and are not excelled in their edible qualities by esculents grown elsewhere.

As a fruit-growing region it is preferable to the far-famed Mesilla Valley, for the reason that the crop is surer in consequence of the lateness of the bloom, which renders it less liable to be destroyed by late frosts, and no fear is entertained from insects or disease to the vine and trees as are peculiar to most fruit-bearing regions. The valleys here spoken of are peculiarly flat and easily irrigated, and at all seasons there is a sufficiency of water for that purpose.

The fact that our climate presents no rigors of either heat or cold, with its boundless extent of gramma and mesquit grasses, which cure in autumn on the ground, retaining their nutritive qualities, and the peculiar configuration of this rocky mountain slope which protects stock from the winds of winter, commends Grant county as an unequalled stock-raising county. Hitherto the only drawback upon New Mexico as a stock-raising county has been the hostile Indians, who at present number about 14,500, all told; but their day has gone; they cower and retire before the march of civilization, and seek a home in the yet untrodden West.

Here there are no miasmatic influences to affect health; diseases of the liver, spleen, bronchitis, phthisis, dyspepsia, general depression of the nervous system are all relieved or cured by residence here. We have a number of hot and warm springs, the efficacy of some of the waters of which have a fine reputation as curatives of rheumatics, syphilitic eruptions and kindred diseases. In this connection it is also proper to state that Grant county abounds in the best of timber, and has more of it than any other county in the Territory.

Another subject of interest to those disposed to invest their capital in building a Southern trans-continental railroad is the item of freight, and as we are not disposed to speak of any other locality than our own, we have to say that Grant county, which may be said to have but a four years' growth, is unequalled in its commercial rise, which the following figures of pounds of import freight for the present season attest:

J. F. Bennett & Co............800,000	J. A. Miller & Co............300,000
H. M. Porter...................800,000	Jno. R. Magruder & Co........350,000
A. H. Morehead & Co..........650,000	B. Rosenfeldt & Co............100,000
J. B, Morrill & Co.............375,000	J. B. Woods.................. 50,000
I. N. Cohen & Co..............200,000	Thompson & Bull..............100,000
R. V. Newsham................ 50,000	J. A. Lucas & Co............. 50,000
G. W. Baily................... 50,000	N. Y. Anchetta & Co..........100,000
Cosgrove & Holt............... 25,000	T. M. Hall.................... 50,000
Van Wagenen & Co............ 25,000	J. R. Adair & Co.............. 50,000
Derbyshire & Bro.............. 25,000	Military supplies for Fort Bay-
M. Amador....................200,000	ard......................1,500,000

The foregoing, it must be remembered, is only an estimate of import freight, to which should be added the export of pig copper, wool and hides, which may safely be calculated at 1,675,000 pounds, and had we railroad facilities, who can estimate the millions of tons of silver, copper and lead ores that would find a market East?

Independent of the foregoing list, there are a great number of small retail houses which make their purchases at the terminus of the railroad, and we may safely add 200,000 pounds for them per annum; there is also a large percentage of the goods consumed by Arizona Territory which pass through New Mexico from the present terminus of the railroad, and for which we may add 1,000,000 pounds.

That the amount of merchandise received in the Territory of New Mexico is not sufficient for the demand is evidenced from the fact that from the first of February to the first of June of each year, the supplies are nearly exhausted, especially the staple articles, which is accounted for from the fact that no freight arrives here until after the first of June. Another item of interest which here presents itself is, that goods purchased in the Eastern markets for Grant county seldom arrive under three months, and in many instances are six months on the road. These great delays are not only annoying to the merchant but costly to the consumer. To this cause may be attributed the fact that large capital is required to conduct business at this point.

Southern New Mexico presents a vast field of mineral resources, awaiting the development which a line of railroad would secure, prominent among which are her mines of gold, silver, lead, copper, iron and coal, scattered over nearly all that portion of the Territory lying between the 35th parallel of latitude and the Mexican line.

The greatest development of her mining interest has thus far been effected in the county of Grant, immediately on the proposed line of what is generally known as the 32d parallel road.

The mineral productions of Southern New Mexico, in rank of their importance, are silver, copper and gold, these only bearing the necessary enormous outlay for working, though doubtless, with the advent of a railroad, copper would soon become the leading article of all her wealth.

Though so far removed from railroad transportation that the high cost of machinery and supplies prevents the remunerative working of any but the highest grades of ore, nevertheless the production of silver and gold has steadily increased until now Grant county alone ships at the rate of $800,000 per annum of these metals, while the enormous amount of ore of lower grades that annually accumulates about her mines is only a slight evidence of what New Mexico could add to the wealth of the nation when a railroad places the great reduction works of the East at her command.

The celebrated "Virginia Mining District," centering at Ralston, near one of the most available passes found by the surveyor, can alone furnish thousands of tons of silver-bearing ore of a class which would pay a large profit above the cost of shipment and reduction in the East, to say nothing of the richer though less extensive districts of Silver City, Lone Mountain and Mimbres.

The copper interests of Southern New Mexico, though first brought into prominence by the Mexican Government during the last century, under their system of convict labor—as witness the celebrated old "Santa Rita" and "Hanover" mines—lay in a dormant condition until within the last two years, when, with the comparative security from the ravages of the Apache, which an increase of civilized population has brought, a renewal of work on those mines and the opening of even more extensive deposits of copper has been accomplished, and now the annual copper product of Grant county amounts to over 600,000 pounds; in addition to which we have the inexhaustible deposits of copper ore in the "Fresco Copper District" of Arizona, adjacent to and dependent for its supplies upon Southern New Mexico.

In the latter district, though of very late discovery, the amount of copper produced in the old primitive Mexican mode is only limited by the wagon transportation that can be obtained to haul it nearly 1,000 miles to reach railroad communication. One company alone in the Fresco District has contracted to deliver 1,000,000 pounds within the year.

Taking into consideration the fact that the cost of freighting this metal to a market is from four to five cents per pound, it can readily be understood that the thriving condition of our mining industry, though under a freight tariff so restrictive, is the best indication of the proportions which it would assume if a cheaper mode of transportation were available, and presents to the mind of the practical railroad manager a story of mineral wealth that is beyond cavil or controversy.

But not only is Southern New Mexico rich in the more precious metals, but iron, coal, fluor spar and fire-clay abound in unlimited quantities, and many of these articles of a very superior quality.

While considering the mineral resources of this portion of our own domain, it is none the less important to notice the fact that we are directly bordering on the States of Chihuahua and Sonora in the republic of Old Mexico, a region capable of yielding its millions of wealth, but which, like this portion of our own land, only awaits the more modern appliances for the reduction of ores, which railroad communication will make cheap and available, to develop a production of mineral wealth, and create thereby a commerce and traffic that will surpass the most enthusiastic estimates.

And now, in conclusion, permit us to ask that if the wonderful rise of Grant county in wealth and population (within four years), so remotely situated from means of rapid transit, is a matter of such vast surprise, what may we not expect with railroad facilities at our doors, or within easy stages of our great mineral deposits, which are still buried, awaiting the means of transportation? So far Grant county, unlike other mineral districts, is not indebted a dollar to foreign capital for an assisting hand. The bowels of the earth have furnished the wherewith to build our towns, mills, furnaces, churches and school-houses, and from an inauspicious beginning we have, with the pick, drill and shovel, clothed our settlements in holiday attire, and present to the world, from the recent heart of a savage country, unmistakable evidences of a high state of Christian civilization. And having, unaided, accomplished this much towards the humanizing influence of a so lately surrounding waste, we ask that the great commercial centres of the Union may provide a means of transit which will enable them to profit by our truly valuable discoveries of gold, silver and copper deposits.

J. A. KETCHAM,
S. H. ECKLES,
A. H. MOREHEAD,
U. C. GARRISON,
J. M. GINN,
Committee.

MEMBERS OF CONGRESS INVITED TO SEATS IN THE CONVENTION.

Mr. E. N. Hill, of Arkansas: I desire to offer a resolution that any Senator of the United States or members of the House of Representatives present be invited to seats on the floor of this Convention.

The question was put and the resolution was adopted.

The President: The regular order of business for this morning will be the report of the Committee on Resolutions.

BRANCH LINE FROM DALLAS TO SAN DIEGO.

Mr. J. T. Trezevant, Sr., of Arkansas: I have a resolution that I wish referred to the Committee on Resolutions.

Resolved, That a branch line from Dallas to San Diego shall be completed and in operation before any work shall be done on its branches.

The President: The resolution will be referred under the order of the Convention.

ADDITIONAL DELEGATES.

The President: I ask leave to report as additional delegates from Kentucky, Henry Burnett, of Paducah; George C. Thompson and W. F. Bradshaw, of the same place. Their names will be enrolled. L. R. Elliot is also reported as an additional delegate from Kansas.

REPORT FROM COMMITTEE ON RESOLUTIONS.

Hon. Jacob Thompson, of Tennessee: Mr. Chairman, the Committee on Resolutions are now ready to report.

The President: The report will be received.

Mr. Thompson: Mr. President, I hold in my hand a preamble and resolutions which have been agreed upon by the Committee on Resolutions, which I will proceed to read:

This Convention of delegates, duly appointed from thirty-one States and Territories, many cities and boards of trade, merchants' exchanges and other commercial bodies, constituting a body of 869 delegates, representing not only a large proportion of the people of the United States, but of the active, producing, business capital of the country, and now assembled to take action upon the construction of a Southern line of railroad to the Pacific, do respectfully represent to the Senate and House of Representatives of the United States in Congress assembled—

That a Southern trans-continental railway from the waters of the Mississippi, via El Paso, to the Pacific Ocean, on or near the 32d parallel of latitude, is imperatively demanded:

1. As a measure of sound statesmanship.

Because it is only by constant intercourse, business and social, that the great States now growing up on the Pacific slope can be permanently bound in a common interest with our Eastern and Southern communities, and it is therefore sound policy and wise foresight to promote the most intimate relations between all sections of our common country—a necessity already recognized by the Government in its grant of bonds and lands to the Union and Central and Kansas Pacific roads, and of lands to other trans-continental lines on the 32d, 35th and 47th parallels, under the belief that private capital would furnish the needful funds to complete these highways; but owing to the great commercial depression, they cannot be built by individual capital, and the responsibility still rests upon the Government to secure the completion of at least one additional trans-continental line.

2. As a means of national defence.

Because it is the duty of the Government to have a line to the Pacific, unobstructed at all seasons of the year, for the prompt transportation of troops and supplies, should trouble arise with any foreign country and the ports and cities of the Pacific coast be exposed to insult or attack. Such line to be sufficiently removed from our border to enable it to be fully protected against the movement of any hostile force.

3. As a local military necessity.

Because the experience of the nation on the Central, Union and Kansas Pacific roads has proven that the rail and telegraph, and the facilities thereby provided, furnish the only sure means of intercepting and punishing the hostile Indians, and unmistakably indicates the adoption of the same methods to prevent constant depredation in Western Texas, New Mexico and Arizona, make life and property secure, and establish there the same law and order that prevail along the present Pacific lines.

4. As a measure of practical economy.

Because, as already shown by the experience of the present Pacific road, the expense of maintaining a military establishment for the protection of the Southern territory against Indian depredations will be largely reduced, first, by enabling the Government to transport troops and supplies at one-fifth of the present cost; and, second, by enabling it to dispense with the services of two-thirds of the present force through the facilities afforded for transportation and the movement of troops, and thereby save from eight to ten millions of dollars per annum, and at the same time provide more efficiently and economically for the care and maintenance of the Indian tribes who are under the charge of the Government.

5. As a commercial necessity to the twelve millions of people inhabiting a belt of country from 400 to 700 miles in width, and stretching along the entire South Atlantic coast, the Gulf of Mexico and Old Mexico to the Pacific Ocean, who have no direct communication with the Pacific, and, by reason of their geographical position, cannot share in the benefits conferred by the present Pacific line.

6. As a direct saving to the people of the entire country.

Because it will give a competing line between the two oceans, both for the large local and through traffic of this country and for the great through traffic of the Sandwich Islands, India, China, Japan, Australia and Western South America, thereby conferring a substantial benefit upon the entire nation.

Because in this manner the people of the United States will best be protected against a monopoly to whom they have loaned $55,000,000 of six per cent. Government bonds and made large grants of land to build the present Pacific line, and for whose benefit the Government is now paying yearly upwards of three additional millions out of the treasury—a corporation that has established arbitrary rates for transportation, and is now seeking to perpetuate itself as a close corporation, and control its lines, and such as it may hereafter build, in its own exclusive interest, instead of making them an open highway such as the people of this country have a right to demand.

7. Because the communication thus established with the rich and productive States of Old Mexico would secure a large and lucrative traffic now diverted to other countries, and would thereby increase the revenues of the Government, while at the same time the connections made with the lines now projected from the capital of Mexico to its northern border would stimulate and develop this trade and enrich the citizens of our own country by the exchange of our manufactured goods for the products of her soil and mines.

8. Because it is the duty of the Government to protect the citizens whose guardianship it assumed under treaty obligations in the

acquisition of the Mexican territory in which they were resident, and also all other citizens who have been induced, by the grants made by the Government to aid the building of railroads, to settle in the territories which those roads were intended to develop.

9. As a prudential and proper act to encourage the people of the South, who may very justly, and with great force, urge that while $175,000,000 of the public moneys have been appropriated in the Northern States and Territories since the organization of the Government, there has been but $19,000,000 expended in the Southern States and Territories.

10. Because not only will this road, as a means of national defence, strengthen the military arm of the Government, and at all times perfect the security of our Pacific coast against attack by foreign powers, reduce the expenses of its local administration, bind our country more closely together, facilitate communication with the Pacific and with Old Mexico, develop new traffic and the agricultural products and great mineral wealth of Texas, New Mexico and Arizona, but it will also, by the demand for manufactures and productions of every description, including iron, steel, cotton, wool, timber and other material needed in the construction of engines, cars, bridges, machinery, buildings, etc., for the use of the road and by the laborers employed in building and maintaining the same, give employment to the furnaces, mills and machine shops of the country, and once more revive and stimulate the depressed industries of all sections.

AND WHEREAS, To secure to the Government and the people these several advantages, and in addition thereto secure the return to the people of thirty millions of acres of land heretofore granted to build the 35th parallel line, and save the building of fifteen hundred miles of road, it is, in the judgment of this Convention, not only the right, but the duty of the National Government to render such aid, properly secured, restricted and guarded, as will secure the prompt completion of the line referred to, and of such extensions as will give to all sections the advantages resulting therefrom; now be it resolved,

1. That a Southern line to the Pacific Ocean should be built on or near the 32d parallel from Shreveport, via El Paso to San Diego, where it will make connection with the waters of the Pacific in a safe and excellent harbor, and connect also with the railway lines now building from San Francisco to the southern part of California, thus securing a continuous line to that great city and port.

2. That there should also be constructed extensions from the most eligible points on the Texas and Pacific road to New Orleans, Memphis and Vicksburg, and from a point near the 103d meridian to Vinita, in order to reach the Mississippi river, and to connect with every road and harbor of the Atlantic coast, and with every railway east of the Rocky Mountain slope.

3. That to insure to the nation the greatest benefits from this line of road, and to prevent its being controlled in the interest of any one party or section of country, there should be established such regulations as will maintain the road from Shreveport to the Pacific as an open highway and as a competing line to all trans-continental railroads, to be used on equal terms by all connecting roads which are now or may hereafter be built; similar regulations to be applied to the branches receiving similar aid to the Texas and Pacific trunk line.

4. That it should be built at the lowest cash cost, in order that the people shall be protected against undue or oppressive charges, and shall be secured in its use at the lowest possible rates required to protect the comparatively small capital actually expended on its construction—a result which can be greatly aided by its construction at this time, when material and labor can be secured at prices much below those that have prevailed for many years past—and that Congress shall at all times reserve the power to protect the people against speculation and oppression in the use of this national highway.

5. That the building of the main line should proceed under such regulations as will insure the construction of the road continuously from the point of its present completion, in Texas, to San Diego, in California, or until it meets an extension of the same line from San Diego.

6. That the construction of such a line and branches can be best secured by the extension of Government aid to the line and branches heretofore mentioned in these resolutions, in the form of a guarantee of interest, not principal, on a limited amount of five per cent. construction bonds, payable in fifty years, so that the entire liability assumed shall not in any event exceed $2,000 per mile per annum, nor the interest on the actual cost of the line and said branches; such liability to be secured by a first mortgage upon all the railway property and franchises of the companies, and upon the lands granted by the United States, and any deficit in the earnings of the line and branches to meet the interest maturing on these bonds while the road is in course of construction, to be met by the deposit in the United States Treasury of one-eighth of the whole authorized issue, and the

sale of the same if it becomes necessary, after applying all net earnings and proceeds of lands and the sums due for Government transportation, mail and telegraph service, to meet the interest so maturing as aforesaid, so that there shall be no outlay by the Government; these bonds to be issued only to the actual amount of cash expended upon the road and branches, and upon the certificate of sworn commissioners appointed by the Government to supervise the building of the line and branches, and their redemption at maturity to be assured to purchasers and holders by providing a sinking fund out of the revenues of the road and branches, to be paid by the companies into the Treasury of the United States, of such amount as may be sufficient to pay off and discharge the entire bonded obligations of the companies, on which the Government has guaranteed the interest.

7. That the President of this Convention be requested to prepare an address to the people of the United States, embodying the views set forth in the preamble and resolutions adopted by this Convention, and that he be authorized to appoint a committee of thirteen, who, with the President of this Convention, shall present an engrossed copy of the proceedings of this Convention, together with the address, to the President of the United States, the presiding officer of the Senate, and the Speaker of the House of Representatives; and to take such further action as in their judgment may be deemed best to promote the objects and purposes of this Convention.

8. That duly certified copies of this preamble and resolutions be also furnished to the Governors of States, mayors of cities, and to the commercial and other bodies represented at the Convention, and that they be earnestly solicited to advocate the plan proposed.

9. That the Secretary of this Convention have the proceedings published in pamphlet form, and also that the newspaper press of the country be requested to publish the same, so that the States, municipal, commercial and other bodies here represented, and those which may not be, shall fully understand the objects and purposes of the Convention, namely: the securing of another highway across the continent that must prove highly beneficial to the Government and the people of every section of our country.

Mr. President, I have only one word to add. After a very close and full examination of this report and these resolutions by your committee of two from every State and Territory represented, we came unanimously to the conclusion that this was the best thing we could do.

DISCUSSION ON THE RESOLUTIONS.

Mr. Anderson, of Virginia: I move that the resolutions be adopted by acclamation.

Several Delegates: Second the motion.

The President: Gentlemen, the motion is to adopt the report of the Committee on Resolutions; Col. Hill, of Arkansas, has the floor.

Col. E. N. Hill, of Arkansas: I believe, sir, that it will be right and proper for this Convention, in presenting those resolutions to the country, to give the reasons in as brief a manner as possible to the country why they should be adopted, and with your permission I will (as I have been engaged for some time in preparing some statistics on this subject) occupy the attention of the Convention for a few moments.

The President: Mr. Hill will come forward and speak from the platform.

Several Delegates: Question, question.

The President: Gentlemen of the Convention, Col. Hill, of Arkansas, has the floor [loud cries of "Question, question"] for the purpose of reading, as he states, some statistics that he has prepared in support of the conclusions to which the committee has come.

Several Delegates: Publish them. Question, question.

The President: Under the rules, Col. Hill has the right to be heard. [Applause.]

Mr. Hill then came forward, and taking a position upon the platform, said:

Gentlemen of the Convention, I do not intend to detain you or to make any efforts at oratorical display, but I think that it is the duty of this Convention to give to the people of the country the reasons why they want these resolutions adopted, and for that purpose I think that carefully prepared statistics, showing the condition of the country, are very valuable in connection with this report, which is to go forth indorsed by so respectable a body as this. I do not intend, gentlemen, to make any exordium or any extended remarks, a few of which I have prepared, but I shall pass immediately, as the Convention seems to be impatient, to the statistics which I have prepared, which have been gathered from the official reports of the Secretary of the Treasury of the United States during the last ten years. In connection with the construction of the Northern roads— the Central and Union Pacific—I think that it is pertinent and proper to examine into the business done by those roads, their revenue, and from what source that revenue was derived. I find that the earnings of the Central and Union Pacific for the years 1872, '73 and '74 were: in 1872, $21,627,535; in 1873, $24,138,736; in 1874, $24,965,359. Of these amounts the Government paid for transporting mails, troops, supplies, etc., in these three years, $18,453,129, an average of $6,151,000 per annum. It would not be necessary to cite evidence here had it not already been done by the able chairman of the Executive Committee, Col. Broadhead, to show that it would cost at least twice that amount to transport those supplies, troops, etc., if the road had not been built. You will observe that the amount annually paid by the Government is rapidly increasing from the year 1871. In the year 1870 it was only $2,677,000.

Several Delegates: Publish it.

Mr. Hill: I will give it to you. In the year 1874 the amount increased to $7,000,000. Now, sir, let us suppose the maximum of Government business has been arrived at; there is an annual saving of $6,151,000, and this, in less than six years, would pay for the loan to the Union and Central Pacific, if the Government were to make them a free gift of it. [Applause long continued and stamping of feet.] Gentlemen, I am very patient and I will allow you to get through with any of your demonstrations.

Several Delegates: Print it.

Mr. Hill: I will not detain you many minutes, gentlemen. [Constant stamping.]

The President: Allow me to suggest that time will be saved by hearing Col. Hill.

Mr. Hill: Gentlemen, I am not going to make a speech, I simply wish to call attention [renewed demonstrations by delegates]—but as the gentlemen of the Convention seem to be very impatient, if they will allow me I will present my statistics to the Secretary to be printed in the proceedings of this Convention. I think that will be the most popular thing I can do. [Laughter and applause.]

Mr. Smith, of Texas: I rise to move the previous question.

Mr. Smoot: Before that question is put I should like to have the Convention give Col. Hill the privilege of making his speech a part of the proceedings of this Convention.

The President: That is already allowed by the consent of the Convention; the remarks which Col. Hill was making are to be entered as being made part of the proceedings of the body. [Applause.]

SPEECH OF MR. HILL.

The following is the speech of Mr. Hill as authorized to be made a part of the proceedings:

Mr. President and Gentlemen of the Convention:—Almost ever since this nation was established with its complicated machinery, it has been a question how far the National Government ought to or could go in giving aid to internal improvements. Political parties made the question an issue upon which many a bitter contest was fought. But even the most strict constructionists—those who held to the doctrine that the Federal Government had no powers but such as were expressly granted by the letter of the written law—even these admitted that the General Government had the power to aid works of a national character. John C. Calhoun will be readily accepted as the most able exponent of the views of the extremists of the strict construction school, who opposed grants from the Federal Government in aid of projected improvements. Yet thirty years ago, Mr. Calhoun, when presiding over a railroad convention, as is the honorable gentleman from Ohio to-day, assembled as is this Convention upon the banks of the Mississippi river, said, while discussing the question of Government aid for a railroad intended to connect the Atlantic coast with the river at Memphis, and the improvement of the navigation of the Mississippi, that it was the duty of the Federal Government to aid in the construction of a road which would connect the ocean with what he called that "great inland sea," and to make that river navigable at all times. His reason for saying this was that both these works were of a national character. How much more so is the one we are asking aid for. The road from Charleston to Memphis was a short one, not over five hundred miles in length, and it passed through the territory of organized States. This one is five times that long, and most of its route is through thinly settled Territories.

As the ever-restless people penetrated farther from the seaboard and began to develop the wealth that was contained in the valley of the great river upon whose bank this Convention is assembled, the policy of those who favored national aid to assist private enterprise in works of great magnitude intended to increase the wealth and prosperity of the nation, rapidly gained favor, and for many years such has been the settled policy of the nation. That it was and is the true policy, no one can doubt who has marked the rapidity with which, through those means, vast and unpeopled forests and plains have been converted into productive fields, dotted with flourishing cities.

This Convention, if I understand its object, has been called for the purpose of inducing the Congress of the United States to lend its aid toward a work that we consider a matter of right and justice to certain sections of a common country, but of infinite national importance.

When it was first proposed to build a railroad "across the continent," the projector was pronounced visionary, and the idea impracticable, but more than twenty years ago the present speaker, after having passed over the ground, thought and wrote that the road could and ought to be built, the principal difficulty, in his opinion, being that the snow would render portions of the road impassable in the winter season, which difficulty he said could be avoided by running the road south of the 35th parallel of latitude.

The exigencies, or the supposed exigencies, of war caused the building of this great highway many years sooner that it would, but for that reason, have been constructed, and the same reasons caused it to be built north of that parallel. We know that but for the ingenuity that devised snow-sheds for the protection of the road-bed, it would often be useless and always in the winter unreliable.

But the building of that road demonstrated several things. It showed not only that it could be built (which was doubted), but the necessity of it. And how was it built? By private enterprise? No; but with the money of the Government. Sixty-four millions of dollars of the bonds of the United States, and one hundred millions of acres of its lands—the last absolutely given, and the first loaned on the most favorable terms—were required to complete this work. I have neither time nor inclination, nor is this the place, to discuss the question of whether this money was honestly or wastefully expended, or whether private parties acquired great fortunes through its construction. All these things have nothing to do with the matter which we are considering. But it is pertinent and proper to examine into the business done by this road, its revenue, and from what source it is derived.

I find that the earnings of the Central and Union Pacific for the years 1872, 1873 and 1874 were, for 1872, $21,627,535; for 1873, $24,138,736; and for 1874, $24,965,359; of these amounts the Government paid for transportation of mails, troops, supplies, etc., in 1872, $5,096,400, or twenty-four per cent.; in 1873, $6,018,988, or twenty-five per cent.; and in 1874, $7,337,741, or thirty per cent. This makes in these three years the sum of $18,453,129 paid by the United States for the necessary transportation of troops, supplies, mails, etc., an average of $6,151,043 per annum. It will be unnecessary (if it had not already been done by Col. Broadhead in his very able remarks when this Convention was called to order) to cite evidence to show that it would have cost at least twice that amount to transport these supplies, troops, mails, etc., if the road had not been built. It is a fact too well known to require proof. You will observe that the amount annually paid by the Government is rapidly increasing. In 1871 it was only $3,775,159; in 1870 only $2,677,822. So that in five years, from 1870 to 1874 inclusive, the amount paid has been increased nearly threefold. But let us suppose that the maximum of Government business has been reached, the annual saving would be $6,151,043, and this saving in less than six years more would pay off the entire amount loaned to these railroads, if what was loaned were now made a gift to them, as the amount of bonds they received was $53,121,632. The roads spoken of, the Union and Central Pacific, have a total length of 2,254 miles. The average amount paid them by the United States for the five years above cited, each year, for transportation was $2,210 per mile; the amount paid in 1874 was $3,225 per mile; the interest on the bonds issued for them is $3,187,267, or $1,414 per mile. It will be unnecessary for me to show the amount of interest per mile for which a guarantee is asked on the Texas Pacific, the figures having already been given.

But to leave this branch of the subject, and touch upon another cognate one. The total amount of bonds issued by the United States to aid in constructing the Union Pacific, Central Pacific, Kansas Pacific, Central Branch Union Pacific, Western Pacific and Sioux City and Pacific was $64,613,512. I have prepared a table which shows the amount of interest upon these bonds from 1870 to 1874, inclusive, and the amount paid each of these years by the United States to all of these roads for the transportation of troops, supplies, mails, etc. It reads as follows:

	Int. on bonds.	Am't paid for Transportation.
1870	$ 3,830,522	$ 4,006,877
1871	3,877,128	5,434,679
1872	3,878,099	7,045,198
1873	3,877,410	8,229,142
1874	3,877,410	9,918,090
Total	$19,340,569	$34,633,986

It will be observed that in these five years the amount of work done for the United States by these roads nearly doubled the amount of the interest on the bonds in their aid. The business of the Government on these roads increased from $4,006,877 in 1870, to $9,918,090 in 1874 — an average increase each year of $1,417,304, or 35 per cent. I would here remark that I am not piling up these figures — and I expect to use a good many more — without an object, which I hope to make apparent before I conclude.

But to pass to other points. I felt very confident that one of the objections that would be made in Congress to the passage of the bill we ask, would be that the South had no right to ask from the General Government any expenditure for its special benefit, and that this road was solely for its benefit; and sure enough, last week, before writing this, while conversing with a gentleman fully equal to the average Congressman in intelligence, on the subject of this Convention, the question was raised, and I informed him that I was prepared to show that if we went into Congress and asked for a donation of the amount necessary to build the Southern Pacific Railroad with termini at St. Louis, Memphis, Vicksburg and New Orleans we could do so, and then claim that justice had not been done us in the expenditure of public money.

To be enabled to make good this assertion, I have examined in detail the reports of the Secretaries of the Treasury of the United States from July 1, 1866, to June 30, 1874, inclusive, a period of nine years since the close of the war. I found the net ordinary expenses of these nine years to be $1,916,781,833, or $212,975,759 average per annum. I then examined the various items of these expenditures for several years, and, where the tables admitted its being done, found what had been expended in the Southern States, including only those in the rebellion, and what in the remainder of the country. In the last fiscal year I found these figures to be:

	Expended North.	Expended South.
Public buildings	$ 3,674,919	$ 178,363
Custom-houses	2,451,381	1,500,000
Light-houses	2,481,479	197,600
Fortifications	1,890,844	374,000
Improvement of harbors	1,841,662	166,257
Improvement of rivers	2,737,257	766,000
Expenditures at navy-yards	2,538,727	117,000
Expenses of collecting internal revenue	5,804,479	1,076,440
Expenditures at mints	1,263,558	3,589
Expenditures at independent treasuries	489,657	13,869
Expenses of transporting—mail service	9,957,192	3,677,808
Pensions	27,238,902	2,811,950
Total for these items	$62,370,057	$10,877,896

Here, in a total expenditure of $73,247,953, we find less than fifteen per cent. expended in the South, and this was an exceptional good year for it. In 1873 the table showed:

	North.	South.
Public buildings	$ 4,817,932	$ 74,900
Custom-houses	2,319,551	683,675
Light-houses	2,789,700	340,500
Improvement of rivers and harbors	6,727,357	1,617,129
Navy yards	1,227,710	143,320
Pensions	24,468,852	2,490,000
Total of these items	$42,351,102	$5,349,524

This year, out of expenditures of $47,700,636, the South had only eleven per cent., and so through every year since the close of the war. A close examination leads me to believe that not over ten per cent. of the amount paid out by the United States for net ordinary expenses in the nine years named was expended in the South. And then it must be remembered that in 1866, the first of these years, the Southern States had just emerged from a devastating war, in which they were the principal sufferers, with $4,000,000,000 worth of property in slaves and fully one-fourth as much in other property destroyed, while the Northern States were rich. The average population for these nine years was, in the North, 28,000,000; in the South, 13,000,000. From this we find that there was expended by the General Government in nine years, amongst 28,000,000 people, $1,725,-103,650, or $61.60 per capita; and in the South during the same time, amongst 13,000,000 people, $191,678,183, or $14.67 per capita. But even this is not all. In one single item of taxes, that on cotton, $70,000,000 was taken from the Southern States, with no corresponding tax upon the Northern ones. And to crown all, a system of internal revenue taxation was conceived, which is illustrated in the following figures, showing how unequally it bears upon the various sections: The New England States, with 3,491,103 inhabitants, pay $4,031,730 internal revenue tax, which cost $165,490 to collect, and there was assessed against them and unpaid $751,000. Missouri, with 1,721,295 people, paid $4,591,856 tax, the collection of which cost 73,431, and there was $511,000 assessed and unpaid. Kentucky, with 1,321,011 people, paid $9,022,636, the collection of which cost $118,773, and there was of the amount assessed unpaid $898,000. Virginia, with 1,225,163 people, paid $7,659,639, collecting which cost $100,032, and there was unpaid of the amount assessed $271,000. To formulate these figures they would read thus:

	Population.	Rev. tax paid.	Per cen'ge on ass'm'ts not paid.	Average tax per capita.	Per capita cost of collecting.
New England States	3,491,103	$4,031,730	18½	$1 15	4.8
Missouri	1,721,295	4,591,856	11½	2 66	1¼
Kentucky	1,321,011	9,022,636	9½	6 83	9
Virginia	1,225,163	7,659,636	2 2-3	6 26	8

Now, what do these tables show? Let us see. They show that the Government taxes the South per capita three or four times as much as it does the North, and expends per capita for necessary expenses four and a half times as much in the North as it does in the South. I think I have pretty clearly established the assertion I made that if we were to go to Congress and ask that " the money be given to build this road, we would not ask more than justice would accord."

But what are we asking? Only that Congress shall guarantee the interest on bonds sufficient to build the road, and for the payment of that interest and principal by the road sufficient guarantees are offered. The bill drawn reads:

Sec. 4. That the acceptance of the provisions of this act by either of said companies shall, *ipso facto*, constitute a first lien or mortgage upon the respective lines of road and telegraph upon which such bonds are hereby authorized to be issued, with the rolling stock, depots, shops, fixtures, and property of every kind appertaining thereto, including the franchises of said companies connected therewith, and all the lands granted in the United States in aid thereof, and so much of the earnings of said companies, respectively, as may be required to provide for the interest, and for a sinking fund, as provided in this act; and it shall be the duty of each company, respectively, upon accepting this act, to file a mortgage with the Secretary of the Interior, duly executed under its corporate seal, to secure the said bonds and the interest guaranteed by the United States, and the sinking fund required to be paid under the provisions of this act; which mortgage shall be in such form as shall be approved by the Secretary of the Treasury and the Secretary of the Interior of the United States; and for the purpose of more specifically providing for the interest on these bonds as it shall mature from time to time, and for a sinking fund sufficient, as hereinafter provided, to redeem such bonds at or before maturity, there shall be set apart by the said companies, and paid into the Treasury of the United States, ten days before the interest coupons on said bonds shall mature, and as the installments for the sinking fund shall become due and payable, as follows:

1. The entire net cash proceeds of sales of lands granted by Congress to aid in the construction of the road upon which bonds shall be issued under the provisions of this act.

2. The whole amount that shall be earned and be due from the Government of the United States for the transportation of troops and supplies, and for its postal and telegraphic service.

3. A sufficient amount from the earnings of the road to make up each interest payment to be provided for, and also to provide a sinking fund, to commence with the year eighteen hundred and eighty-five, and to continue until the year nineteen hundred, equal to one per centum, and thereafter two per centum per annum on the whole amount of bonds so issued and outstanding; the payment for account of fund, with its accretions, to be invested annually in these bonds by the Secretary of the Treasury, when they can be purchased at par in gold; and when they cannot be so purchased, then in United States bonds, at current market value, until such payments, with the accretions of the fund, shall equal in value the par value at maturity of the bonds issued by and outstanding against each company under this act; and all of said bonds, the interest of which is guaranteed under this act, purchased for the sinking fund, shall, when so purchased, be cancelled with the Government indorsement thereon, by the Secretary of the Treasury; but the company issuing them shall continue to pay the interest on all such cancelled bonds into the Treasury of the United States, for the purposes of the sinking fund, until such fund, with its accretions, shall, as aforesaid, equal in value the par value at maturity of all outstanding bonds entitled to the benefit of the fund.

The second clause, above quoted, says, "the whole amount that shall be earned and due from the Government of the United States for the transportation of troops and supplies, and for its postal and telegraphic service," shall be reserved by the Government to pay the interest on the bonds guaranteed by the Government. This in itself will be more than sufficient to fully provide for the interest. To show this, I will have to refer to some things I have previously said. It will not be asserted that the business of the Government in transporting troops, supplies, and for postal and telegraphic services, will be less on the Texas Pacific, with its several termini, than it has been on the Central and Union Pacific, and I have already shown that in the five years from 1870 to 1874 the amount paid by the Government to those roads for services rendered was $34,633,986, an average of $6,936,797 per annum, and that in four years the necessary Government expenditures on these roads increased from $4,006,877 in 1870 to $9,918,090 in 1874, nearly two and a half times. A very large proportion of the amounts expended in these years (what the exact proportion is can easily be arrived at by an examination of the accounts of the United States Treasurer) was for business seeking the nearest point by railroad transportation to the very countries (New Mexico and Arizona) through which the Texas Pacific would pass; and the expenditure to arrive at the place of destination, after quitting the railroad, has been fully as much as that on the road.

The largest possible amount of bonds that can be guaranteed under the proposition is $90,000,000, the annual interest on which, at five per centum, would be $4,500,000. The business of the Government in 1874, on trans-continental railroads, amounted to $9,918,090—more than twice the sum required to pay the interest on the maximum amount of bonds that can be issued. At least half that business would necessarily go over the Texas Pacific road, and that alone would pay the interest, as the Government is authorized to retain *every dollar* of the money earned from it by the road for the transportation of troops and supplies, postal and telegraphic service. As the necessary expenditures of the Government for services on the Pacific roads have increased so rapidly since their construction, it is fair to presume that this increase will continue in about the same ratio, and if so, the Government expenditures alone will not only pay the interest on the bonds, but will, before their maturity, provide a fund for their redemption.

I have up to this time discussed the question before us from a purely Southern stand-point. Is any one, however, so short-sighted as for an instant to suppose that the building of the Texas Pacific would only benefit the South? If there be any such, I pity their inability to comprehend the advantages to be derived from it. First of all, it will cheapen all rates of transportation across the continent, because it will cause a monopoly to cease to exist. The cheapening of rates, with the rapidity of transit, would divert much of the trade between Western Europe and Eastern Asia across this route, causing it to pay toll for crossing the American continent. This of itself would be of incalculable benefit to the whole country. Again, it would open for settlement and development a vast territory, rich in everything that adds to a nation's wealth. What railroads have done for the country east of the Mississippi river they will do for the country west of it. Fifty thousand miles of railroads have been required to people that section, and transport the products from its forests, fields and mines. The country west of the river will in time require as many miles of railroad as the country east of it. As the roads of the East have been subsidized, so must those of the West.

I will not, however, detain this Convention to discuss these questions. We met here to urge upon our National Legislature the propriety and necessity of giving Government aid to a line of road that will most materially assist in the work of extending the great Republic, a solid phalanx of States, from ocean to ocean. Gentlemen of the Convention, the resolutions offered here to-day—the unanimity of the action of this body—will certainly secure the object for which we met. We may consider the Texas Pacific, with termini at St. Louis, Memphis, Vicksburg and New Orleans, an accomplished fact. Observe on that map how, from the main line, these branches extend to the North and South, embracing the whole country within their extended arms, which seem to reach as do the arms of a loving mother to clasp all her children in one fond embrace. Are they not emblematic of the fact that hereafter no dissensions can arise to mar the harmony and blot with blood our future history ? Do not they speak with a voice as loud as that which shall one day waken the dead from their tombs, that the work of conciliation and fraternity has been accomplished—that there are no more "bloody chasms" over which Americans are to clasp hands—that the great American Republic is once more united *now and forever ?*

When this work is finished, as it will be surely and speedily ; when the grand objects for which we are here to-day are attained ; when every portion of the country east of "the great river" is bound with an iron band to the golden shores of the Pacific, it will be pleasant to us to reflect that we were here, and aided to secure such grand results. But then and *now* we should accord honor where honor is most due. We should remember that but for the untiring energy, the acknowledged ability, and determined will of the Hon. Thomas A. Scott, there would be even no prospect of this road being built for years to come. When Moses, on Mount Pisgah, had viewed the rich land promised to his people, he raised his hands to ask a blessing; but powerful as he had been, the assistance of Aaron and Hur was required. Our promised land is before us; we stand upon its borders ready to enter in and take possession. That this is so we owe, as I said before, to the energy, ability and will of Thomas A. Scott. Let us, then, one and all, "hold up his hands" in the work, each of us to the best of his ability. Gentlemen, I have done.

Mr. Smith, of Tennessee: Mr. President, there are a thousand orators here; we have not time to hear them, and I want the previous question, and move it.

The question was put and the motion was carried.

Mr. Anderson, of Virginia: Does that cut off debate?

The President: There can be no more debate. The question is on the adoption of the report.

Several Delegates: Question, question.

The President: The question is on the adoption of the report of the Committee on Resolutions; the previous question has been called for and sustained.

Mr. Filley, of St. Louis: Mr. President, there seems to be no objection on the part of this Convention to the resolutions; there seems to be almost an unanimous opinion in favor of their adoption. I trust, at this stage of the proceedings, we will not put a gag upon this Convention. While I favor the resolutions as presented, and am opposed to any amendments, yet I believe the minority should be respectfully heard, and voted down if occasion demands. [Renewed cries of "Question."]

Mr. Harrison, of Texas: I have an amendment.

The President: The previous question has been ordered.

Mr. Harrison: The previous question has not been sustained.

The President: It has been voted on.

Mr. HARRISON: I wish to read the resolution: "Resolved, That there be also recommended a connection of the Texas Pacific Railroad with the seacoast of Texas." This is conspicuously just, since Texas is the only State that has granted a subsidy to the road, and it is the only State that has a seaport terminus to offer.

Mr. MARSHALL, of Mississippi: I rise, if possible, to second that resolution; and in doing so, I wish to make a remark. I do not believe that this respectable body is prepared to vote on those magnificent resolutions which have been read to us by the Hon. Jacob Thompson this morning. I do not, for my part, propose to gag any man. I want to hear every delegate who has anything to say. I have looked at that diagram up there, and I have listened to the various reports and propositions that have been read here, and I have wondered why in all this matter Galveston itself was not named. We are just about to adopt these resolutions by acclamation, and I wonder why St. Louis has not been spoken of, but has been passed in silence. The citizens of this place have extended to us their hospitality, and have spoken to us in the generous acts of a great city. We have heard it intimated, sir, that even Col. Scott has been in disguise in the views which have been read to us, and I want Col. Scott and his friends to be sounded to the bottom. I want to know that they introduce these resolutions which have been read to us, thoroughly, honestly and candidly. I want to know if he is willing, as a gentleman—and I believe he is willing—to risk his reputation for hundreds of centuries on the veracity with which he speaks in his own communication for the execution and carrying out of the resolutions Mr. Thompson read to us; but, at the same time, I am not willing that these resolutions shall be adopted, though I think they will be, by acclamation, until we get the views of some of the thousand orators on this subject; until they have an opportunity to be heard in all candor. [Applause.] Sir, I am from home, and a good ways from home. I am all the way from the city of Vicksburg, which I represent on the floor of the Convention, or a part of it; from the State of Mississippi, a grand and glorious country, which in all her sorrow and sadness does not sit there with a single thread to stitch up a shroud or a shirt, but with only a plow to turn up to the glad sun the generous soil, and make herself, by the aid of this road, another great and glorious and bright gem in the galaxy of States of which the whole continent may be proud. I want, as a Mississippian, and as a citizen of Vicksburg, because we have constant communication with St. Louis and Missouri, I want to be generous, free from any soil, any stain, any suspense, or any doubt.

I want to be manly, brave and courteous, and I want this thing in regard to this railroad to be carried out in such a manner that every man on this floor, from little Maine, way up in that corner of the diagram, to Wisconsin, shall feel proud of what has been achieved here, and that in order that we may all go home to execute the great purpose for which we are convened, I do not wish to array any part of the country against the other, and, therefore, I do beg this Convention may listen patiently, though it may take two or three days, generously, and with toleration, sir, to a discussion of this matter. Sir, commerce is the soul of civilization, and transportation is the soul of commerce. With these words, I submit— [Loud cries of "Question."]

Mr. Harrison: I have the floor.

The President: The gentleman will forward his amendment.

Several Delegates: Question, question.

Mr. Harrison: Gentlemen, I am not to be put down. Mr. President, I just wish to say that Texas has granted to that road twenty sections to the mile, and gentlemen can see how far this road runs through Texas; gentlemen can look upon this map and see that for thousands of miles Texas has given this road twenty sections to the mile—more sections of land to the mile than it has given to all of her own roads, all of her local roads. And it at the same time is the only State along the whole line of this road, until you get to New York, that offers salt-water connection and deep-sea navigation; and yet, while mention is made of connection eastward and southward, the committee have not recommended that Texas on her seacoast shall have a single connection. Look at that map! Suppose, sir, that there is a line from the intersection at Vinita of a road running to Galveston. Look at it, gentlemen of the Convention! Is it not on the natural line of trade? It is the only line of the heavy shipping. [Applause.] We have a road now running from Galveston to Austin, and a line from Austin to that intersection [indicating on the map] will not be any more than a line from one road to Shreveport. Why shall we not have it? I appeal to you, gentlemen of the Convention, to add that amendment to the resolution of the committee. The Texas delegation will stand, at least, as Joshua did, and it shall command of you to stand still, because it can say to you, and will say to you, that unless you make this concession you shall not have a foot of her land; no foot of land will she give. She will give it to the Galveston branch, and by adding twenty to sixteen makes thirty-six sections of land to the mile, and that will build her road in spite of you.

SEVERAL DELEGATES: Read the resolution.

The President then read the resolution offered by Mr. Harrison, of Texas.

MR. GARNER: Mr. President, I have no objection to Galveston, but I wish merely to state that Texas was represented on the Committee on Resolutions; that committee made an unanimous report, and I wish to lay the amendment on the table, and on that motion to move the previous question.

MR. STEMMON, of Texas: I offer the following as an amendment to the report, or as a substitute for the amendment offered by the gentleman from Texas (Mr. Harrison): Strike out the word "Shreveport," wherever it occurs in the resolution reported by the committee, and insert "the Mississippi river at such point as Congress may prescribe."

THE PRESIDENT: I think that resolution is out of order. It is not germain to the amendment as offered by the gentleman from Texas (Mr. Harrison). [Applause.]

A DELEGATE: I have an amendment to offer to the original resolution.

THE PRESIDENT: It is not in order. There is now one pending, and it is not in order unless it is an amendment to the amendment.

ANOTHER DELEGATE: I move to lay it on the table.

THE PRESIDENT: That will carry the whole report if the motion prevails.

MR. MARSHALL: Will it be in order to move that the Convention go into Committee of the Whole, under the five-minute rule, to discuss this question? Let the previous question be regarded as agreed to and go into Committee of the Whole on the report and the amendment to the report, with the understanding that at the hour of one o'clock we will come to a vote and allow any gentleman to speak five minutes on the subject, and that we will vote at one o'clock precisely on the amendment and the report.

THE PRESIDENT: It is undoubtedly in order for the Convention to make such an order. Gentlemen of the Convention, a motion is made that the Convention resolve itself into a Committee of the Whole to consider the report and amendment, under the rule prescribing five-minute speeches to delegates, with the understanding that the Convention will vote on the report and the amendment at one o'clock precisely.

The question was put, the roll of States being called, and the vote resulted: ayes, 14; noes, 16, as follows:

YEAS—Alabama, California, Georgia, Illinois, Iowa, Louisiana, Minnesota, Missouri, New York, Pennsylvania, Tennessee, South Carolina, Texas, Wisconsin—total, 14.

NAYS—Arizona, Arkansas, District of Columbia, Indiana, Kansas, Kentucky, Michigan, Mississippi, Nebraska, Nevada, New Jersey, New Mexico, North Carolina, Ohio, Virginia, Wyoming—total, 16.

The announcement of the vote was received with applause.

MR. SMITH, of Tennessee: I rise to inquire whether it would be in order to move that all speeches be limited to five minutes? If so, I make that motion.

The question was put and the motion was carried.

THE PRESIDENT: Gentlemen, the question is now on the amendment offered by the gentleman from Texas (Mr. Harrison).

A DELEGATE: I am not from Texas, but I do think that Texas should have an opportunity of explaining the change the member from Texas wishes to make, and I propose that he take the stand and in five minutes explain what he wishes. I have had some conversation with delegates from Texas, and I think it important that they should have an opportunity to explain their wishes to the Convention. I hope the gentleman will take the stand and address the Convention.

ANOTHER DELEGATE: I rise to a point of order. It is, that this Convention has already adopted as a rule that all resolutions shall be referred to the Committee on Resolutions. That committee has reported, and it is too late now for the offering of any resolution. These resolutions must go to the Committee on Resolutions before they can be considered by the Convention.

MR. MARSHALL, of Mississippi: I then propose as an amendment—since it seems to be not rulable, according to the gentleman's understanding, for gentlemen to go on the platform without a formal resolution—that Col. Harrison be invited to the stand or table, where he can be heard five minutes.

The President: The question of order is raised to the effect that the present amendment is out of order, on the ground that the Convention adopted a resolution requiring that all resolutions offered be referred without debate to the Committee on Resolutions. The Chair is of the opinion that that applies only to the resolutions offered prior to the time when that committee made its report, and that it is in the power of the Convention to amend the report of the committee.

Mr. Anderson, of Virginia: I understand the motion now before the Convention is the amendment of the gentleman from Texas to the report of the Committee on Resolutions.

The President: That is it.

Mr. Anderson: I desire, sir, to say one word on that question, Mr. Chairman. I intend to vote for the amendment of the gentleman from Texas [applause], and I desire, sir, to name but two reasons in favor of that vote. Virginia desires and intends to vote for that amendment, first, because she thinks it is just to Texas, and, second, because she thinks it is politic so to do.

Mr. Hale, of Texas: I desire to make this statement. Of course the amendment of the gentleman (Mr. Harrison) I shall favor, and shall vote for it, but I desire to add here my own opinion in regard to it. The resolution reported by the committee, as well as the amendment of the gentleman from Texas, encumbers this whole question with entirely too many outside issues. [Applause.] If the Government could do everything we want done, all these things might be added, but I am of the opinion that when we go before Congress to accomplish the one grand object of this Convention—the construction of the Texas and Pacific Railroad—we should go there with that question and that alone. [Applause.] Otherwise we might have a thousand branches, and every man would want a road to his own door, or even to run to the kingdom of heaven. [Laughter.] I want one, of course, in that direction [laughter], but at the same time we cannot encumber this question with every road that a man wants, and I am therefore opposed to it because we want too many branches; and if you do have your branches, I shall vote for the branch from Galveston, like my friend from Texas.

Mr. Wright, of California: Mr. President, I shall vote for the amendment, but only for one reason, and that is the last reason given by the gentleman from Virginia (Mr. Anderson); that is, because it is politic.

Mr. Harrison, of Texas: Mr. President, can I be permitted to point out some localities on the map?

The President: The gentleman can occupy the stand five minutes. [Mr. Harrison then came forward on the platform.]

Mr. Harrison: Gentlemen of the Convention, I will not make a speech, but I will point out to you some localities upon this map which I think you will have in your eyes when you vote. Here is Galveston [indicating a point on the map] with a fine commodious harbor. There is Austin, the capital of the State, with a railroad now running from Galveston to Austin. There is Vinita [indicating].

Several Delegates: Oh, no.

Mr. Harrison: A line of intersection from this point to Galveston would be as short as the intersection from Vicksburg or Shreveport to Monroe. Memphis already has her connection, one of her own selecting.

A Delegate: She built it herself.

Mr. Harrison, of Texas: Texas is giving twenty sections of six hundred and forty acres from that point [indicating] to this one. You can see how far it is. I have not got time to take a pencil and make the calculation. It is almost an empire of land that Texas is giving to this road—the only State, gentlemen, that has given it one single section, and the only State in which a salt-water terminus can be found.

Mr. Turner, of California: Where is California, Colonel? Isn't there any salt water there?

Mr. Harrison: That is already fixed.

Mr. Leach: Does not California give anything to the Texas and Pacific road?

Mr. Harrison: I am speaking of this side of the mountains.

Mr. Leach: You say Texas is the only State that has given anything?

Mr. Harrison: I admit the correction. California is giving it land—any amount of it; I don't know how much—but, gentlemen, I think justice to Texas requires that she should have more from this road than a mere line of passenger depots stationed at different points through the State where people can get their dinners; and I think not many would get their dinners on that route. This passes beyond the settlements of Texas, and people would not go that road. But you see how straight this road from Galveston is. There we have shipping direct from Europe, sufficient to accommodate all the trade of the West. I beg of you, gentlemen, to look upon this map and cast your votes with that in view.

Mr. McCarty, of Vicksburg: I desire to ask the Colonel, before he leaves the platform, if Galveston has not at the present moment a railroad connecting with the railroad that you speak of?

Mr. Harrison: Yes, sir.

Mr. McCarty: Then if she has got a railroad connection at the present time, why does she seek to overload this project and make the tail of the dog a good deal larger than the dog itself? [Laughter.] Now I will ask the Colonel another question. We hear a great deal here very strongly put by gentlemen from Texas with reference to Texas having given twenty sections per mile to this road; that is admitted. It had to be done by her for the purpose of building that road. The State of Texas, through its Governor and Legislature, said they would give twenty sections, but they wanted the road. That is all they asked; and now these gentlemen come here and ask us to overload this project with another, giving connection with Galveston —a connection that the State of Texas, in its official capacity, through its Governor and Legislature, never asked for.

Mr. Topp, of Memphis: I did not come up here to oppose any gentleman's scheme, especially from the South, but I wish to say, in regard to this last amendment, that I oppose it, and will give you my reasons. The first argument presented by the gentleman from Texas is this—that Texas has given twenty sections per mile. Well, sir, I have this to say with regard to that gift, that without this road, it ain't worth three dried apple d—ns. [Great laughter.] Another reason is, and I want you gentlemen of the Convention to remember it, that Texas is the only State in this Union that comes in owning every foot of land, and that has enough and more than enough to build all her roads, whereas in all other States the land belongs to the General Government.

Mr. Turner, of San Francisco: I will detain the Convention but a single moment. We all desire this road to be built; we are all glad to have it go to Galveston, Memphis, Vicksburg, St. Louis, New York, Charleston, and everywhere. It is a question of policy and wise action. Now we could pass this resolution here, but we wish this bill to be successful in Congress. Take my word for it, you cannot pass the bill in Congress if you load it down with this additional resolution. [Applause.] Look at it a moment; it involves the construction of five hundred miles of additional railroad through the noble State of Texas; that involves a cost of $20,000,000 additional of money. Congress will not pass this bill if it is so loaded down. Let it remain as it is, and then it will be passed by great effort, great labor and great diligence. We hope it will be passed; we believe it will be passed. The gentleman from Texas effectually kills the road—kills the main proposition—by this addition. God bless the State of Texas and her beautiful lands; she got them from the General Government and she is welcome to them; that is all right.

Several Delegates: No, no.

Mr. Turner: She fought gallantly for them; the people of the whole country helped her; the Lone Star State we love and admire. We never can forget the Alamo.

A Delegate: You did not help her; she did it herself.

Mr. Turner: We will drop that; it is a side issue. It seems to me it is better to defeat the resolution in kindness, hoping some day to go further. Let us stick to the resolutions as reported, stop where the resolutions do, and we can accomplish all that the gentleman desires; passing this resolution, we defeat the whole matter. [Applause.]

Mr. Higgins, of Texas: Mr. President, I had no idea of making any remarks on this question, but, sir, when the gentleman from San Francisco (Mr. Turner) says that Texas derives her land from the General Government—

Several Delegates: He took that back.

Mr. Higgins: Texas, sir, derives her land by the blood of her own sons.

The President: She derived them from Mexico. [Laughter and applause.]

Mr. Higgins: She won them on the plains of San Jacinto by the blood of her citizens. It was there, gentlemen, that Texas won her lands, and not from the General Government, and her lands pertain to her; they belong to her under the annexation treaty. Sir, we retain our lands under that treaty. We have the right to these lands to-day, and no power on earth can take an acre of that land from us; when it goes, it goes with her own free will. We granted this subsidy, sir, to the Pacific Railroad; we did it, sir, not only for the benefit of Texas, but for the benefit of the whole Government. The State fought, sir, for this great thoroughfare by giving this grand donation to the road, and we thought we were benefiting not our own State only, but the other States of the Union, and that act remains to-day as a solemn fact; but, sir, if you deprive us of the right that remains to the original State—if sir, by the action of Congress, you deprive us of the right that pertains to us as a State—we will certainly, sir, as a State, as an independent, sovereign State of this Union, reclaim those lands and bestow them in the direction where they belong.

SEVERAL DELEGATES: Time, time.

MR. SNOWDEN, of Pennsylvania: It seems to me, Mr. President, that the gentleman from Texas, who has just taken his seat, has not represented the State he is supposed to represent to-day, in the statement he has uttered. Does he mean to say that the State of Texas will withdraw her grant of land for the building of this great highway across the continent, because, in the wisdom of this Convention, it was not deemed prudent to load down the measure with small branches from one point to another?

SEVERAL DELEGATES: No, no.

MR. SNOWDEN: Does he mean to belittle this great enterprise with little jealousies and little rivalries, and to say that because this Convention will not recommend a road from Galveston to some point, or from Waco to some point in Texas, that therefore the State of Texas will resolve to take back her land? I say I do not believe it. I believe that the people of the Southwest desire one great highway to the Pacific, and I know and believe that highway will be built, and can be built, by the people of the country uniting in such action as will accomplish the result. [Loud applause.] But, Mr. Chairman and gentlemen of the Convention, if you load this measure down with branches from one point to another, then I say this Convention, assembled as it is from the different States of the Union, will have utterly failed in its purpose. You can pass just such resolutions as you choose, but when you come to ask Congress to do all the work the gentlemen in different localities seem to desire to have done, you ask Congress to do what never will be done, and you destroy the great work that your people have been elaborating for years, and you inflict on the State of Texas and the country irreparable injury. [Loud applause.]

Mr. Jones, of Kentucky: Mr. President, I rise, sir, to make a a suggestion to the gentleman from Texas, rather than to speak to the amendment altogether. Now, sir, like many gentlemen that have spoken, especially like the gentleman from Virginia, I am disposed to vote for the amendment, and say further, sir, that, having the honor to be a member of the present Congress (honor or dishonor, whichever it may be) [laughter], I, sir, desire to cast my vote and to give my influence towards the amendment of the gentleman from Texas. Texas, sir, is in one sense the wheel-horse of this great enterprise. But, sir, we should be cautious how we attach amendments to the resolutions already read, and I would beg my friend from Texas to bear in mind that the resolutions do not constitute the bill which is to be offered to Congress in behalf of this great enterprise. [Applause.] These resolutions will be considered, as a matter of course, but the bill may be differently worded, and therefore I would suggest to my friend in all good faith, and with the highest allegiance to the South, and to the State of Texas particularly, to withdraw his amendment. [Applause.] For this reason, Mr. President: if it be possible, according to the complexion of the next Congress, to insert your amendment to give you a road to Galveston, we can do it just as well without your amendment being attached to this resolution as with it. I, for one, would go for it in the Congress of the United States. But it is politic, Mr. President and gentlemen of the Convention, as has been said by many gentlemen who have spoken, not to load down these resolutions—not to make them a bugbear to Congress. At the inception of the question let us go cautiously. I would ask the Convention to take the resolutions as they are, without any amendment [applause], and when they are presented to the Congress of the United States, if it is possible, I would say to the gentleman from Texas who desires the insertion of this amendment to give them a terminus of this road where I think there ought to be one, that we can give it to you just as well without that amendment being inserted in the resolutions as we can with it; therefore, for prudence and for policy, I would suggest to my friend to withdraw his amendment.

Mr. Harrison: Mr. President, may I make an explanation? The gentleman asks me to withdraw my amendment.

The President: The gentleman can decline or insist, whichever he chooses. The gentleman has no right to occupy the attention of the Convention under the rule.

Mr. Harrison: I decline to withdraw it, sir.

Mr. Stemmon, of Texas: I desire to state, Mr. President, that I am a Texan and I am in favor of Galveston, as a matter of course. However, I am opposed to the resolution of my friend, Mr. Harrison. I have, however, but a few words to say. We have in our delegation here, sir, an old San Jacinto soldier, a man who fought at San Jacinto, and we appointed, sir, a committee of Texas people and Louisiana people, and a good many from Arkansas, as we came along together; we appointed a committee of fifteen, of which this old San Jacinto soldier (who was also a General in the late unpleasantness) was chairman, and we agreed that any man who mentioned the claims of any locality in this Convention, to be considered by the Convention, should receive, at the hands of that committee, thirty-nine lashes. [Laughter and applause.] I do not propose to visit that on my friend over there. I beg, however, as the gentleman who preceded me has expressed the wish, that he will withdraw his resolution, and I wish to make this further remark, and I desire this Convention to remember it, and that is, that Congress will not be bound by what this Convention may say, but will exercise its own judgment. Why, sir, the act of Congress chartering the Texas and Pacific Railway Company, makes it commence at Marshall, Texas, and run to San Diego. The resolution of this committee—friends of mine have endeavored to explain it to me, but they do not seem to understand it yet—the resolutions of the committee say commencing at Shreveport, Louisiana. Now I wish to call the attention of the Convention to the fact that if you make it other than a Texas corporation, your enterprise—why, sir, you will affect this magnificent donation made, and which the gentleman over the way (Mr. Topp, of Tennessee) characterized as not worth three dried apples. [Laughter.]

GEN. PRESTON, of Kentucky: Mr. President, I recognize the force of the views presented by the gentleman from Texas (Mr. Harrison). Texas, sir, won these lands before the United States had anything to do with them. Her people derived title to them by the highest of all human documents—their own blood. [Applause.] This was anterior to her connection with the United States, and she holds them to-day by the sacred faith of the treaty of San Jacinto, and that must be inviolable to us. I beg the gentleman from Texas to understand that the remarks I am about to offer can spring from no unkindness to the State of Texas. We all recognize the liberality of the munificent grant of that State, and we can see the anteriority of the title it holds in connection with that grant. But our committee has reported; if we add this amendment, as is apparent from the temper of the Convention, we will be apt to complicate affairs, and I concur in the opinion of the gentleman from Kentucky (Mr. Jones) that it might produce great embarrassment. Now we are on the verge of coming to a vote. Let us consult as to how that vote shall be cast to best subserve the object we have in view. I must consult my own delegation, of which I am chairman, for the subject is of such importance that I will not exercise the authority with which they have clothed me, without first ascertaining their individual views. However strong may be my sympathy with Texas for many causes, I will not say more than that I think it would be advisable not to hazard a vote upon this amendment. I think the gentleman from Kentucky (Mr. Jones), who is now a member of Congress, has expressed the true sentiment in regard to the matter, and I trust the gentleman from Texas will withdraw his amendment.

Mr. Harrison: It would gratify me exceedingly to comply with the request of the distinguished gentleman from Kentucky, as no one reveres or admires him, or the gentleman from Virginia, more than I do; I appreciate their expressions of good-will, and am thankful for them, but, in justice to my State, I must insist on my amendment. It will take no longer to vote it down than to withdraw it.

Mr. Anderson, of Virginia: I could not hear the gentleman from Texas. I wish to know whether he withdraws his amendment.

The President: He insists on his amendment.

Mr. Anderson: I rise, then, Mr. President, to ask the gentleman, as one of his friends, to withdraw his resolution. [Applause.] I have had a consultation with the delegation from Virginia, and I find that that delegation consider themselves committed to the report of the committee, and I am under instructions now to say that they will cast the vote of Virginia against the gentleman's amendment. [Applause.] I therefore unite with the gentleman from Kentucky in calling upon the gentleman from Texas to consult his best interests and withdraw his amendment, as, if he insists on it, he will force many of his friends to vote against it.

Mr. Pierce, of Indiana: I think it is obvious at this time to every member of the Convention, that the consumption of time in this manner is worse than folly. If our vote is to commend itself to the country, and secure that consideration and respect which we have a right to demand, I think we should vote down this amendment and adopt the report of the committee.

A Delegate, of Texas: I move that we postpone the vote on this question until three o'clock.

Mr. HIGGINS: As a delegate from Texas, I move that we postpone it till doomsday.

Mr. GARNER, of Tennessee: I move to lay the amendment on the table.

Mr. KIDD, of Texas: As a representative from Texas, representing the votes, I think, of a majority of the delegation from that State, I have this to say, sir, that we ask that no particular favor be extended to us on the part of this Convention. What we demand is the main trunk line, and when that is made we can meet it. Texas asks no other favor.

Mr. THOMPSON, of Texas: Mr. Chairman and gentlemen of the Convention, I am from Texas; I have lived in Texas nearly twenty years. I represent the northern part of Texas, and I want to say to you that Texas is divided on this amendment. There is a large portion of the people of Texas who do not wish to trammel this great enterprise by tacking on to the report this amendment. [Applause.] I shall vote against the amendment and for the main line. I do not want to trammel Congress with all these propositions.

Mr. SUMNER, of Texas: I wish to say to the Convention, that I am a delegate from the whole State of Texas, and it is very evident to me that the incorporation of this amendment in the report will have the effect to defeat it or very materially damage the general result. [Applause.] As a member from Texas, I shall vote against the amendment. [Renewed applause.]

Mr. WEST, of Texas: Mr. Chairman and gentlemen, I came here —[cries of "Question"] I came here at the call of the Executive Board of St. Louis, to assist in building a main trunk line from Fort Worth and San Diego. I take it that the object for which we are assembled here is to make peace and concord between the upper and lower portions of this country. I am a native of South Carolina. This is my second visit North. My first visit was on foot from Richmond to Gettysburg on a mission of war, with a musket in my hand; my second visit is to St. Louis, and I trust in God it is a mission of peace. The delegation from Texas had a meeting this morning; my friend Col. Harrison presented his resolution in that meeting, and I voted against it. Individually, my sentiment was against it, and for the sake of harmony and union I believe it should be voted down. I say this in due deference to the views of the gentleman from Texas, and in deference to the views of a gentleman whose name I have been taught to worship since William C. Preston taught me my first lessons in South Carolina College. For the reasons which I have stated, and a hundred others which my age and other things would suggest, and in deference to the many gray hairs which I see before me, I bow to what I believe to be the express desire of this Convention, and shall vote against the amendment individually.

Mr. Soussy, of Georgia: I have heard a gentleman say that he represents the whole State of Texas. I think I represent the State of Georgia, and I may say that Georgia wants to vote to build up Texas; Georgia wants this great national line; and although I stand here nominally to represent Georgia, I stand here also representing this nation. [Applause.] I do not want to speak more than a minute or two, but I do want to come to some conclusion and not allow the delegates from Texas to take up so much of the time of this Convention. I want to come to a vote, and with that purpose move the previous question. [Applause.]

The motion for the previous question was carried by the following vote:

Ayes—Alabama, Arizona, Arkansas, California, District of Columbia, Georgia, Illinois, Indiana, Iowa, Kansas, Kentucky, Louisiana, Michigan, Minnesota, Mississippi, Missouri, Nebraska, Nevada, New Jersey, New York, New Mexico, North Carolina, Ohio, Pennsylvania, Tennessee, South Carolina, Texas, Virginia, Wisconsin, Wyoming—total, 30.

The President: The question now is upon the adoption of the resolution offered as an amendment to the report of the committee.

The question was put and the amendment was lost by the following vote:

Ayes—Alabama, Arkansas, Georgia, Illinois, Iowa, Louisiana, Minnesota, Missouri, New York, Pennsylvania, Tennessee, South Carolina, Texas, Wisconsin—total, 14.

Nays—Arizona, California, District of Columbia, Indiana, Kansas, Kentucky, Michigan, Mississippi, Nebraska, Nevada, New Jersey, New Mexico, North Carolina, Ohio, Virgina, Wyoming—total, 16.

The President: The question now is upon the adoption of the resolutions reported by the committee.

A Delegate: I move that the vote be taken on the resolutions *seriatim*.

Several Delegates: No, no.

— 134 —

THE SAME DELEGATE: I have the floor, and I will be heard.

THE PRESIDENT: Debate is out of order, the call for the previous question having been sustained.

MR. JONES, of Kentucky: I move that the resolutions be adopted by acclamation.

THE PRESIDENT: The order is to take the vote by States.

The roll of the States was called and the resolutions were adopted by the following vote:

AYES—Alabama, Arizona, Arkansas, California, District of Columbia, Georgia, Illinois, Indiana, Iowa, Kansas, Kentucky, Louisiana, Michigan, Minnesota, Mississippi, Missouri, Nebraska, Nevada, New Jersey, New York, New Mexico, North Carolina, Ohio, Pennsylvania, Tennessee, South Carolina, Texas, Virginia, Wisconsin, Wyoming —total, 30.

INVITATION TO HON. RICHARD W. THOMPSON TO ADDRESS THE CONVENTION.

MR. ST. GEM, of Missouri: Mr. President, I notice on the floor of this Convention the Hon. Richard W. Thompson, of Indiana, who was a distinguished member in the Convention of 1849, and who addressed that Convention together with Thomas H. Benton and Stephen A. Douglas. I move that the Hon. Richard W. Thompson be invited to address this Convention.

MR. GARNER, of Tennessee: Will the President announce the vote?

THE PRESIDENT: The vote has been announced; the resolutions have been unanimously adopted. Allow me to suggest to the Convention that a motion has been made to invite the Hon. Richard W. Thompson to address the Convention. Is it the pleasure of the Convention to hear him? Taking it for granted that it is, I have the pleasure of presenting to you the Hon. Richard W. Thompson, who will now address you.

SPEECH OF HON. R. W. THOMPSON.

MR. PRESIDENT AND GENTLEMEN OF THE CONVENTION:—I did not come to this city with the expectation or purpose of making a speech. I have been a long time identified with this great work. I was a member of the Convention which met in this city in 1849, when we declared to the country that the national interests required the construction of a railroad to the Pacific Ocean. [Applause.] There were some differences of opinion among the members of that Convention, but the great idea which we expressed to the country was that which I have announced. The Congress of the United States has recognized that idea by repeated acts of legislation. The people of the country have acquiesced in it, and it has become a part of the settled policy of this Government that whatever is necessary to be done in order to develop our national commerce, and to make us the great leading nation of the world, it is the duty of the National Government to do. [Applause.]

If, in the construction of the works which have been already made by the grants of national subsidies, the public necessity has been fully answered, we could not ask of the Congress of the United States that they should give us additional assistance. But there is nothing more easily demonstrable than the fact that the roads already constructed do not answer that necessity. [Applause.] The country requires something more—the whole country requires something more—and the great question for the American people to decide now is what that something shall be. If we desire to control the great and desirable commerce of India, and compel the great commercial nations of the earth to be in any degree contributory to us, we must answer all the demands of that commerce by doing whatsoever shall be required to be done [applause]; and if its wants are not accommodated, in my opinion the National Government has no right to stop short of their accommodation. [Applause.] But it does not matter to me, sir, whether, in doing that, Texas or Louisiana or Arkansas or Mississippi or Missouri is aided, because by building such a work the entire nation is benefited. [Cries of "Good!" and applause.] I am not disposed to look at this question in its local or sectional aspects. I have heard enough in the course of my life of the diverse interests of the different sections of this country. [Loud applause.] I don't know of sections. There is, sir, to my mind, no visible line between them. [Applause.] We are all one people, for weal or for woe. [Applause.] And if but the other day there was an estrangement between us, to-day, sir, the bright sunshine of peace has dispelled it [applause], and we are assembled here like a band of brethren to administer for the interests of the best and most powerful nation upon earth. [Applause.] Let us, therefore, sir, not stop to consider whether this section or that section is to be benefited, but let us do whatsoever is necessary to be done to develop the vast commerce of this country. [Applause.]

In the Convention of 1849, which met here, and which was composed, perhaps, of not so many representative men as there are assembled here to-day, but some men distinguished for eminence and for their services to the country, I then expressed the thought which I am about to utter now—that, in my deliberate opinion, there is no railroad to the Pacific Ocean which can be constructed, answering all the ends of such a work, but one in or upon the 32d parallel of latitude. [Applause.] My mind from that day to this has undergone no change, but the more I have thought of it, the more I have read about it, and the more I have seen, the stronger and stronger have become my convictions that I was right at the start. [Applause.] And the reason is this: It is utterly impossible to overcome those difficulties which nature has thrown in the way on the Northern line. You cannot contend against her storms. You may surmount her mountain peaks by the intervention of human ingenuity; you may overcome many of her embarrassments, but you cannot hold her storms in the hollow of your hand. [Applause.] And she will pour down her snows upon your railroad trains just so long as you shall attempt to defy them. But when you come into the region of the country along the 32d parallel of latitude, you have the finest climate in the world. [Applause.] There are no snow-storms to overcome, and every week and every day, and every hour in the year, your steam horse may pass from one extent of the Union to the other. Your steam horse can never be arrested in his course. Therefore, sir, you have answered the ends of commerce far better by the construction of such a work than upon any other line which can by any possibility be adopted.

Now, then, the plain, practical question for the American people to decide is, is such a work national? Now the idea which fills my mind in reference to the action of this Convention this morning is this: If you will look at that line of road from San Diego to the East, you will find that when it reaches Shreveport it fails to accommodate the interests and necessities of a large portion of the country. Hence, your Committee on Business and Resolutions were compelled to give to that line which might have some local aspects a national feature. Therefore they extended a branch to Memphis, so that by communication with the roads which pass through Tennessee and Kentucky, North Carolina and Virginia, it might assume a national aspect in that direction; and again, by a road to Vicksburg, and another to New Orleans, taking in the whole southern extent of country, making them what we are ourselves—prosperous by means of facilities of railroad intercommunication. [Applause.] There is something grand in the idea, and there is something which makes it even more peculiarly grand in the time in which that idea is sent forth to the world. [Applause.] We are here really upon a mission of peace. These Southern States are just as much entitled as the Northern States to the protection and fostering care of the Government. [Applause.] Whatever they may have been yesterday, to-day the old flag is ours, and we all honor it. [Applause.] And wheresoever there is a portion of the people of this country who are unable of themselves, whether by misfortune or otherwise, to aid in the development of the great agricultural, manufacturing and commercial resources which they possess, I hold that it is the duty of their countrymen elsewhere, who have the means, to come to their assistance. [Applause.] The South cannot build railroads; we know it. She has the enterprise, the intelligence, the honor and the chivalry, but they do not build railroads. [Applause.] The wealth which she possessed is gone. We are rich. We have our immense fields with their vast products and our extended commerce; and every dollar that we add to their wealth but extends ours. [Applause.]

Now, sirs, it so happens that Providence has provided that along upon the 32d parallel of latitude that great article of cotton alone should be produced. How far the cotton regions extend towards the Pacific I do not know. It may be that with irrigation in the valley of the Mesille it may extend all the way, and I trust in God it may; but we know that the vast fields of Texas are annually increasing her cotton crop, and I believe that out of the increased product of that great crop we may be enabled to secure a better and a more extended control over the commerce of the world than by any other of the products of our soil. [Applause.]

I read in history that the old jealousy of England towards this country exhibited itself in the expenditure of four or five hundred millions of dollars to raise cotton in India to rival ours in the markets of the world; and I read also in the history of the present that in this she has failed, because Providence has not given to India either so desirable soil or climate for the production of that article as it has to us, and we are enabled to-day to go into the markets of Liverpool and sell our manufactured cotton cheaper than she can herself. [Applause.]

Now if we should succeed by the extension of this railroad to the Pacific Ocean, in increasing our cotton product one or two hundred fold, we will have demonstrated to England that her expenditure in India is profitless, and instead of our buying from her the manufactured article, and exchanging the raw material for it, she will have to buy the manufactured article from us which we have made out of our own raw material. [Applause.] And, sir, the cotton of India will have been wasted, and the India people will be turning their attention to the development of that great wealth which civilization for centuries has been seeking to acquire. And then, when that time shall come, the grand problem will be solved, and it will not only be demonstrated that Columbus was right when he said, "If you want to go to the East you must start westward," but it will demonstrate that Providence has preserved this cotton, virgin as it was, for a race of people fused from all the nations of the earth, who by their intelligence, their energy and their enterprise, would be enabled to rise up and to become the controlling power of all the world. [Applause.] And then, if we shall be true to ourselves, we shall not only carry along with us our commerce and our flag, but we shall carry along to all the nations of the earth the great idea of man's capacity to govern himself. [Applause.] And we shall carry our Christianity and our civilization, and it may come to pass in the course of the future, when you and I, sir [pointing to Gen. Preston], have passed away, and when our children shall take the places which we fill, it may come to pass that by means of these very Pacific Railroads which we are now proposing to build, we shall have belted this entire earth with our influence, until the light of our example shall have been shed upon the pathway of every nation upon earth, and we will be blessed by coming generations for having preserved as their inheritance the vast work of our fathers. [Loud applause.]

I said to you at the outset that I did not come here to make a speech. I am a practical man, long since retired from active life, enjoying my own domestic quiet. But there have rushed into my mind since I came here a class of thoughts which I would not hush if I could. Years ago in active life I met a class of gentlemen in the great struggle for political ascendancy, from whom I have been separated for many long years. I find them here to-day. To these men I extend the hand of fraternal greeting. [Applause.] I say to them that although circumstances may have called us apart for a while, we are now with our arms interlocked pursuing that grand highway of national honor and reputation, by which alone this nation can be built up. [Applause.] And, sir, let the remnant of your life and mine [pointing to Gen. Preston]—for we have spent its early years in the service of the country—let the remainder of your life and mine demonstrate to our posterity that when we have gone we have left to them a glorious work to be achieved—the work of taking care of those institutions which our fathers formed, and of planting deeper and deeper in American soil the pillars of the old Union, that they may rise up higher and higher towards the heavens, and that the light which shall go out from them shall become with each revolving season brighter and brighter until all the earth shall recognize man's capacity to govern himself. [Loud and prolonged applause.]

SPEECH OF COL. ROBERTSON TOPP.

Mr. Topp, of Tennessee: Gentlemen of the Convention, I rise to make a request which I hope nobody will oppose. It is this: you do not know me, and I do not know many of you; but I have studied and thought about this thing, and have prepared what I think is a most excellent argument upon the whole subject-matter, although you, perhaps, may differ with me in that respect. I intended to have delivered it to the Convention, but now I want the privilege of doing as they do in Congress, where they manufacture a great many public men; that is, that you will consider the speech as spoken, and that I may have it published with the general proceedings. I trust you will allow me to do that. [Laughter and applause.]

The President: Leave will be granted, there being no objection.

The following is the address of Col. Robertson Topp, of Tennessee, the publication of which was authorized in the official proceedings:

We have met in Convention for the purpose of considering an improvement of much interest to this city, to this valley, to the people of the Southern and Western States, and I should think to the people of the whole Union.

The object, as I understand it, is to suggest some speedy and efficient method for the completion of a grand trunk railway from a point in Texas, on the 32d parallel, to the Pacific Ocean, and at the same time give aid for constructing railways from St. Louis, Memphis, Vicksburg and New Orleans.

The cities named are selected because all the roads east of the Mississippi below St. Louis converge upon one or the other of those cities, and the aid proposed is to enable them to connect from the west bank of the Mississippi their respective roads with the main trunk, at such points of intersection as to them may seem best.

No amount of wild lands will furnish means to do this; it requires money, especially in a wilderness country. We propose to ask Government to aid these enterprises by loaning her credit, by guaranteeing the payment of the interest on bonds issued.

This assistance is asked because the Government is the principal proprietor of the land, because the main trunk line for 1,500 miles is through a wilderness, and because the physical obstacles to be encountered in the expansive and deeply overflowed bottoms of the Mississippi are so great and so costly as to place these enterprises beyond the reach of individuals. The roads sought to be aided are thought to be so important as to justify demanding the helping hand of the Government.

Permit me to state the proposition in another way. The Government, by princely donations and subsidies, has aided in constructing the Union and Central Pacific, and Kansas Branch, and have likewise granted munificent subsidies for a still more northern road from the head of Lake Superior to Puget Sound. Notwithstanding the murmurs, blackened complaints, charges of fraud, etc., etc., concerning these subsidies and the management of these roads, I think the Government in granting aid acted wisely and well, as this was the only possible way to cause that great wilderness country in the West to be settled. If not settled and developed, of what value is it?

The Union and Central Pacific have caused this in some degree, and opened a magnificent thoroughfare from ocean to ocean. It is worth tenfold its cost; its value cannot be measured by dollars and cents; it should be considered invaluable, and so will be the road from Lake Superior when constructed.

This finished road opens up a great and convenient thoroughfare to the upper and northern half of this country. It is not, however, the nearest, best or most convenient route to the lower or southern half of the United States. It should be remembered that this is an expansive country, more than twenty degrees in width. Having aided out of a common fund to make this road, we demand assistance to build the roads that suit us. Is there anything unreasonable in this?

In time to come other Pacific roads will be required. It has taken more than fifty thousand miles of railways to answer the commercial wants of the people between this great river (from its head to its mouth) and the Atlantic and Gulf coasts.

These roads afford admirable facilities with the cities on the Atlantic and the Gulf, and through them with the great marts in Europe. The country between this river and the Pacific coast is larger, perhaps intrinsically more valuable, and in time to come will require as many railways. Besides, there lies beyond the trade with the Orient—with three hundred millions of people—whose track has marked its pathway in the history of nations as plainly as the milky way in the firmament above us. As the Government is the great landed proprietor, owns all the country, it is but right that she should lead in the enterprise to develop the same, leaving to individuals and communities to fill up the gaps with such minor improvements as may hereafter be needed. This is precisely what was done when they aided in constructing the Illinois Central, the Union and Central Pacific. If it was right then, is it not so now?

I see it in the papers and hear it in a thousand ways, that Jay Gould, who is said to control the Union Pacific, with his associates, are busily engaged to thwart this enterprise, by sowing the seeds of distrust, by fighting the friends of levees against the railroad, by planning to concentrate the Eastern end of his road on this city, so as to make a Southern road unnecessary; and it is even charged that he will expend the means of his road with a lavish hand in *subsidizing* members of Congress to defeat aid to a rival road, or any other Pacific road.

I do not credit these clamors. I have always understood that Jay Gould was an eagle-eyed, clear-headed, deep-thinking, talented man. So thinking, I do not believe that he would engage in the contemptible tricks imputed to him. I did not comprehend his movements exactly until some one handed me, this morning, this pamphlet, containing the speech of Mr. Benton, who, with the aid of his scientific friends, the buffaloes, had not only discovered the best route, but that this city was in the exact centre—not half a mile to the right or left.

Having read this speech, no doubt Jay Gould and his associates are shaping their course to prepare for coming events. He sees this city with its immense area of country to support it, and that its trade, manufactures, commerce, wealth and population are looming up in such grand proportions as to force the conclusion that ere long it will become the second, if not the first and principal city on this continent. Seeing and knowing this, is it surprising that they should make their Eastern terminus here, that they may share a part of this mighty traffic? If in this just and honorable interpretation I am mistaken, and Mr. Gould or any of his friends are here for the miserable tricks and purposes imputed, I beg leave, in a kind, quiet and private way, to say to them, look at this intelligent audience. You will see that you can neither dupe nor mislead such men; that being so, the best thing any of you can do (I speak it kindly) will be as quietly and as secretly as possible, on tip-toes, to slip out of the room, and in some back alley-way get out of the city.

With regard to levees—they are a national necessity, and concern the cotton manufacturers of the United States and of Europe, who desire the best staples of cotton; and all those who have mules, corn and meat to sell are quite as much interested as those who grow cotton. I am not in the councils of the nation. If I were, and discovered any members who had heretofore advocated appropriations to the Union and Central Pacific, and otherwise championed that road, opposing this, I should not hesitate to ask them how much they had been paid to take such a miserable and degraded course.

I repeat, however, that I give no credence to such charges. Our danger lies in another quarter—in dissensions among ourselves; in one section asking too much, and denying the just claims of others.

At the last session of Congress a bill was introduced which ignored the claims of Memphis, and through her the just claims of Tennessee, North Mississippi, North Alabama, the Western Carolinas, Kentucky, Virginia, Maryland and Delaware, whose system of roads concentrate in a large degree at Memphis. When asked why this discrimination? the reply was, You have connection through the Cairo and Fulton Railroad. As that road is controlled by St. Louis, would it not have answered them as well as us without aiding to build another? Besides, to be plain, we did not choose to subject ourselves to the caprices or cupidity of a rival in trade. We had not forgotten the adage handed down to us from the time of the Trojan war, "*Timeo Danæos et dona ferentes.*" Beyond this we were seeking connection with a road three degrees south of the line proposed to us, and as our right we demanded the nearest and most direct route, and such we shall continue to do. In this connection I am pleased to be assured that the objectionable features in the bill of last session will be remedied. That being so, there can be no contest between us; unitedly we can act. On this principle I stand here pledged and prepared to co-operate and work with you for success, if that be practicable.

I have heard it bruited about since I came here that there is another formidable obstacle to success in another quarter altogether. It is said that the leaders of both parties, in Congress and out of it, have changed their politics; that they are now opposed to subsidies; that it is a dangerous system, well calculated to corrupt Congress. I have not much respect for platforms; they are foolish things to fool foolish people.

If this anti-subsidy clamor comes from those who have grown great, rich, prosperous, populous and fat from subsidies, so fat that they are in danger of being smothered in their own grease, it reminds one of an old thief, hoary with a long life of villainies and peculations, who, in the last agonies, joins the church and takes the sacrament, hoping to deceive his Maker and neighbors. It comes too late—deceives nobody. It is, in my opinion, a pernicious, demagogical doctrine, without reason or manliness. With regard to corrupting members of Congress, I do not credit such charges. If true, however, you have the corrective in your own hands. Exercise the elective franchise intelligently, elect those who are too wise to be duped, too manly to be bribed, too honest to betray their trust. As this subsidy question may assume an important aspect, being on the eve of a Presidential election, when every demagogue is looking out for popularity and place, I trust you will pardon me if I depart from discussing the precise question before us for the purpose of combating this heresy, and that we may more properly tread the path of duty on the present occasion.

The word *subsidy*, as construed by lexicographers, means aid, assistance. It may be by legislation, by furnishing arms, men, ships, credit, money or lands, or all of these. If subsidies are wrong in one respect they are wrong in all, and common honesty requires that those who have pledged themselves to this new doctrine shall in good faith practice it in all things. It will be remembered that Mr. Clay and other advocates for protection to manufactures advocated it as a temporary policy only—"*Protect manufactures in their infancy.*" As this protective subsidy policy has been in operation for fifty-nine years, grinding and oppressing those not specially protected, will not thinking people say it has lasted long enough and must be repealed? Suppose they begin with *iron*, the duty on which costs $2,000 per mile on every mile of imported railroad iron. What will Mr. Kelly and the representatives from Pennsylvania say to this? Suppose they next name *copper*. What will the representatives from the copper regions on the lakes say? Suppose *salt* is mentioned. What will those who champion that interest, from New York and other localities, say? Suppose woolen and cotton fabrics, bunting, spool-thread, suspenders, gaiters, lastings, cobourgs, in fact everything mentioned in the tariff act, from absinthe to zinc, are proposed to be overhauled, how long would it be before Washington City would be found insufficient to accommodate the vast crowd of Yankees that would rush to the Capital? The compulsive result would be they would change their politics and say that they did not mean that doctrine to apply otherwise than to oppose subsidies in land and money to railroads. Railroads being in bad odor just now, that would be cheap patriotism.

Looked at in that light only, it would be a practical outrage upon the Southern States.

This land-subsidy system commenced with Illinois in 1850, and it has been extended by various acts to all the States of the West, until there are no more roads to build, and no more room for subsidy roads in some of the States.

The effect of this system has caused Illinois and other Western States to progress in population, wealth, power and development a full century in advance of what they would have done had no such subsidies been afforded. Can that be a bad system which has caused such mighty developments, and that without costing the Government a cent? And are you, gentlemen from Illinois and other Western States, who have reaped such a golden harvest from this system, prepared to deny its benefits to others? Can the managers of the Union and Central Pacific, after receiving such mighty aids in land and money, hold up their heads, look honest men in the face, and justify themselves in opposing similar aid to others? If they do, could the annals of effrontery find a parallel? This doctrine of anti-subsidy cannot be maintained on principle.

It is a well-known fact that the greater part of the valuable public lands are to be found in the States and Territories west of the Mississippi. Out of these, railroad companies in those States and Territories have received immense donations, in some instances almost sufficient to pay for the construction of their roads.

To shut down on that doctrine now, that they may use the balance to give it to emigrants, and thereby increase the population, power and wealth of those States, is asking subsidy in another shape with a vengeance as mean as it is deceitful. Giving away lands to control immigration. What is that but a bonanza—subsidy under an anti-subsidy name?

If the Northern men who have been pampered by subsidies, under the name of *protection*, for fifty years, until they are bursting with plethora, sanction it, what is this but another proof that avarice is insatiable and meanness inscrutable? If this doctrine comes from politicians, is it not evident that public men have degenerated, and that they clothe themselves with this mantle that they may skulk responsibility? What does a doctrine which refuses to do anything, improve or advance any interest, develop any wealth, promote any enterprise, lead to, but clogging the wheels of government?

If the wheels of government are to be clogged by a doctrine which virtually negatives all useful legislation, will not the people inquire, Why collect three hundred or more legislators who have nothing to do beyond voting "a trembling contribution" for themselves? This doctrine leads to that. Away with it, and contemplate, if you please, the different views, the better men, and better days of the republic.

Beginning with George Washington, is it not a well-known fact that throughout his long and valuable life the improvement of his country was the predominant wish of his heart? His public life needs not the embellished trappings of declamation to brighten and sustain a name and fame which is consigned to immortality.

Think of Mr. Hamilton, of whom his countrymen may say, as was said of Coriolanus, "He hath so planted his honors in their eyes and his actions in their hearts, that for their tongues to be silent and not confess so much, were a kind of ingrateful injury."

Think of Mr. Madison, of whom it may be said, as Mr. Burke said of Lord Chatham, "A great and celebrated name, a name that keeps the name of this country respectable in every other on the face of the globe. *Clarum et venerabile nomen gentibus.*"

To come nearer the men of our own times.

Think of Mr. Webster, the great Northern star, "of whose true, fixed and resting quality there is no fellow in the firmament," whose capacious mind, like some great maelstrom, engulfed all knowledge and science of government, or rather like the fabled Neptune, who, with one wave of his trident, caused states and communities, like naiads and sea-nymphs, to follow in his wake and dance attendance in his train. What would he have said of such a doctrine as this?

Think of Mr. Clay, who for thirty years stood steadfast to his principles, like unto a rocky promontory stretching out into the sea, and, like it, as heedless of the angry surging of the waves at its base; whose genius and eloquence lifted him as far above the level of ordinary men as Mont Blanc above the plains beneath. What would he have said of such a doctrine?

Think of Mr. Calhoun, the darling of the South, whose bright mind enabled him to reduce to simplicity every subject, no matter how complex, which passed the crucible of his vigorous investigation. To this was added lofty patriotism, dauntless courage, and more than Cato's virtue. What would he have thought of such a doctrine?

Have we stumbled on an age of mediocrity, when our public men may be compared to a "gouty Briareus, many hands and no use; or purblind Argus, all eyes and no sight?"

In further illustration of these views, permit me to allude to some important events intimately blended with the history of the past, which are well calculated to lift us to higher and nobler considerations of duty on the present occasion.

It is not quite a century since our fathers dissolved their connection with the mother government, and resolved to be free and independent. This *resolve* involved them in a long, bloody, terrible and expensive war with Great Britain, which demanded the subsidies of the lives, fortunes and honors of every man, woman and child in all the land; and nobly did they respond by staking all, by risking all.

I shall not dwell upon the actors or incidents of that event. It has become the theme of orators, been decorated with the wreath of the muse, and has assumed its place in the undying pages of history, and there it will remain in all coming time, enshrined in the hearts of our countrymen, so long as liberty has a votary on earth. This was our first subsidy; it has been eternized and canonized. At the close of our revolutionary war, and to the beginning of this century, our possessions, as a nation, were bounded on the east by the Atlantic, on the west by the Mississippi, on the north by Canada, on the south by the possessions of France and Spain. In 1803 the entire country west of the Mississippi, including the very spot where we are standing to-day, with both banks of the Mississippi at its mouth, were in the hands of a powerful European nation.

The men of that day did not believe it was either wise or prudent to permit, if it could be avoided, these vast possessions west and south of us to remain in the hands of a foreign nation that might become an enemy, line this river on its west bank, from its source to its mouth, with frowning batteries, and shut out our commerce from the ocean and the markets of the world. They avoided this possibility by purchasing the country known as Louisiana from France. They called on the people for a subsidy of fifteen million dollars, at that time an enormous sum of money, to pay for it, and nobly did they respond to this demand.

This was our second subsidy of magnitude. Now look over those vast regions, the magnificent States that have been carved out of it, and tell me whether there is a man living who would deny the wisdom and justice of that measure.

In 1812, for the vindication and maintenance of our maritime rights on the high seas, it became necessary to declare war against Great Britain. In the prosecution of that war, on land and at sea, our gallant soldiers and seamen displayed undaunted courage, and in many memorable actions

"Bore their country's honors high,
Resolved to conquer or to die."

This war demanded heavy subsidies from the purses of the people; again nobly they honored the draft. Tell me, my countrymen, could any one be found base enough to begrudge their share of it?

In 1819 we purchased Florida from Spain. This gave us more than twelve hundred miles of frontage on the Atlantic and Gulf, and an immense valuable territory if developed as it should be—more valuable to us than Cuba ever was to Spain. This—if we include the Indian wars—to defend it, cost another heavy subsidy.

In 1845 we purchased Texas from herself. That purchase cost us a war with Mexico. You know the history of that war, its incidents and cost. I should do injustice to you and myself if I omitted saying that that war, from the first battle at Palo Alto to the final surrender of the capital of Mexico, reflected a blaze of imperishable glory upon the American name. Growing out of that war and as a part of it, and by treaties, we acquired our vast possessions on the Pacific slope, including California, New Mexico and Arizona; and by a later treaty with Russia, Alaska. This last-mentioned war and these last-mentioned acquisitions have cost us in subsidies fabulous sums of money. But who among living men can gauge their value, or properly estimate their importance to us? These are our jewels acquired by subsidies. Which one would you pluck from the casket and throw away?

That you may form some faint, distant conception of their importance, permit me to invite you to place before you side by side the map of Europe and of the United States and ask you to examine them.

After examining the bounds of each, and the area of each of the States that constitute Europe, you will turn your eyes to the imperial proportions of the United States, stretching from the commerce-lashed shores of the Atlantic and Gulf to the calm but majestic Pacific, and then from the line of Britain's possessions,

"Where our green mountain tops blend with the sky,
To the waves where the balmy Hesperides lie."

You will perceive that in area we are larger than all Europe south of the Ural mountains. If you will turn your eyes to these maps again, and compare them with reference to navigable streams, lakes, bays, harbors, inlets and ocean boundaries, you will perceive that we are endowed with greater facilities for commerce, internal and external, than all the States of Europe combined. If you will consult the physical geographies and statistics of the two countries and compare them with reference to soil, climate, varied productions, water power, mineral wealth, particularly iron, stone coal, copper, lead, zinc, gold, silver and other precious metals, you will perceive that, in these particulars, which contribute so much to the material advancement of all countries, we are quite equal to all the States of Europe together. In present population, wealth, manufacture, mechanic arts, high culture, commerce and capital there can be no comparison. Ours is a new country, not yet a century old; theirs the result of many, many centuries.

Looked at in the lights before us, after giving the States of Europe full credit for their great deeds and noble actions; their triumphs in arts, arms, conquests, in all that is greatest, brightest and grandest —forgetting, if you please, in generous magnanimity, any and all things that may have saddened and darkened their annals—are we not justified in concluding that these States, in time to come, under one flag and a common country, may reasonably hope to equal in material power all the States of Europe combined? Without subsidies these mighty results could not have been accomplished. Again I ask, which of these stars would you strike from the firmament of our glory?

In conclusion, permit me to ask that you will be just to the gentleman who will have the chief burden of building this road. Instead of aspersing his character and motives, let us aid by holding up his arms and cheer him in his noble work.

Let us gather a little of inspiration from a recent event. In one of our large cities a house was on fire and many thousand citizens had rushed to the scene of the disaster. A wild, frenzied and appalling scream was heard inside the burning building. In an instant a noble fireman was seen ascending the giddy height on a ladder; just as he had reached the last round on the ladder, a fearful amount of flame and smoke burst from the roof and windows; the fireman halted. A noble-hearted man perceiving what was the matter, in a loud and manly voice, high above the tumult, shouted out, "Cheer him, boys; cheer him!" Cheer after cheer went up from the vast crowd. The fireman, catching courage from that cheering, rushed in, came out with a little girl, and saved her.

Governed by this, let us cheer on Mr. Scott in a voice that will be heard from the Atlantic to the Pacific.

Mr. Dan. Voorhees was loudly called for, but did not respond.

MISCELLANEOUS BUSINESS, &C.

Mr. Broadhead: I wish to offer the following resolution:

Resolved, That the Secretary of the Executive Committee appointed by the citizens of St. Louis, together with the Secretary of this Convention, be instructed to prepare, under the direction of said committee, the proceedings of this Convention for publication in pamphlet form, and to publish such number of copies as they may deem advisable.

The resolution was adopted.

Mr. Haven, of Louisiana: I move that the Convention tender a vote of thanks to the gentleman from Indiana (Mr. Thompson) for the able speech delivered by him before this Convention.

The motion was carried.

A Delegate: I move that the thanks of this Convention be tendered to the various railroad companies for the transportation of the delegates of the Convention, and also to the Western Union Telegraph Company.

The motion was carried.

The President: I will announce to the Convention that tickets of admission to the Rink, in accordance with the invitation read on yesterday, are now in the hands of the officers of the Convention for delivery to the members on call.

Mr. Kountz, of Pennsylvania: I have sent to the Chair a resolution which I desire to have read.

The President: In the opinion of the Chair, inasmuch as the subject has been disposed of by the action of the Convention in the adoption of the report, the resolution is not in order, but it will be read for the information of the Convention if it is so desired.

Mr. Kountz: Then I will withdraw the resolution, sir. I move now that we adjourn *sine die*.

Mr. Filley, of Missouri: Mr. President, there is a resolution pending, which the Chairman of the Executive Committee will put, in regard to a vote of thanks to the officers of the Convention.

The question was put and the vote of thanks was carried unanimously.

Mr. Stearns, of California: As there has been no provision made for publishing and distributing the pamphlets of the proceedings of this Convention, which we have ordered, I move that each delegate now come forward and make a deposit with the Secretary, giving his name and address, and that when these pamphlets shall have been published that they shall be forwarded to each delegate in proportion to the amount of money that he pays. [Applause.]

Mr. Bowman, of Kentucky: I move that the thanks of this Convention be tendered to the citizens of St. Louis for the very hospitable manner in which they have entertained this Convention.

The motion was carried.

Mr. Filley: I would like to make an announcement in reference to the excursion arranged for the delegates to the Convention, on to-morrow, that the boats will be ready promptly at half-past 9 o'clock, and the delegates who have not been furnished with tickets will find them at the wharf-boat to-morrow morning.

Mr. Snowden, of Pennsylvania: I move that the thanks of this Convention be tendered to the officers of the Convention.

The motion was carried.

RESPONSE OF PRESIDENT MATHEWS.

In response to the vote of thanks to the officers of the Convention, President Mathews spoke as follows:

Gentlemen of the Convention:—A motion has been made and seconded for a *sine die* adjournment of this body, but before putting that motion allow me briefly to congratulate myself and you upon the successful conclusion of our labors. [Applause.] If our proceedings have not been without debate, that debate at least has been without acrimony, and leaves no sting. [Applause.] But our proceedings have been marked not only by harmony, but by unanimity. We stand, gentlemen, committed by the unanimous voice of these delegates, representing so many and such various influential interests throughout the whole country, to the prosecution of the single enterprise of constructing this great highway to the Pacific coast; and when I say "to the single enterprise," I mean to emphasize that fact. I mean that we are committed to no other, and that as we desire this above all others, so, in order to insure its completion, we must not be caught in any entangling alliances with doubtful schemes. [Applause.] Let us all bear in mind, gentlemen, that at this juncture in our national history, more, perhaps, than at any other time since the days of its original purity, the public mind is aroused and the public conscience is sensitive to everything which bears the appearance of perverting public power, and of turning the national treasury into private courses.

Our claims we believe and know to be just and right. Let us stand on the merits of our enterprise; it is able to stand by itself. [Applause.] Let us not, for the sake of lobby influence or votes in either house of Congress, make bargains with schemes that well-intentioned men must oppose as seeking to turn the taxes of the people into the pockets and profits of private speculators. Let us go to the national seat of government, let us go to the national law-makers, let us go to the national guardians of the public treasury and present the just claims of our well-considered enterprise. We may fail to-day, we may fail to-morrow, but early and ultimate and complete success is as certain as that the people of the United States have the intelligence necessary to govern themselves. [Applause.]

Gentlemen, on behalf of myself and those who have been associated with me as the officers of this Convention, allow me to return my and their grateful acknowledgments to you for the honor you have done us. I repeat at the close of this Convention what I anticipated at its beginning, that experience has shown that this Convention will not only be heard but will be felt, and felt in the weight of its character and the wisdom of its recommendations. To have been called upon to represent it as its presiding officer is an honor far beyond my expectations and far beyond my deserts. [Great applause.]

Gentlemen, the question is whether you will now adjourn without day.

A DELEGATE: May I ask the indulgence of the mover of the resolution for an adjournment *sine die*, that the Convention request that Gen. Preston respond, on behalf of the South, to the good wishes so cordially expressed by the Hon. R. W. Thompson. [Cries of "General Preston."]

In response to these calls Gen. Preston came forward and spoke as follows:

REMARKS OF GENERAL PRESTON IN RESPONSE TO THE SPEECH OF HON. R. W. THOMPSON.

MR. PRESIDENT AND GENTLEMEN OF THE CONVENTION:—Although I felt honored by the call, I declined to obey; but as we are about to close our meeting, and as you assign me a duty that addresses itself so powerfully to my head and to my heart, I feel that I can no longer decline your call.

I certainly listened with the most peculiar pleasure to the gentleman who has received, for the noble words he has spoken, the spontaneous thanks of this great body of gentlemen, assembled from the New England States, from Pennsylvania, New York, the Carolinas, Louisiana, Kentucky, Texas, and other of our sister States—an unanimous compliment that must make him carry home with him the proud satisfaction that this day he has done a good deed. [Applause.] What is that good deed? It is the wise words he has uttered in a manly and kind spirit, and I hope that with similar sentiments I can say for the Convention who here call upon me to speak in their behalf, that whatever defeat befell the South in battle, they felt that their motives were pure, and therefore stand here with no sense of inferiority to mortal man. [Applause.] They claim no superiority, but admit no inferiority to any gentleman in the land. [Applause.] When welcomed with hearts like these, they feel anew that equality is the only ground upon which freemen can unite, and were we to stand on any other ground we would be false to the moral sentiment of our country, so that we would debauch the public spirit, until the republic would perish under the power of an established monarchy. [Applause.]

Our sense of honor may be sometimes called Quixotic. It may be that the word "honor" sometimes provokes a smile, as if it were a foolish element in modern society. But what is honor? I will not give it the witty but base definition of Falstaff, for I hold that public honor in America is made up of sound common sense and exalted self-respect. [Applause.] Charles Francis Adams has recently given us an admirable admonition of its decay and danger, but in the old spirit of honor and fraternity that breathed from the lips of the gentleman from Indiana this day, my heart leaped, as it were, across the gushing waters of the Ohio and restored old memories, when no words but those of friendship were uttered as the soldiers of our States marched along the great plains of Mexico to win the very soil which this railway is to traverse, and when the troops of Louisiana and of Massachusetts marched under the same flag, where Southern statesmen directed us in the path of empire. And, let me say, it is within my personal knowledge that no more devoted friend to peace and concord, no firmer advocate of harmony, no more wise or sagacious statesman was found to represent his State in Congress at that time than Richard W. Thompson, of Indiana. [Applause.] I therefore feel it is a pleasant duty to respond to your call in behalf of the Convention. The thoughts uttered were well conceived and the words well weighed, so that I feel I will have the support and approval of this body and of every Southern gentleman present when I affirm in your presence that we receive the kind and timely words of the gentleman from Indiana with profound thanks, and accept them in the true spirit of manly candor with which they were so eloquently expressed. [Applause.]

The President: The Chair will state to the Convention that the Memorial Committee will be appointed hereafter. Are you now ready for the question? The motion is that this Convention adjourn without day.

The motion was put and carried, and the Convention thereupon adjourned *sine die.*

MEMORIAL COMMITTEE.

After the adjournment of the Convention the President of the Convention, Judge Stanley Mathews, appointed the following committee to prepare an address to Congress, in accordance with the resolutions adopted by the Convention:

James O. Broadhead, Missouri; Wm. Preston, Kentucky; John H. Kennard, of Louisiana; R. W. Thompson, Indiana; Morton McMichael, Pennsylvania; Peter Cooper, New York; Jas. R. Anderson, Virginia; Wm. Johnson, North Carolina; D. Felsenheld, California; Henry G. Smith, Tennessee; A. G. Clapton, Texas; Joseph E. Johnston, Georgia; C. K. Marshall, Mississippi.

The committee above named met in Parlor No. 5 of the Southern Hotel, on Friday morning, the day after the adjournment of the Convention, when the following proceedings were had:

Col. Broadhead called the committee to order, and stated that, although he was named as chairman, he felt that the members should elect at that time a permanent chairman.

On motion of Gen. Wm. Preston, of Kentucky, Col. James O. Broadhead was elected permanent Chairman, and Judge Kennard, of Ohio, Secretary.

The Chairman then stated that the object of the meeting was to consider what the duties of the committee are according to the following resolution adopted by the Convention:

"That the President of the Convention be requested to prepare an address to the people of the United States, embodying the views set forth in the preamble and resolutions adopted by this Convention, and that he be authorized to appoint a committee of thirteen, who, with the President of this Convention, shall present an engrossed copy of the proceedings of this Convention, together with the address, to the President of the United States, the presiding officer of the Senate, and the Speaker of the House of Representatives, and to take such other action as in their judgment may be deemed best to further the objects and purposes of this Convention."

RESOLUTIONS OF THE COMMITTEE.

Gen. Preston offered the following resolution, which was adopted:

Resolved, That the Chairman is requested, as soon as practicable, to obtain proof-sheets of the contemplated address of the President of the Convention to the people of the United States, so that said copies may be forwarded to each member of the committee for information and comment, and to correspond with them in relation to the address, to the end that the true intent and purpose of the Convention may be carried into full effect.

The following resolution, offered by Gen. Anderson, of Richmond, Va., was also adopted:

Resolved, That the Chairman be authorized and requested whenever, in his discretion, he deems it necessary, to convene the committee at such place as he may deem proper, and that three members of the committee constitute a quorum at any meeting so convened.

Gen. Anderson also offered the following resolutions, which were adopted:

Resolved, That the Chairman is requested, at his convenience, to appoint a sub-committee (of which he shall be a member), which sub-committee is hereby authorized, at their discretion, to appear before the proper committee of the Senate and House of Representatives to explain and advocate the measures adopted by this Convention, and that the Senators and Representatives from their respective States be requested to procure proper facilities for a fair hearing of the sub-committee by the committee of Congress.

Resolved, That the Chairman of this committee be authorized to supervise the publication of the proceedings of the Convention, with the Secretary, and see that they embrace the proper official action of the Convention.

On motion of Judge Kennard, it was

Resolved, That the Chairman of the committee be authorized and instructed to append, when the address is completed, the names of each member of the committee to the same.

The committee then adjourned.

APPENDIX.

THE BANQUET.

In the evening a banquet was given in Masonic Hall, which several hundred delegates attended. Music was furnished by the Kunkel Brothers' band, and Porcher's Restaurant furnished the following

BILL OF FARE.

OYSTERS, RAW.

Burgundy (White).   Chablis.

POTAGES.

Cressy and Royale.   Sherry.   Old Brown.

HORS D'ŒUVRES.

Bouche a la Reine.   Celery en branche.

FISH.

Red Snapper a l'Hollandaise.   Potatoes a l'Hollandaise.
Sauterne.   Vin de Graves.

RELEVES.

Filet of Beef pique a la Perigueux.   Turkey a l'Ambassadrice.

ENTREES.

Chicken Croquet, Tartare Sauce.
Quails a la Dauphine.
Sweet Bread with Green Peas.
Breast of Goose a la Very.
Vol au Vent a la Financiere.
Filet Mignon of Ducks, sauce a poivrade.
Lamb Chops a la Soubise.
Tenderloin of Veal a la Marechale.

Burgundy.   Pommard.

COLD ENTREES.

Boned Turkey truffes garni d'athelets.
Pates truffes a la Lucullus d'athlets.
Mayonnaise of Fowls a la Lucullus d'athlets.
Hams a la Gelee de champagne,
Piece of Beef en Belle Vue.
Chicken Salad.

VEGETABLES.

Spinach a la Parisienne.   Bean panaches.
    Green Peas a la Francoise.   Tomatoes aux Mirepoix.

CHAMPAGNE.

George Goulet.   Piper Heidsieck.   I. Imperial.

ROAST.

    Pheasant.   Snipe.
       Teal Duck.   Saddle of Venison.
          Lettuce Salad.

DESSERT.

Corbeille of fruit.   California grapes.
California pears.   Malaga grapes.
Oranges.   Apples.
Pyramids of macarons.   Pyramids of rings.
    Pyramids of oranges glaces.

ICE CREAM.

Vanilla.   Lemon.   Pistache.
    Assortment of fancy cakes.

WINE LIST.

Sauterne—Vin de Graves,   Sherry—Old Brown,
    Chablis.   Burgundy,
                                                       Pommard.

CHAMPAGNE.

Geo. Goulet.   Piper Heidsieck.   Cook's Imperial.

After the last course had been served, Col. Broadhead, Chairman of the Executive Committee, who occupied the head of the centre table, rose and said:

Gentlemen, I shall not detain you with any preliminary remarks. I rise for the purpose of announcing the first regular toast, "The President of the United States," which will be drank standing and in silence.

The toast was drank in accordance with the announcement of the Chairman.

THE CHAIRMAN: The next toast is "The Congress of the United States," which will be responded to by the Hon. T. L. Jones, of Kentucky.

RESPONSE OF HON. T. L. JONES.

MR. CHAIRMAN AND GENTLEMEN OF THE BANQUET:—I have been called upon to respond to the toast of "The Congress of the United States." All will admit, I think, that the Chairman has imposed on me a very heavy responsibility, for to respond properly to that sentiment, I would have to embody in my single person all the iniquities and the good deeds which have been performed by that body within the last many years. [Laughter.] But I beg of you to bear in mind, gentlemen, that I have become a member of Congress since the Credit Mobilier and other scandals which are connected with the Congress of the United States were perpetrated. [Applause.] I desire to say, however, that perhaps the Congress is as much sinned against as sinning.

But, jesting aside, I suppose I am expected to say something in reference to the great subject which has called the Convention which is now assembled in this city together; and I beg leave to say that if I had the power to control the action of the next Congress of the United States, I would instruct it to do its best to further the great project of the Southern Pacific Railroad. [Applause.] I suppose the reason I have been selected to respond to this sentiment is, that it has leaked out somehow or other that I am a railroad man [applause], and a Southern Pacific Railroad man. [Renewed applause.] I congratulate my countrymen, I congratulate the projectors of this great enterprise, and I congratulate the city of St. Louis especially, that this Convention is possessed of so much talent, so much experience, so much reputation, statesmanship and practicability as was evinced in the Convention to-day. [Applause.] With an experience of no few years, I am proud to be able to say, having attended many national conventions, that I have never seen a body composed of more of the intelligence and reputation of our country than that which has assembled this day in the city of St. Louis. [Applause.] I congratulate my countrymen of the South especially that the land of my birth, the land which I love so much, the land which has been prostrated for these many years, has a sure prospect of a great work being accomplished which will place that section of the country upon an equality with the North [great applause]; for, while I am a Southern man by birth, and allied to the South by every sentiment that can absorb the heart of man, yet I am no less a patriot, no less a lover of my whole country. [Applause.] In the spirit of patriotism I am here, ready to say that my efforts in the Congress of the United States shall be directed to the building up of the South, and placing her upon an equal footing with the States of the North. [Applause.] And I have the highest authority for the vote which I expect to give in the Congress of the United States, for the aid of the General Government to this great enterprise. I was brought up, to use a familiar phrase, at the feet of the great Gamaliel of the South. I represent, I believe, to a very great extent, the political principles of South Carolina; and although the great statesman from that State and from the South, in his latter days, had, perhaps, some scruples in regard to appropriations by the General Government for internal improvements in the States, I think I can point to him as the first and the most illustrious apostle of the principle that the National Government should make appropriations for internal improvements within the States. [Applause.] I here say, without the fear of successful contradiction, that the very first movement which was ever made in the Congress of the United States, looking to the construction of public works and internal improvements within the States, by the General Government, was upon the report, in 1816, of John C. Calhoun from South Carolina. [Applause.] He moved, in his motion to establish a Bank of the United States, that from the dividends arising from the stock of the Government in it, a special fund should be set apart for the erection of public works in the States; and his words on that occasion were: "Let us erect a perfect system of roads and canals which will bind together the republic in indissoluble links." [Applause.] We have, in later times, just as high, and perhaps higher authority—I point to the statesman of Massachusetts, Daniel Webster. [Applause.] It was but yesterday that I happened to look at his patriotic speech in advocacy of a motion that the Government of the United States should purchase the Louisville canal, not only for the benefit of the States in its neighborhood, but for the benefit of the commerce of all the States and every State in the Union. [Applause.] His language ought to be imprinted in letters of gold. Said he, on that occasion, "I am for improvement in the East as well as the West. There are no Alleghanies in my politics." [Applause.] That sentiment is a fitting epitaph to be inscribed on the tomb of that glorious patriot from the North. [Renewed applause.] He said he desired, as the consequence of great national roads and highways, to bring the Far West so near to the East that "he could see the smoke of their dwellings, and hear the stroke of their axes." [Applause.]

Then, sir, when we have such illustrious examples as these to inspire and encourage us in this great undertaking, why should we hesitate? Why should any Democrat who adheres to a strict construction of the Constitution, in these times when the South is lying prostrate, as it were, at the feet of the country, begging for aid, any longer withhold the assistance of the Government in such great enterprises as the one now proposed? [Applause.] But this is no Southern enterprise; this is no sectional project; it is one which is to bring prosperity not only to the South, but to the middle States and to the North. It is one the benefits of which, when accomplished, will be felt by every State in this Union. The North will experience its benefits as well as the South. I pity from my soul the narrow-hearted and contracted policy of those men who stickle, with conscientious scruples, for the Constitution of the United States, at the aid of the General Government being given for such an improvement as we are met here to advocate. [Applause.] I beg of you to consider for one moment how great have been the appropriations to the North in comparison with those to the South; and that, in the last ten years, the Government of the United States has appropriated six millions of dollars for internal improvements in the State of Massachusetts alone, while it has not appropriated that much to all the Southern States of the Union.

But this is no time for argument. All I can say to you, in conclusion, is, that being a member of the present Congress, I shall endeavor to induce my fellow-members to look to the resolutions which you may pass in your Convention, and give the aid of the General Government to this great enterprise which you are called together to lend your voices to. [Great applause.]

The Chairman announced as the next regular toast "Our Sister Republic," which was responded to by Gen. Wm. Preston, of Kentucky.

RESPONSE OF GEN. PRESTON.

GENTLEMEN:— In responding, under the unexpected call of the Chairman, to the sentiment in regard to our sister republic, the song which has just been so charmingly sung suggests appropriate ideas, from the impression it evidently made upon the sensibilities of this great audience. The theme was the pleasures of peace, and I trust that the melody of the musicians is an auspicious prelude of the future relations of our country with her sister republic. We should always remember that together we exercise sovereign dominion over the chief habitable regions of North America, and that we are responsible to the world for the success of republican institutions within our vast territories. By our own efforts we have established our independence, and disenthralled America from two of the most powerful monarchies of Europe. Mexico modeled her system of federative republics upon that established by the constitution of the United States, and with governments of the same cast, and self-government for its cardinal principle, we ought hereafter, and, I trust, will live in just and honorable amity.

It is true that more than a quarter of a century since, when one of the States of Mexico was dissatisfied with the centralization of the government, Texas resisted by arms, and we having annexed that State to our Union, a war ensued. I see around me at this banquet men then in the prime of youth, whose names will pass down to posterity as first signalized in that war, and as founders of our Western Empire. I see one near me (General Sherman) who, then a simple captain of artillery, established, under Kearney and Fremont, our flag upon the golden coasts of the Pacific, but who, after mightier campaigns, is now the General of the Armies of the United States. I see another, then only the Colonel of a Mississippi regiment, who at the critical instant on the decisive field of Buena Vista, when all seemed lost, by timely maneuver, saved the battle, and secured the very territory to our country which we now endeavor to develop and civilize. The victory of Taylor was not forgotten by his country, and his son-in-law, who gave such opportune aid, is now uniting with us, to complete it by bearing the blessings of commerce and civilization, not only to the territory we won, but the Republic against whom we were then arrayed. Other men mentioned in history are present, without regard to former hostility of opinion, and we see around us, in the midst of these splendid festivities, soldiers, statesmen, merchants, engineers, and the most distinguished men in the peaceful professions and industrial pursuits of our country, all earnestly united to secure the completion of the great railway. It will unite us not only with the Pacific States, but will open a new trade between the cities of the Valley and our sister republic; a nation of more than ten millions of people, with a commerce of sixty millions, will pour the rich stream of its trade, far richer than the placers and bonanzas of California, and diffuse its blessings throughout our whole country.

I know that there are those who may hesitate in indulging such splendid hopes, but they ought not to consider themselves wise, because they are timid; or conservative, because they have never examined this mighty question. They should remember that when the statesmen of the South and the Democracy of the North gained these future seats of empire, the ablest intellects were warped by hasty judgment or the prejudice of party, and that under such influences, one of the greatest statesmen, and probably the most splendid orator of America, Daniel Webster, is reported to have said that

APPENDIX. 163

the whole territory acquired by the annexation of Texas and the treaty with Mexico, was not worth a good Massachusetts farm.

When, therefore, we see the enterprising and thoughtful men convened on this occasion, when we remember that posterity will pass impartial and just judgment on the great and humble, no man of sense or virtue should condemn as unauthorized or impracticable the great railway we propose. The principles of past statesmen are to be revered as monitors, but not to be worshiped with superstition. The most striking characteristic of the mind of America is progress, and no party can successfully sit down with the apathy of an oriental sultan and declare that the world cannot be improved, or the wisdom of our fathers equalled. If it does, others will push it aside and assume control.

But time has rolled on, and the memories of the war with our sister republic are almost effaced. Since that period she has signalized her history by driving from beyond her borders the triple armies of England, Spain and France, sent during our civil war to establish an empire under Maximilian on our southern frontiers. The unfortunate Emperor perished in the attempt. The country has necessarily been greatly disturbed, but I believe that from the fact of the disparity of our condition now that Mexico will have in the generous nature of my countrymen a surer guarantee for future peace than if we were more nearly matched in power. The government under *Lerdo de Texada,* at this time, is, I am informed by General Sherman, conspicuous for its effort to observe international obligations on our frontiers, and good order within its boundaries, though the long line of uninhabitable territory renders it a difficult task for both countries. This railway, when completed, would give a stronger guarantee of peace than a multitude of soldiers, and its cost to our country, even if the Texas and Pacific Railway were to become bankrupt and throw the whole expense of construction on our central government, would not be greater than the annual cost of supporting three or four regiments on our southern frontier.

Let me, in conclusion, say that the occasion allows at this time only a few crude and desultory remarks, which may, however, I hope, suggest some inquiries hereafter. It is well known to practical miners that the great deposits of gold and silver, stretching along the Rocky Mountains and the Andes, the metallic spine of America, are richer in Mexico than within our territories and Pacific States. It is a fact well known that within the contemplated connections of our road in Northern Mexico, the mountains are marvellously rich in gold and silver. No wisely organized labor; no skillful and powerful machinery; and no able associations for the development of that wealth, yet exist. It far transcends the mineral riches of California and the Pacific States. The gold grows richer with the altitude of the mighty Mexican mountains as you ascend, and the silver, as the shafts sink below the surface of the earth. In the striking language of the Mexican miners, "the gold springs to Heaven and the silver sinks to Hell." "*Usque ad Cœlum et usque ad Orcum.*" There lies, darkling in the matrices of nature, wealth beyond the dreams of avarice. There repose, from immemorial ages, fabulous treasures awaiting the future labor of man; there is gold and silver far richer than India and the East will ever yield, and there is the "BACK COUNTRY" for St. Louis and the cities of the valley to civilize and develop.

And now, gentlemen, allow me, finally, to say that I sincerely hope we may be firmly united by the strong bonds of justice, friendship and peace to our sister republic, and that Mexico will feel assured of the lofty purposes of the men assembled in this Convention to secure our commerce and friendship, so that there may be between us perpetual peace.

The Chairman announced as the next regular toast "Trans-continental Transit," which was responded to by Col. Thos. A. Scott, of Pennsylvania.

RESPONSE OF COL. THOS. A. SCOTT.

MR. CHAIRMAN AND GENTLEMEN:—I beg leave to thank you most kindly for the very cordial reception you have been pleased to extend to me as the President of the Texas and Pacific Railway Company. I respond with pleasure briefly to the toast just read by the honorable Chairman.

I believe that the true solution of cheap transportation across the continent will be found in the construction of a great national highway on the 32d parallel that will connect every road east of the Rocky Mountains, and every harbor of the Atlantic coast, and every city in the Eastern States with the waters of the Pacific Ocean—a road that we desire to be built under the closest governmental supervision of its expenditure, and for cash, thereby securing the lowest possible cost, and providing for the Government and the people a line that can and must afford to carry for all time, at the most moderate rates possible for a highway of its character.

This great road should be so guarded that every line that may connect with it now or hereafter shall have the right to use it as an open highway on equal terms, and the Government should also reserve to itself the right to so regulate rates as simply to provide for the capital invested therein, and prevent undue charges or speculation by any party or from any quarter.

I want it distinctly understood that the bill asking for Congressional aid should provide that no bond shall be issued or its interest guaranteed by the Government unless it is actually required to accomplish these results, and that the residue of the first mortgage bonds shall be retained in the treasury of the United States for the future improvement of the road and the consequent benefit of the people, so that they never can be made an object of speculation or barter for individual benefit. By pursuing this plan, I believe that the Government of the United States never can be called upon to advance a single dollar of its money to secure the results that are desired to be attained.

These results, in connection with the development of the great territory which the road will traverse, the heavy traffic it must secure from the countries of the East, as well as our own country and the adjacent States of Mexico, will be in my judgment beyond the estimate of any gentleman now present, however enthusiastic he may be upon the subject.

I have been requested by gentlemen of the Convention (to which I am not a delegate) to prepare such a statement as would be proper to come from the executive officer of the Texas and Pacific road for the information of the Convention. I have prepared that statement this afternoon, and will transmit it to the President of the Convention for its consideration, and therein I have set forth fully all I can say on the subject of this great road and upon the questions to be affected by it.

I believe the action of the great body of distinguished men present from twenty-eight States and Territories, earnest in their desire to secure this road on a basis that all good men can approve, will satisfy the public generally, and, I trust, the Congress of the United States, that the Southern line to the Pacific will meet a need which the Government itself has the greatest interest in supplying, and that it cannot act too promptly in connection with the economies of its own administration, while at the same time providing for the best interests of the people who may in all time to come find it to their interest to use it, through the practical question that comes home to every man —moderate charges for transportation.

Again thanking you, gentlemen, for the kind manner in which you have been pleased to receive these brief remarks, I leave the subject for the action of the Convention and the future action of Congress, trusting and believing that the final results, whether I happen to be officially connected with them or not, will be productive of great good to our entire country.

The Chairman announced as the next regular toast "The Centennial," and called upon Mr. Morton McMichael, of Philadelphia, to respond. Mr. McMichael being absent, the toast was responded to by Mayor Fox, of Philadelphia.

RESPONSE OF MAYOR FOX.

Mr. President and Gentlemen:—I am sorry that circumstances have made it necessary that I should take the place of one who would have done justice to the toast, "The Centennial," one of the greatest subjects of the age; but I will endeavor to give you some facts which will possibly interest you. We have on foot, at this time, in the city which I represent, one of the greatest projects that has ever been conceived of on this portion of God's earth. We have invited all the nations of the earth to come to our country and participate in its beauties, to witness its grandeur, and to see what a young and vigorous people can do in the short space of one hundred years. We have invited nations which are thousands of years old, to come to our land, that we may show them something of the vigor and energy, power and prosperity of a great, free and independent nation. [Applause.] If it were possible, Mr. Chairman, for me to present to you and this great audience something of the magnitude of the preparation that has been made, you would be astonished (as I myself was, although a participant in it) at the greatness of the undertaking.

But, whilst that is the case with that great project, it is not the only one we have before us. We have invited and attracted, from all quarters of the globe, the greatest men of progress, the finest scintillations of genius, and are about to show them a grand exhibition of all evidences of the nation's prosperity and wealth. They are coming to our land, and we ask that this wonderful project which has been occupying this Convention to-day shall be kindred to it. We ask that you shall make a highway to Asia—one by which we can reach all portions of the earth at all seasons, and bring to our shores some of those things which contribute to our happiness and to the happiness of the civilized world. [Applause.] When we are able to show to the nations of the earth this American people's prosperity, and as we now have an opportunity in a free country, in a land of independence, to show what we can do and what progress we have made, it behooves us to do all we can to promote the success of what I promise you will be the last exhibition of the sort that we will have for a hundred years. [Applause.] Take it to yourselves, take it home with you, and see whether you have not got something in the shape of a patriotic obligation imposed upon you to do all you can for fostering this great enterprise. [Applause.]

The Chairman announced as the next regular toast "The Great Southwest," which was responded to by Gen. George B. Hodge.

RESPONSE OF GEN. HODGE.

GENTLEMEN OF THE CONVENTION:—How could Kentucky fail to respond to a call from her child, Missouri, when that appeal is made in behalf of an enterprise which is to benefit the whole country? Kentucky will aid you in constructing this great road. She has no selfish wrangling to indulge in as to its termini or the immediate points to which it will run. Well she knows that wherever the main channel of the stream may run, its overflow, like the Nile upon the delta of Egypt, will bestow its beneficent effects upon her and her soil. She knows that it is the grandest enterprise which has ever occupied the thoughts of men—no less than to grasp the trade of that great hive of nations, the East Indies; she knows that it has been the dream of commerce, back from a time whose date o'erawes tradition, to control that trade. For it is a remarkable fact that wherein has passed the trade of the Indies, there, for the time being, has been displayed the highest civilization, the most advanced statesmanship, the greatest wealth, the most successful improvements of man. Thousands of years ago it passed in caravans across the arid wastes of Syria, making its desert lands to blossom like the gardens of Gul in their bloom; and although in lapse of time its channel has been diverted, it has left enduring monuments of its passage in titanic cities, whose gigantic ruins dwarf the architecture of to-day into insignificance. When the discovery of the mariner's compass enabled navigators to push boldly out upon the ocean, that trade was diverted around the Cape of Good Hope, and England, which for six hundred years had maintained only a precarious struggle for existence, and averted subjugation and conquest from the continent of Europe only by reason of her isolated position as an island, seized the trade, and became for two centuries the arbiter of the destinies of the world, we will create a feeling in favor of an independent government of the people, which will benefit mankind and create happiness in all portions of this great world. [Applause.] No such opportunity has ever been offered to show to the nations of the earth the greatness of our country as that which is afforded by this centennial national exhibition. It happens to be held in a distant State, eleven hundred miles from here; but the people of the State and the city in which it is held have offered great facilities for all the other States to exhibit their productions to the people of the world. We have in that city the greatest bell ever heard of. Its tones have been ringing from the time it first proclaimed liberty throughout all the land. From that day to this it has been sending its music to the remotest corners of the earth. [Applause.] The very building in which the greatest instrument that ever was framed is kept is in that city; but we are only the custodians of it; it belongs to the nation, to you and to me, and to every man—to the highest and the lowest. We also have in that city the greatest railroad man that ever was born [great applause], and we look upon him, not as a Pennsylvanian, but as the nation's benefactor. [Renewed applause.] He is ever opening up avenues and creating opportunities for prosperity to the American people from ocean to ocean. No man in the land has a greater mind for projecting and carrying out great enterprises than the Hon. Thomas A. Scott. [Applause.]

This nation is likely to be put upon trial at that grand exhibition, which will bring it into contrast with the old nations of the earth—even of the Orient; and it is upon the exhibit we make that the reputation and good name of this country is to be judged. Therefore it behooves every portion of this country to bring forward its contribution so as to add to the magnitude, the wealth and the power of the exhibit we may make. I desire to say that every man here and every man in the whole land ought to be deeply interested in this grand enterprise, for the honor of the country is involved in it. If we do not come up to the measure of a proper exhibit, in accordance with what we have boasted of, we will suffer in reputation, and we will deserve whatever discredit grows out of it. Therefore I appeal to you, my fellow-citizens and countrymen, to take up this subject for yourselves, to look into it and see what constitutes this enterprise, and whether some obligation as an American citizen and patriot does not devolve upon you individually. We regard it as the grandest movement of the age. In the present condition of Europe there will be no exhibitions in the coming century; they are disturbed, unsettled, and unable to maintain the peace of their portion of the world;

making that magnificent but truthful boast that the reveille of her cavalry trumpets and the morning drum-beat of her infantry met each hour the rising sun as he swept on his diurnal course around the globe. Columbus sought a new channel for it, and, in seeking, found a world.

You propose again to divert its channel, until the star of empire, which westward takes its way, shall meet the tide of wealth and commerce advancing from the East in the midst of your own beloved land. Your energy proposes in the future to turn this magnificent commerce, not over arid and sandy wastes, not across stormy seas and forbidding, rock-bound headlands, but over a land beneath skies bright and radiant as an angel's smile, to make the great journey one long and jocund delight, amid flowers and tropical vegetation, luxuriant in its gorgeous development as are the hearts of the noble people of the beautiful South which invites you. I pledge Kentucky to the enterprise.

The Chairman announced as the next regular toast "The Pacific Slope," which was responded to by Judge George Turner, of San Francisco.

RESPONSE OF JUDGE TURNER.

Mr. Chairman and Gentlemen:—I am proud and happy to have the privilege of saying a word for our young empire which is just growing up on the Pacific slope. It is but a quarter of a century since your flag floated for the first time upon the margin of the Pacific Sea, but it has been reserved for that young country to realize the sentiment of your own New England poet, who said:

> "At first our land was but a shelving strip,
> Black with the strife that made it free;
> But now you see her banners dip
> Their fringes in the Western sea."

[Applause.]

Why, it seems but a few moons since Balboa, the leader of the Spanish cohorts, standing for the first time upon the shores of the Pacific, exclaimed, in language familiar but immortal: "Spectators of two hemispheres, I call you to witness that I take possession of this new land in the name of the crown of Castile, and my sword shall defend what my hand has won for it!" But Brother Jonathan was too bright and valorous for the Spanish cohorts. You are the rulers of that mighty empire to-day; you have there three grand States; you have there seven vast Territories; you have it banded to you by a band of iron.

Gentlemen, in 1861 I crossed those very plains in an overland stage-coach, at the behest of our Government, in the discharge of official duty; and when I crossed them, after sleeping twenty-three nights in a stage-coach in order to reach my destination, if an angel had stood before me and said that in ten short years I would cross that same country in a palace-car, I would have said, "You are a fallen angel!" [Applause.]

But, while we have one line of railroad, we want another. Such beneficence as was shown the Central and Union Pacific roads is unequalled in the history of the world. Oceans of money were given, volumes of liberal legislation were enacted, and all that the country could do to aid in its construction was done. It is built. It is well. But another line is wanted. [Applause.] Down yonder to the southwest is that grand country of New Mexico, the greatest wool-field in the world. There is the valley of the Rio Grande, 600 miles long and 50 miles wide—the Rhine quadrupled over and over again. There is the rich land of Arizona, with its mountains of gold and its valleys of silver. There is Southern California, a land so rich that "if you tickle it with a hoe it will laugh in a harvest." [Applause.] There is the land where the apple, the peach and the pear ripen alongside of the grape, the pomegranate and the fig, where ripe fruit falls every day in the year—a country where that sentiment is true which the darkies sing of heaven,

"Oh, de streets am paved wid gold over there."

[Applause.]

Now, gentlemen, you and I, Californians and Eastern people, Southern and Western people, are interested in a competing line—a line that shall afford no monopoly; a line that shall be a double opportunity for our country. Let this line be built, and let us have another iron pathway for our commerce. All liberal-minded men will say "this is a consummation most devoutly to be wished."

And in conclusion, gentlemen, allow me to say, give us this road, and we will quadruple the population of California in a few short years; give us this road, and we will make you the Emperors of the Pacific Sea; give us this road, and China will lay her riches at your feet, and we will bring to you the wealth of Ormus and of Ind.

I thank you, gentlemen, for your kind attention. [Applause.]

The next regular toast was "The Southern Atlantic States," which was responded to by Judge John H. Kennard, of New Orleans.

RESPONSE OF JUDGE KENNARD.

FELLOW-MEMBERS OF THE CONVENTION AND FELLOW-CITIZENS:—A quarter of a century ago, that gifted son of the State of Mississippi, the immortal S. S. Prentiss [applause], standing upon the banks of the Susquehanna, upon an occasion most eventful in the history of this country, commenced his speech with these memorable words, "Fellow-citizens: On the banks of the Mississippi river, at New Orleans, I have said 'Fellow-citizens;' on the banks of the grand Ohio I have said 'Fellow-citizens;' here, upon this spot, to-day, I say 'Fellow-citizens;' and, thanks be to God, a thousand miles north of us I can still say 'Fellow-citizens.'" [Applause.] I recognize my presence here, not as a compliment to me individually; I recognize it in this way, that this great Convention, representing thirty States of this mighty Union, demands that the city of New Orleans, whose Chamber of Commerce I solely represent here, has a right to be heard upon this question. [Applause.]

Inasmuch as the hour is late, and our time is short, I propose to address myself to the business which has called me to this stand. All I have to say is this, that we, the people of New Orleans, that we, the people of Louisiana, are not here forgetful of the grand sentiment which underlies that speech of S. S. Prentiss; we are here recognizing that we are but a fraction of this great country; but, at the same time, we propose to assert what claims we have upon the national treasury of this Government.

No people within the limits of these United States have been more disposed to recognize and aid, by all the means in their power, the grand efforts that have been made by the railroad king of the United States to span this expansive territory of ours. [Applause.] No people in the United States are to-day more cordial supporters of the grand enterprise which is now going forward at the mouth of the Mississippi than the people of Louisiana. Notwithstanding the fact that many of us believed that a more certain outlet to the sea was through a canal, still, now that the wisdom of Congress has passed upon the matter, we are a unit in favor of the great experiment which your distinguished fellow-citizen, James B. Eads, is making near our city; no people in the United States shake him more cordially by the hand, or wish him better success than we. [Applause.] We recognize Mr. Eads as one of America's proud boasts. We recognize him as a man who, by reason of the work which he has done in erecting this immense bridge which spans your mighty river, deserves, if he were to die to-morrow, the epitaph of "immortal." [Applause.]

The desire of Louisiana is to have the main trunk of the Texas Pacific Railroad built. If, in the wisdom of Congress, it is decided to subsidize—as we hope will be the case—any branches of the main trunk, we, the people of the city of New Orleans, representing 250,000 people—the largest city south of the Ohio river—contend that we have a right to have our branch to the city of New Orleans recognized and subsidized. [Applause.]

THE CHAIRMAN: The regular toasts of the evening having been gone through with, volunteer toasts are now in order. [Cries of "Voorhies."]

A DELEGATE: Mr. Voorhies is absent, but Col. Wilson, of Indiana, with whom Mr. Voorhies studied his profession, is here. [Cries of "Wilson."]

Judge Wilson, of Indiana, in response to these calls, spoke as follows:

RESPONSE OF JUDGE WILSON.

MR. CHAIRMAN AND GENTLEMEN:—I am sorry that Mr. Voorhies is not here to respond to your calls in person. Mr. Voorhies was one of my students; I taught him what little law he knows. [Laughter.] He came to me with the name of D. W. Voorhies—Daniel Webster Voorhies; and I suppose he thought when he came to read law with me, that he would go to Daniel Webster when he died [laughter], but I soon convinced him to the contrary. He is one of my pets that I feel very proud of. [Laughter.] He is a boy who has got the soubriquet of "the tall sycamore of the Wabash." He is a pretty smart boy, considering his advantages. [Laughter.]

Now, gentlemen, we are here in the interest of the Texas and Pacific Railroad. We want that railroad; we cannot do without it; we must have it. I am not a very old man [laughter], but I rode after the first locomotive that ever was imported into the United States. It was called the "John Bull," and ran between Albany and Schenectady in 1831. We went fourteen miles an hour, and supposed that we had attained the *ne plus ultra* of speed and were annihilating space. [Laughter.] Now we are whirling through the country at the rate of sixty miles an hour. [Applause.] This road is a necessity; we have got to have it. That is all there is of it. And we will make these politicians give it to us. [Laughter.] I tell you when the politicians understand that a demand of this sort is backed by the people, they will be very willing to give us the Pacific road. [Applause.] They are a miserable set of creatures who always respond to a demand when the people are behind it. [Laughter.] They have no independence of themselves. Then we say we must and will have the Texas and Pacific Railroad, and we will run it through Texas, Arizona and California to San Diego. That is the road we want, and no other. We want no Southern Pacific Railroad, for that means the Central Pacific of California, a miserable monopoly—one that will gobble us up and all our children. [Laughter.] We want an independent line, and a competing line, from the Pacific to the Atlantic [applause], and we will have it. We want a road independent of the Central and Union Pacific Railroads. In the language of Col. Benton, when this line is completed we can revolutionize the commerce of the world. [Applause.] We can come from Liverpool to Hong Kong in forty days, while the nearest England can come to putting goods into Hong Kong is fifty-three days; therefore we have thirteen days the advantage of any line that can be made to Hong Kong in China. Then let us have the Texas and Pacific Railroad. That is what we want, and we must and will have it. [Applause.]

In response to numerous calls, Hon. Mr. Claiborne, of Tennessee, spoke as follows:

RESPONSE OF MR. CLAIBORNE.

Gentlemen:—Twenty-three years ago I first put my foot in St. Louis, as a small lieutenant, and it seems to me the strangest thing in the world that this evening I should be speaking to the most intelligent audience I have ever seen gathered in this city. I feel my inability to talk in the presence of such men as those who have preceded me, but the State of Tennessee, I assure you, has men that can talk, and talk good, sound, practical sense, too.

The State of Tennessee feels the greatest interest in this movement, and I hope the Convention now assembled will not adjourn until it has put the seal upon its action, and that it will be responded to by the Congress of the United States instanter. [Applause.] I desire to say on this occasion, as a Southern man, feeling all the disabilities which the South has labored under of late years, being compelled to work hard for my living, that the State of Tennessee to-day owes to Thomas A. Scott, of Pennsylvania, as much gratitude as she owes to her own illustrious Jackson [applause]; for, gentlemen, he comes to us as an angel of mercy, stretching out his hands to help men who cannot help themselves. [Applause.]

It is no new thing for me to favor a Southern Pacific Railroad, but the interest which I have always had in such an undertaking is increased when I see other men taking a like interest in it. In the country from the mouth of the San Francisco to the borders of Texas, I spent twelve years of my life, and it is the most astonishing thing to me to find that where, twenty years ago, I was detained ten days by a horse stampede, caused by a wolf, at the mouth of Cherry creek, there is now a city of thirty thousand inhabitants. It is also a matter of wonder to me that railroads have gone over snow-clad mountains in that country which looked like barriers inaccessible to human progress and enterprise.

Gentlemen, the State of Tennessee has an interest so great in this matter that it is impossible to calculate it. We have in the bowels of the State of Tennessee the richest iron ores in the world. We have, on the banks of the Tennessee, iron from which boilers have been made that never exploded and never will, we have forests which contain the finest character of timber, and we have a water-power that puts to blush all others you can mention; therefore you can see that it is greatly to her interest to develop all these vast resources. All thinking men in Tennessee are earnestly looking this way, and they hope and pray that your action will be such as to secure the desired result. I hope the greatest harmony will prevail in the Convention, and that resolutions will be passed in so grave, dignified and marked a manner that your action will be responded to promptly at the next session of Congress. [Applause.]

Mr. Pierce, of Indiana, was next called for and responded as follows:

RESPONSE OF MR. PIERCE.

GENTLEMEN:—I am not in the habit of public speaking. Those gentlemen who are present and know me at home are aware that I very seldom attempt to address my fellow-citizens. But I did not hear any one respond on behalf of my State except Judge Wilson, and I did not think it due to you nor to ourselves that this Convention should adjourn until some one had declared to you the sentiments of the State which I in part represent; therefore I have responded to the call which has been made upon me.

Indiana is the great central State of the central portion of the nation. The city which I in part represent is the great focal point of the railroad system of the West, and we have an interest in the success of this project as great as that of any portion of the United States. We care nothing about terminal points; we care nothing about any question except that in connection with a railroad which shall be built from the Mississippi to the Pacific Ocean, and the State of Indiana will do all she can to aid this great enterprise. At present our people have not had their attention called to it very much, but when we hear our Southern neighbors and friends engaged in a struggle to carry a road through that great Southern productive region, we will endeavor to hold up their hands. I have the fullest faith that our State, in a short time, will instruct her members of Congress to do all in their power to induce the General Government to do all that is necessary to secure the completion of the enterprise.

Gentlemen, we who have come here are delighted with the reception we have had in this great central city of the West. We have been well entertained and dined and wined—some of us, perhaps, a little too much of the latter [laughter] ; I am one of them [renewed laughter] ; and we will go home with our hearts full of gratitude and good will towards the city of St. Louis. [Applause.]

Between the addresses the Owl Quartette Club entertained the guests with choice vocal selections. At half-past eleven o'clock the remaining delegates left the banqueting hall to the tune of "Home, Sweet Home."

THE STEAMBOAT EXCURSION.

[From the St. Louis Dispatch, Nov. 26.]

The excursion tendered by the citizens of St. Louis yesterday to the delegates of the National Railroad Convention, through the Committee of Arrangements, as will be seen by the number that participated therein, was well attended and thoroughly enjoyed. We propose now to detail something of the manufacturing and other items of interest that attracted and commanded the attention of our guests, and proved to them where the importance of St. Louis, as the central and commanding city of the continent and of the Mississippi basin, asserts itself, not only as the leading city in population, but also in manufactures, and ranking fourth in population and third in manufactures in the country.

Steaming up the river past the numerous steamers and wharf-boats from whence our commerce is carried to the head-waters of the Missouri, the Mississippi, the Illinois, the Ohio, the Arkansas, Tennessee, Cumberland, Red and other rivers, and which connect with the great and augmenting auxiliaries of our commerce — the railroads — our strangers had a panoramic view of its importance, and were struck with its extent and magnitude.

Passing under the arches of the magnificent structure that spans the river, and unites the iron links of the continent, giving dispatch to passenger and freight traffic, expediting the mails and military and subsistence transportation of the Government, and giving impetus and power to our home manufacturing interests, by conveying the raw materials, iron, coal, coke, etc., unobstructed throughout the season, and rendering it impossible, while the proud structure stands, ever to burden the poor, or subject the domestic demands to excessive but necessarily extravagant prices for fuel, such as existed before its completion; the constant stream of traffic across its wagon-way soon develops to the observer what composes the commerce of St. Louis—

cotton, tobacco, grain, meats, hides, wool, ores, metals, merchandise and manufactured products. Add to this the freight which crosses in the cars upon the track underneath, and that which floats upon our river, and thus the panorama is complete; and we take in the smoke from stacks and chimneys of factories, locomotives and steamers as an index that where there is so much smoke there is also fire, and industry, business and wealth.

GENERAL MANUFACTURES.

St. Louis has gained since 1870 fifty-one per cent. in value of manufactured products. The product of 1873 is estimated at about $210,000,000, and that of 1874 at about $239,600,000. While every other leading manufacturing city shows a loss, St. Louis alone gains. So we go marching on to that commanding position which nature intended, and which not only location, but the acknowledged stability and capital of our citizens promotes, and which is perhaps slowly, but none the less surely and successfully done.

IMPORTANCE OF THE SOUTHERN PACIFIC.

Thus when the Committee of Arrangements, on the 27th day of October, made an appeal to our citizens to consider the importance of the Convention, as follows, it struck the key-note to activity and aroused those who had previously given the matter little if any attention:

"A National Railroad Convention has been called to convene in this city on the 23d day of November next, to aid in securing the long-delayed rights of the south half of the continent for a railway to the Pacific. Its importance is not confined to the interests of this city, or it would be incumbent upon it to provide the means to build it, but to the people and the agricultural, mineral, manufacturing and commercial interests of the great belt of States and Territories adjacent to it and between the Atlantic and Pacific oceans. It is, therefore, of national importance, and entitled, like the two other Pacific railways, to national recognition. An appeal of this nature to Congress from a single city or State, unaided by other States and Territories in interest, would have but little weight. Therefore the co-operation of other States and Territories has been invited, and already from the Governor of this and other States have emanated recommendations and indorsements of the Convention and the appointment of full delegations of prominent and intelligent gentlemen to attend it in furtherance of its objects.

"It is by such honorable and potent methods that citizens can promote its objects and make it a success; yielding not only in the present, by the presence of the large and intelligent delegations that will be in attendance, but securing for the future such needed communications, by the southwest route, as will directly inure to every business interest of the city, and add still further empires of territory and trade tributary to St. Louis, the third manufacturing city in the country and the largest in wealth and population of the Mississippi basin. It was by such methods that the attention of Congress has been directed to and secured for the improvement of the Des Moines and Rock Island rapids and the mouth of the Mississippi —improvements that will revolutionize the carrying trade of the river.

"These improvements have been secured through the co-operation of our Merchants' Exchange and other commercial bodies, by conventions held for such purposes at New Orleans, Memphis, Keokuk and other cities, and have so aroused public opinion and secured the co-operation of members of Congress as to command respect and secure appropriations.

"Unfortunately, for years, while other enterprises flourished by that reason, we were deprived of a very large proportion of our representation in Congress. Happily we are not so situated now, and as the political power has advanced to the West, we are in a situation to demand instead of supplicate for rights so long deferred. We can appreciate the additions to our trade territory by the opening up of roads to and through Arkansas and Texas and towards Mexico.

"When we shall enter, with our southwest system of railways, the empire of Mexico and its capital, thus attaching it to our trade and manufacturing interest, and so on to the Pacific, our merchants and manufacturers will appreciate the increase of trade, and the Government will have unobstructed communications for its mails and materials of war and subsistence; so that the interests of the Government, as well as of commerce and manufactures, will be subserved, and are therefore of common interest.

"St. Louis now, and has for two years, enjoyed increased prosperity, and such an increase and augmentation of trade as to overcome the effects of panic, and leave it less affected by reason thereof than any other commercial trade-point. St. Louis is advancing by reason of such improvements, faster than ever before, and its material prosperity is recognized throughout the country. This gives credit and prestige. It is incumbent, therefore, to promote every such public enterprise of this nature, and by such attention to the presence of so important a convention, show our appreciation of it in such a way as to impress favorably our guests and the national legislators who will be in attendance, and afford every convenience for the holding of it.

"If cities and communities in interest do not encourage and promote their own interests, who will? Thus we appeal to every manufacturing, trade, shipping and professional interest to take direct action, and by their presence at the meetings of the general committee, and co-operation therewith, to secure the desired result; and we desire that you shall consider this a personal appeal. The result of this assemblage will have its power to promote or retard this enterprise."

NOT AFFECTED BY THE PANIC.

It may strike singularly upon the commercial ears of such trade centres as Chicago, New York, Boston and other large cities, that during the very worst of the panic the progressive march of St. Louis was not delayed; that the consumption of raw materials, sugars, molasses, etc., of

BELCHER'S SUGAR REFINERY,

which we are now passing, was not decreased, but rather very largely increased in both manufactures and sales. Sales at Belcher's in 1870, $4,135,250. In 1874, $6,500,000.

And so, too, with the magnificent stove works, now in sight, of the

EXCELSIOR MANUFACTURING COMPANY,

which produces the celebrated charter oak stoves, the furnaces of which burn by night as well as day, and worked on extra instead of reduced hours. The immense structure, the

ST. LOUIS ELEVATOR,

with its 2,000,000 capacity for grain, and capacious warehouse room, and economical contrivances for loading and unloading bulk and rolling freights, vies with the several elevators upon the opposite side of the river, in making St. Louis a grain market, which, upon the completion of the improvements of the upper rapids, and the mouth of the river, will make the necessary stages of water, whereon can float, at such a reduction of freights as will enable freighters to carry, and shippers to ship, the products of the great

Northwest to the ports of the world at a price not higher than is now charged, or is in the season of navigation charged for inland freight across the country to New York.

	Receipts of the City for the years	
	1870.	1874.
Corn, bushels	4,708,838	6,991,677
Wheat, bushels	6,638,253	8,255,221
Oats, bushels	4,519,510	5,296.967

We have passed the old little low stone houses which in their day were occupied by the merchant princes, the fur traders, and where the steamers from the head-waters of the Missouri brought annually cargoes of buffalo hides and furs. This is one among the few trades that is on the decline, and which, from the proximity of railways to the old hunting regions, must continue to decline.

OUR FLOUR MILLS,

several of which we are now passing, whose smoke-stacks and steam-pipes indicate their locality—one of the leading industries, and aggregating for mill products a value of over $23,000,000 per annum.

TOBACCO TRADE.

Below and in close proximity to the bridge, the towering tobacco house of Peper appeared, and near it Catlin's, and just below, Hudson's. The receipts of the number of hogsheads doubled last year, with a consequent increase of the manufactured product.

We pass the old water-works engine house, which once supplied the water for our city. It is a thing of the past, and no longer commensurate to the demands of a metropolitan city, claiming, and by all usual sources of statistical knowledge having a population of nearly 500,000 people—as likely to exceed as it possibly might be less by 5,000 or so.

BARRELS.

The manufacture of barrels is no insignificant branch of industry, reaching out to the forests of adjacent and our own State for the raw material, and supplying our millers, packers and oil manufacturers.

OUR LUMBER INTEREST

loomed up for itself, lined as the upper part of the levee is by the extensive yards of our dealers, who, be it known, saw their own logs, which they get off their own land, in the Northern pineries, and float or tow hither in immense rafts, and deliver from their yards by rail or boat or for transportation to the interior. It may strike our

PORK PACKERS

that they too have a direct interest in any large gathering of representative men, brought hither from all parts of the country, and particularly from the South and Southwest, where so much of their cutting goes. We are now passing some of the packing houses, and we wish that some of the packers were with us to explain the magnitude of their business, for here is an opportunity to speak to millions of readers and hearers, through the press reporters and distinguished guests from abroad.

	1870.	1874.
Number of hogs received	310,850	1,126,586
Packed	$11,443.845	$22,000.000

We must not overlook, as we pass Cass avenue, that new and important industry, the

ST. LOUIS TIN STAMPING COMPANY.

That branch of business, until recently monopolized by France, and which, to a limited extent, existed in New York and Pittsburg, is a St. Louis industry now, like the

MALLEABLE IRON WORKS

in sight, above Eastern competition; and like the immense

CHAIR AND FURNITURE WORKS

we are passing, rendering the importation from any Eastern city unnecessary and unprofitable for that sort of manufactured goods. It is a trade of immense product and defying Eastern competition. Here we see more stove works, and also the

ST. LOUIS NUT AND BOLT WORKS,

of which our member of Congress, Hon. Wm. H. Stone, has the management, and which, too, defies competition and supplies a needed industry. In this locality some of the

HAME AND SADDLETREE

factories are located, the latter of which St. Louis has long enjoyed, upon the plains and for Government work, an enviable reputation.

STOCK-YARDS.

We are passing the stock-yards upon the St. Louis side of the river, and looking over to the eastern side we see the buildings and long white sheds of the National Yards.

St. Louis is justly proud of both of these great promoters of her stock business, and with the railway connections she now enjoys, has advantages for the cheap, speedy and safe handling of this, one of her leading branches of trade. Receipts of cattle, for 1870, 201,422 head; 1874, 360,925. And now we come to one of the foremost of her industries, the rolling mills of

CHOUTEAU, HARRISON & VALLE.

It was in the early fifties that the sagacity of James Harrison, the father of the present Edwin Harrison, who has been one of the active members of the Committee of Arrangements and entertainers of the Convention, with prophetic vision for the future of St. Louis in her iron industries, built in connection with this firm, and their interest in the American Iron Mountain, these vast works for a merchant mill and rails. This was when the ore was carted from the mountain to the river landing and brought thence by steamer hither; and twenty-five years is about passed or passing, and St. Louis is fixed as one of the leading iron marts for ore, pig or manufactured articles in the country.

We shall wait until we reach South St. Louis, however, before we reach the vast and, we may say, regal evidences of this industry. And so we look at the location, and engine-houses, settling reservoirs and forcing works of our

NEW WATER-WORKS.

Its capacity, when completed, was equal only to the then present demand, some 20,000,000 gallons per day, showing how literally we underrate our growth. It was calculated to have been sufficient for years, and has the past year been nearly doubled in capacity. Just below the

STAND-PIPE

of the water-works, which we see upon Grand avenue, is situated the incomparable grounds and improvements of the

ST. LOUIS MECHANICAL AND AGRICULTURAL ASSOCIATION,

the St. Louis Fair Grounds, whose amphitheatre, tracks and exhibition buildings are beyond anything of the nature in the country, and compare favorably with any in any country.

We must not overlook, as we turn to go down stream, the

POWDER MAGAZINES

of the Laflin & Rand Powder Company, which the indefatigable, genial and public-spirited S. H. Laflin represents here—he that is chairman of the Finance Committee and is one of the Committee of Arrangements, and who so ably and continuously aided the chairman of the latter committee, Mr. Chauncey I. Filley, to make a success of the local arrangements of the National Railroad Convention, of which the Committee of Arrangements had entire charge and the entire responsibility for success or failure, to so arrange all the local details as should honor our guests and be no discredit to our citizens. If there have been citizens who failed to appreciate the importance of this Convention before its meeting, there are none now who deny its utility, its significance, its distinguished *personnel*, its power for good, its favorable impressions upon our visitors in the knowledge that they take home of our present greatness and *our future*.

OUR NORTH AND NORTHEAST CONNECTION.

We must not overlook our great trunk line to the North and Northwest, the St. Louis, Kansas City and Northern Railroad. It stretches its iron way across the Missouri river at St. Charles and Kansas City, and reaches into the heart of Iowa. It is one of the great arteries of our commerce, bringing to us the surplus of the welcome products of Iowa, and distributing thence our manufactures and merchandise. We have mutual interests with our Iowa friends on board and those left at home, and we appreciate their presence and the unanimous "Yes" that they gave in the Convention to the resolution favoring the Texas and Pacific Railroad. This, from a State having over 3,000 miles of cross-railway lines from the Mississippi to the Missouri, and in direct connection with the Union Pacific and Northern Pacific roads, speaks the honest and unprejudiced sentiments of the North, and an appreciation that cross-lines, local roads, alone are not sufficient to promote the agricultural interests of her people, but that they must have, and aid and support the building, by all honorable means, North and South lines, and Southwest lines, whereby the surplus products of their State may find a Southern market and outlet, not alone to and through to New Orleans, but eventually to the consumers of Texas, Arizona, and to the City of Mexico.

And what applies in this instance to Iowa as well applies to Minnesota and Michigan, which were also ably and well represented at the Convention and upon the excursion. Our interests are common, and they are general. The presence of none were more heartily welcome or appreciated.

We must not overlook, on our way down, the furnaces and smokestacks of the

ST. LOUIS GLASS-WORKS,

another important and prominent industry—one that has all the raw materials incident to its manufactured articles abundant in our immediate vicinity—sand, coal, lead, and all, in fact, but soda ash, which comes cheaply and direct by ocean and river, from England, through our Custom-house.

Neither must we overlook our

PUBLIC BONDED WAREHOUSES,

for importing goods, nor private bonded warehouses, occupied with the imports of our dealers.

St. Louis is one of the principal and important interior ports, doing a direct importing business, and one that was instrumental in procuring the passage of the bill in Congress creating interior ports of entry. New York unjustly assumes that the creation of these ports was a direct blow at her ascendency as a port of entry.

The fact is, that imports and exports seek the cheapest channels upon heavy and bulky articles, and the speediest and cheapest on the more expensive and lighter commodities, and thus it is that the great water highway, the Mississippi, reaches out and gathers in upon her waters the bulky imports, and the competing cities of Philadelphia, Baltimore, and eventually Norfolk, Charleston and Savannah, will also reach out in connection with their trunk lines of railways, in competition, not alone for imports, but will vie with New York, Boston, Mobile and New Orleans for tributary traffic and exports.

WHITE LEAD AND OIL WORKS.

We see now another leading industry, the white lead interests, united with the production of castor and linseed oils, promoting thereby the production of both flaxseed and the castor bean, and giving employment to a large number of people agriculturally and mechanically.

	1870.	1874.
Receipts of lead	18,903,120 lbs.	35,301,520 lbs.

Near by we see one—yes, several—of the huge

IRON ESTABLISHMENTS,

such as manufacture the motive power of the steamers we are on, such as make its engines, boilers, etc., etc. And this excursion and the Convention yields something of interest to this class of manufactures, for engines are not alone confined to the use of steamers, but as motive power for factories, which are multiplying in the South, for plantation uses, sugar-houses, gins, etc., and it can be of no disadvantage to see our capacity to produce them, nor to afford our guests some information respecting them, for it is a noted fact, acknowledged by foreign experts who have examined into the matter, that steam motive power can be and is manufactured in this city in competition, both in quality and price, with any produced upon the Clyde, and which fact enters largely and profitably into the further fact that, with the cheapness of iron, together with its peculiar quality, hulls, both for river and ocean traffic, may be produced here in competition with the ship-yards of the old world, and thus another great industry is added, as will be seen as we approach South St. Louis.

We pass the

OLD SHOT TOWER

as we proceed down stream, before reaching the bridge, the lead for which comes out of the soil of our own State. This is an old landmark. Across the river, in adjacent proximity, lie the old passenger and freight depots of the many trunk lines leading to the East, North, Southeast and South.

There, too, centers a vast coal interest, and coke furnaces, and rolling mills and numerous elevators, all auxiliaries to our commerce.

We must not overlook the important manufacture of saws, circular and otherwise.

THE ST. LOUIS SAW WORKS,

established in 1849, and supplying, through their branch houses, Chicago and New Orleans.

Also the old established

OMNIBUS AND STREET CAR WORKS,

and turning out in quality and quantity the equal of any establishment in the country.

So, too, with the well-known

WAGON, AMBULANCE,

and plains freighters' wagons establishment of Espenschied's, which supplies not only large Government contracts, but has a noted reputation from this to and beyond the Rocky Mountains.

CHAINS

which were once solely produced abroad are now largely manufactured here.

ORGAN BUILDING

is another well established and thriving industry.

PICKLES

are represented by five leading houses and factories.

PLANING MILLS

and sash and door factories are mostly in this part of the city, and immense establishments, shipping to all adjacent States and Territories.

PLANING MILL MACHINERY

is represented by the Manufacturers' Union Company.

AGRICULTURAL IMPLEMENTS

are represented by the immense manufacturing establishment of Kingsland & Ferguson, Semple, Birge & Co., Manny & Co., and some half-dozen other manufacturers, whose annual displays at the Fair are a credit to the city, and a leading article of manufacture.

BREWERIES.

Some thirty or more first-class establishments produce and ship their manufactures throughout the West and South. Of late bottled lager has become an article of trade, and is put up by two or three brewers, and finds ready market in the East and elsewhere.

As we repass under the bridge we must follow, in thought, the iron rails that connect the East and the West, the North and the South, at that great common junction and place of arrival and departure,

THE UNION DEPOT.

There centres the traffic of the continent, made possible, practical, economical and convenient by reason of the uniting link, the bridge.

And while we pass the central part of the city and look back to 1849, when the fire swept out of existence the structures that lined the levee from a block below the bridge, down through and back through the leading business streets of the city, the bulk of the business houses—added to which calamity was coupled the destruction of life by the cholera of that season—and almost any other city, at that early period of her commercial life, would have paused in her career of prosperity.

But a year had not elapsed before the last traces of the fire had disappeared, and new structures, in those days considered magnificent, and suited to the commercial uses of the far future, but which now, in comparison with the magnificent stone and iron structures for commercial purposes that are being, and have in the few past years been built, seem to the present eye as did the little old stone structures of that day, insignificant and suited only to the lesser and bulkier and cheaper classes of our rapidly augmenting traffic.

COMMERCIAL PILES.

St. Louis is rearing monuments of stone and iron for commercial uses.

IN BUILDING COMMODITIES,

brick, stone, iron, walnut, pine, cypress and hard woods, St. Louis has no superior.

The soil on the outskirts of the city is a natural brick soil, and requires but gathering under cover, and rolling and pressing, as is done by the several

HYDRAULIC PRESS BRICK COMPANIES,

and hand and other brick companies, preparatory to the kiln. So the capacity of production is only limited by the demand, and this, it is remarkable to state, was so unexpectedly large during the panicky months as to get ahead of the supply.

Marble, sandstone, limestone and granites are profusely scattered throughout the State, and yield such building materials as compose the structure of the new Chamber of Commerce, the Lindell and Southern, the Singer building, portion of the new post-office in course of construction, the

BLOCKS OF RESIDENCES

throughout the city, and the fine suburban residences which are so frequent and attract the eye, and give prominent notoriety to the total absence of frame dwellings or warehouses, which by law are prohibited within the city limits.

And this gives force and pertinent position to our magnificent

STEAM FIRE DEPARTMENT,

admirably managed, paid by the city, and their volunteer aids, the

UNDERWRITERS' CORPS,

and this connects our vast, responsible and prosperous

FIRE INSURANCE COMPANIES,

doing business by means of their capital, under and through the restrictive laws of the several States, in every State in the Union that it is desirable to do business in.

And so, too, with our large and safe, vigorous and ably managed

LIFE INSURANCE COMPANIES.

Local pride of the South and West clings to the early defined purposes of both our life and fire insurance companies, so that it is unnecessary to pay tribute to Eastern companies, and that the very large premiums resulting from this business should be retained in the West, where it originates, for the best interests of the West and the people who originate it. And before we pass along to the southern part of the levee, we must have our say regarding that indicative pulse of our manufactures and commerce, our

BANKS AND BANKING CAPITAL

and business. A recently compiled statement (semi-annual), to June 30 last, thus represents it, as filed with the Secretary of State : Capital at $19,510,812.76 ; deposits at $41,147,116.00 ; loans and discounts at $45,309,998.00 ; aggregate of Exchange purchased by banks from January, 1874, to January, 1875, $274,385,761.00. Instructive figures, that represent something of the solidity and financial ability of St. Louis and the State.

It is this kind of

POWER

that enables St. Louis to go it alone, to prosper in hard times, to increase in material progress. But, after all, the very satisfactory increase of trade and manufactures for two years past has resulted very largely from the opening up of railroads into Arkansas and Texas. Thus have the buyers from Arkansas, Northern Louisiana, Texas, the Indian Nation, Arizona, New Mexico, etc., etc., been brought to the very doors of manufacturers and jobbers, and hence the vast increase of traffic and the interchanges of commodities, including that great staple, cotton, which has of late, through the enterprise of our merchants, together with a very large influx of cotton experts and dealers from the South, who, looking upon the advantages existing here, have taken up their residence, and are among the active and leading cotton factors here ; and while we are upon this subject we will not await the return trip and landing of the boat at the St. Louis Cotton Compress Company, but anticipate it with the statistics pertaining to that branch of our business, and which has made a market attracting domestic and foreign buyers, and promising material increase for the future.

Going back to years ending in September, the receipt of bales was:

1870	11,372
1872	32,421
1873	59,709
1874	103,741
From Sept. 1, 1874, to Sept. 1, 1875	136,806
From Sept. 1 to Nov. 15, 1875	46,145

	Storage capacity, bales.	Compress capacity, bales per day.
Peper Warehouse	15,000	300
St. Louis Cotton Compress Company	25,000	1,000
Evans Bros.' Warehouse	10,000	650
Mammoth Warehouse	25,000	600
Factors and Brokers' Warehouse	20,000	500

There has been no more energetic worker in behalf of the cotton trade and of the Convention than Mr. Miles Sells, one of the Committee of Arrangements and Finance.

The increase of the cotton trade is no more remarkable than has been that of our

DRY GOODS JOBBERS,

which was marked for 1874, and so far this year has continued in a marked degree in quantity and value, notwithstanding the material reduction in values.

This same increase of trade permeates the

BOOT AND SHOE

trade, added to which of late has been the manufactured product of our own manufacturers and dealers, which in fine work, both for men and women's wear, is becoming noted for quality and durability. And in this connection one of the leading and early friends of the Convention is John B. Maude, of Appleton, Noyes & Co., who was also upon the Committee of Arrangements and one of the liberal and energetic promoters of the work of that committee.

We are now passing the

MERCHANTS' EXCHANGE.

This, too, has been a prominent building, but it has accomplished its object as a meeting place for the merchants of St. Louis, and, like all old improvements, was not constructed for the "future great" city, but for the city as it was.

The President of the Merchants' Exchange is Mr. D. Pitt Rowland, one of the live, young and representative merchants of the city, who, from education and position, mingles in the progressive circles, and therefore of necessity, as well as of inclination, was an active co-worker for the Convention, and found time for thirty days to give his presence at the meetings of the Committee of Arrangements at the Post-office, and thus counsel and arrange for the details and success of the purposes and objects of the Convention. He will soon marshal the members of the Exchange and welcome them in the

NEW HALL.

This is the finest chamber in the country, and is not surpassed in the world. Its rooms have been visited by the members of the Convention, and its extent, conveniences and equipments were the subject of general commendation.

We go down past the wharf-boat of the

MISSISSIPPI VALLEY BARGE

Transportation Company. The importance of these hulls, with their low upper-works, cannot be readily understood, nor is the fact generally known or conceded that the Mississippi steamers and barges bear a commerce greater than that of the American commerce of the ocean. The comparative cheapness of barge transportation is yet to have its full effect. Circumstances have been such as not to fully develop its benefits, or as they will be upon the completion of the upper rapids improvements. Then, as stated by Chauncey I. Filley, in one of his recent letters in relation to the Convention, will the shippers of the upper rivers, upon a sure and sufficient stage of water throughout the navigable season, be enabled, in hulls of their own, or furnished like the canal-boats upon the Erie or Champlain canals, or the lakes and Hudson river, and motive power supplied by towing companies, to ship the surplus cereals of the Northwest to this city, or New Orleans, or a foreign port, at such rates of freight, with ordinary competition, as will be cheaper than any other line or mode of conveyance, and realize to producer and shipper the saving of the present inland freight across the country.

The capacity of a tow of five barges is about ten thousand tons—equal to one thousand freight cars. The economy of barge transportation is thus, on comparison, seen. A tow could take 780,000 bushels of corn, which would require twenty-six hundred cars—eight hundred and six (806) trains, of thirty cars each; eight hundred and six locomotives to move them one hundred miles, or eight thousand and sixty locomotives to move them one thousand miles.

Then there are the monster

FREIGHT AND PASSENGER STEAMERS,

like the Great Republic and Howard, and the splendid

MEMPHIS AND VICKSBURG

Packet Line, with Commodore John A. Scudder in the management, who, with Capt. J. N. Bofinger, upon the part of the steamboat interests, have been active and efficient co-operators in the interests of the Convention; as has Capt. I. M. Mason, a representative man in the

NORTHERN LINE PACKET COMPANY,

and President of the Board of Trade. So the steamboat and barge interests, hence to St. Paul and to New Orleans, Vicksburg and Memphis, were active promoters of the Convention, and thereby of the interests of their several lines.

WOOD AND PAPER BOXES

are in large demand, and each branch of the business occupies many large concerns.

PATENT MEDICINES,

representing some of the leading staple remedies and proprietary medicines, are of St. Louis production, and a score or so of houses are exclusively engaged in the business of making the same.

PLOWS.

Manufacturers are mostly below the bridge, and are represented by several prominent firms, who manufacture all kinds of plows for the Western and Southern markets.

BROOMS

have become an article of manufacture of no insignificant amount, and occupy a dozen or more manufacturing firms.

THE ST. LOUIS BRUSH FACTORY,

with some ten or twelve manufacturers, turn out of the coarser and staple article of brushes nearly the whole mercantile supply of the city.

PAPER BAGS

are manufactured by Bemis, Bro. & Co., and this trade has become one of magnitude, and yearly increasing, to so many uses are such articles put.

HEMP BAGGING AND ROPE

are represented by two prominent factories. Hemp is a leading staple of Missouri.

HARDWARE JOBBERS.

This is an important trade of the city, which has as many prominent firms, in proportion to its size, as any city in the country. Among those who took an active interest in the Convention, and are always ready to encourage public enterprise, were two representative houses—the Simmons Hardware Company, and McCombs, Keller & Byrnes.

COTTON AND HAY PRESS

manufacturer, Peter K. Dederick, does a liberal trade.

WINDOW GLASS

manufacture is an article of recent introduction, and embraces one of the finest factories for the production of French window glass in the country, ready sale for which is found at home.

THE CRYSTAL PLATE GLASS COMPANY,

at Crystal City, some twenty miles below the city, has its chief office in this city, and can produce plate glass of equal thickness, clearness and size with any foreign article. It has superior sand in abundance in close proximity to the furnace doors, and of superior quality and inexhaustible in quantity. The sand is an article of commerce and sale to other cities, and is largely exported for foreign works.

DUPLICATES.

It is a noticeable fact that nearly if not quite all of the prominent manufactures—except the Sugar Refinery—of the northern part of the city has its duplicate or triplicate in the southern part. In

THE GLASS WORKS

the southern part now takes the lead, while three years since the northern part had the only glass works in the city; now the Illinois Glass Works is represented and sells most of its product here. The Lindell Glass Company, the Western Glass Company and the Mississippi Glass Company have come into existence, and are adding slowly to an industry that, from the existence of the leading and bulky materials in our own State and neighborhood, must soon make it one of the leading interests of the city.

FIRE BRICK AND CLAYS

of unequalled quality, and surpassing the German for many purposes, underlie the western suburbs of our city, and employ a large amount of capital and labor in the manufacture of brick, tile-pipe, etc., etc., while immense amounts of clay are sold to distant manufacturing cities for pots, retorts, etc., etc.

In the same neighborhood is the

SILVER REFINERY,

reducing about $3,000,000 of ores, silver and gold, per annum.

THE COTTON FACTORIES

are in the lower part of the city, and afford to our jobbers a limited supply of yarns, cotton batting and domestics, which are put upon the jobbing market by our jobbers at Eastern rates, affording a profit, and saving the transportation on the raw material East and on the manufactured article back, and giving the benefit of the labor to our own city.

This was a fact presented by Hon. Chauncey I. Filley to the New Orleans Mississippi Valley Commercial Convention, over which he presided in May, 1869, not only as applicable to cotton, but to wool, leather, walnut wood, iron, etc., etc., which could and should be manufactured in the South and West, and thus save the freights East and West, and give employment to our laborers. The increase in cotton factories throughout the South is remarkable, and the product finds ready sale.

THE ST. LOUIS WOODEN WARE

works was at one time the only and leading factory in the valley. Now Samuel Cupples & Co. produce a vast amount of wooden ware, and the products of our factories are distributed throughout the valley.

WIRE.

It is only within a few years that this important industry, formerly monopolized abroad, has been successfully introduced. It is now made in sufficient supply, by three wire factories, of the coarser and fence wires, and of the finer and finest kinds, and of superior quality, from our tenacious native ores, to supply the market and drive out the foreign article almost from the trade.

STONE WARE

and tiles, and sewer pipe, &c., are represented by two leading factories. With an abundance of clay of superior quality for the manufacture of ironstone or white granite wares, and of the common white or delf ware, St. Louis will become some day the center of an immense manufacturing interest in this line. It now offers to experienced workers and capital in this line a profitable and extensive field. The freight from the Staffordshire potteries or the potteries of the East afford ample protection and a wide margin for profit.

As we remarked above, nearly every industry of the upper part of the city has its duplicate in the lower part. Here we find the immense

STOVE WORKS

of Bridge, Beach & Co., with its celebrated patterns so well known throughout the West and South, and here we find another rolling mill,

THE HELMBACHER FORGE AND ROLLING MILLS.

Its productions are varied and large, and employs a large number of hands. Another and comparatively new industry is the

ST. LOUIS RAIL FASTENING WORKS,

whose products find ready market, and a much needed addition to St. Louis products.

We must not overlook the

MISSISSIPPI IRON WORKS,

which produces entire store fronts, columns, caps, sills, ornamental work, garden seats, vases, girders, shutters, etc. Iron has become one of the substantial and accessible materials for building purposes, and is used in the prominent dry goods structure of Samuel C. Davis & Co., upon Fifth and Washington avenue, a St. Louis built and owned structure; and near by are the magnificent stone structures occupied by Dodd, Brown & Co., and Crow, Hargadine & Co., which three firms represent the leading enterprising jobbing dry goods concerns of the city, and with Wm. Barr & Co. and Scruggs, Vandervoort & Barney, the leading retail houses, took an active interest in welcoming the delegates of the Convention.

THE CARPET TRADE

is advancing rapidly in the quantity and value of the business, and the variety and richness of the texture which is now demanded. Bray & Co. we found representing the interests of the Convention,

APPENDIX.

and looking to the entertainment of the city's guests, and in this, as in all public enterprises, are active co-workers. Bray and Barney were of Laflin's finance committee.

And now we go down past the Arsenal, leaving the Pittsburg Coal Company's road and coal piles upon our left, and sighting the Iron Mountain road upon our right—that great artery of the city into and through Arkansas, and into Louisiana and Texas, by the southern extension to Little Rock and Texarkana, and reaching Marshall, Shreveport, Dallas, Galveston and Sherman; then by way of Columbus and the great Southern and Atlantic Coast connections, Mobile and New Orleans are made. We have passed the river connections of the Missouri Pacific and the Atlantic and Pacific roads, which three roads, with the St. Louis, Kansas City and Northern Railway in the northern part of the city, compose the four great trunk line feeders of the city upon the west side of the river, and for which the city, county and State have in bonds issued, and taxes levied and paid, for and on account of the several roads, or had up to the year 1871, the last official record we can lay our hands upon, nearly $49,000,000. This much has the city, county and State done for

PUBLIC IMPROVEMENTS,

and without which to-day our commerce would be comparatively nothing, as competing cities with iron lines of communication entering into and tapping our trade connections, would have, as for a few years they did, fairly monopolized the trade, and driven us from the field. Thus the completion of our trunk lines became a necessity. The issue of bonds for the railroads was as follows:

State, by bonds issued	$ 23,701,000	
State, by interest on same	15,150,321	
		$ 38,851,321
City of St. Louis, by issue of bonds	$ 1,995,000	
County of St. Louis, by issue of bonds	1,700,000	
City and county taxes levied	2,450,000	
Interest paid by city and county	3,914,700	
		10,059,700
		$ 48,911,021

Few States or cities have done more than this, and yet there are those whose city never advanced or invested a dollar in railroads, and in the past built up by Eastern capital and capitalists and in the present owned by the same, boast of the energy and wealth they display—brag of the shadow, and have no fee simple in the substance.

Of the above $48,000,000 St. Louis city and county paid over one-half, as prior to 1866 the city and county paid over one-half of the entire taxes of the State, and in 1871 about one-third.

We now approach the

ORE DUMP

of the Iron Mountain road, and of the ore beds of Iron Mountain and Pilot Knob, from whence, in bulk, ore is shipped by barges to the Ohio and other rivers. This is an important traffic. Upon the east side of the river the stack of the new

BESSEMER WORKS

and buildings appear; and we approach South St. Louis with its numerous

BLAST FURNACES, ZINC MANUFACTORIES

and rolling mills. Here the coal and ore meet, and the heaviest of the industries of St. Louis looms up to the view of our distinguished guests. Here the cheapest facilities, East or West, exist for the manufacture of pig and blooms, and with the addition that is now being made to the Vulcan Iron Works, the raw material for iron or steel will be made into rails or bars or rods, thus giving additional employment and additional advantages to these works, and making them independent, in a measure, of a market and consumers of their pig metals.

THE ZINC WORKS

comprise three manufactories, and use what was formerly thrown away by the miners of lead ores, and for which now they realize the full if not an excessive value.

THE IRON BOAT YARD

is a feature of South St. Louis, and has already turned out several iron steamers. This industry is one that must flourish and become important. The increase of bulk transportation which will follow the improvement of the rivers, will demand strong, light and roomy hulls. A change is going on from wood to iron hulls, and for river or ocean use the Western Iron Boat Yard will, at no distant day, have an active demand beyond its capacity to furnish.

THE GROCERY TRADE,

from its bulky and weighty nature, naturally seeks water-ways as the cheapest channel of conveyance, and the receipts of sugar, coffee, molasses, etc., show a gratifying gain. The receipts at this port for the years 1870 and 1874 were as follows:

	1870.	1874.
Coffee, bags	113,950	153,919
Sugar, hhds	23,289	36,337
Sugar, bbls	10,597	56,420
Sugar, boxes	56,255	80,836
Sugar, bags	114	39,774

REAL ESTATE.

The reduction in value of building lots in the city has been of no disadvantage. Real estate has, in fact, been too high. The opening up of the many street railway lines has had its effect to reduce inside and advance outside or suburban property. This enables the building of a class of houses suitable to mechanics, operatives, and persons upon small salaries.

This is giving impetus to manufactures and population long needed. Within the five years 7,465 permits for substantial stone and brick structures were issued, including 1,801 during 1874, costing $10,269,280; or since 1870, $34,412,466, up to 1875.

Gen. Frost, representing the real estate interest, was an active member of the Committee of Arrangements, and also of the Banquet Committee, and in both positions devoted his time and energy.

PARKS, PUBLIC AND PRIVATE.

St. Louis has long enjoyed one of the finest private botanical gardens extant—Tower Grove, the property of Henry Shaw, Esq., which is thrown open to the public throughout the week, and by card on Sundays. The liberality and public spirit of the above named gentleman, in his donation of Tower Grove park to the city, was an act of distinguished liberality, and an incentive to the creation, the past year, of three other public parks. Forest Grove park is one of the largest in the country. It is directly west of the central part of the city, and is being improved upon a liberal scale, commensurate with the wants of our city. Lafayette, Washington, Missouri, O'Fallon, Carondelet, Hyde, and others of lesser importance, are appreciated breathing places, around which are clustering private residences that beautify and adorn.

DRY DOCKS AND WAYS

interest strangers but little. They are interesting, however, and with a mammoth steamer raised clear of the water, give a better conception of the hull and steamboat building than can be learned from floating steamers. And now we re-embark, after having witnessed a run at the Vulcan, and plow our way up stream.

Lunch and convivialities commence, and the dry toasts and wet toasts, and oratory, and the American eagle soar throughout the cabins, and we come to the St. Louis Cotton Compress Company. After viewing it, we proceed up stream. and the convivialities continue, and the guests from North and South and East and West are of one common mind and purpose—that we are one people, one nation, never to be divided, but to grow and expand in territory, and in the great fundamental precepts our forefathers taught us to revere and worship.

And we must break in here in response to an inquiry as to where our huge water-mains were produced, and we point in the direction of Shickle, Harrison & Co., who, for quality and price, produce a cheaper and better article than formerly was furnished from the East, Pittsburg and Philadelphia.

We answer another interrogatory as to where our car wheels and freight cars are built, and we direct the attention of our questioner to the Missouri Car Company; and we go back to the early days in the fifties again, when Palm was building locomotives here—just a little too soon for his own interests—and before the demand was sufficient to justify the establishment of, or a continuation of, locomotive works here.

We pass the outlets of some of our great

SEWERS

that so effectually drain our whole territorial limits. The grand sewer system of St. Louis was commenced about 1852. The results have been to make St. Louis, as statistics prove, the

HEALTHIEST CITY IN THE WORLD.

We have been asked what were those large brick buildings in different parts of the city, so similar in construction. They are the

PUBLIC SCHOOLS.

There are above fifty of them, and are unequal to the demand. Our public schools are one of the particular features of St. Louis institutions that we are proud of. The student that goes through them from bottom to top will take with him into actual life all the education necessary, and better than many get in high-sounding colleges in the rural districts of many States.

ADIEU.

We approach the wharf-boat, and some of our genial guests and courteous citizens are preparing to separate. Acquaintances and impressions have been made that will last a lifetime. We have been impressed with the intelligence and unusual amount of talent and representative men that were delegates to the Convention.

No such representative body of men ever met, to our mind, in convention for purely commercial purposes before. Where so many have been distinguished at home as Executives of States, Senators, members of Congress, judges, generals, legislators, it would be invidious to particularize, and the roll of the Convention and the reports of the proceedings will show each and all. The forthcoming pamphlet report of its proceedings will be sought for, and will preserve the record of proceedings that in after years will be cherished as a memento of participation in an assemblage that will have the effect upon the public and popular mind to carry conviction and success to and through Congress, and to give to the Southwest her just due—a highway, free at all seasons of the year from snow, to the Pacific.

To the Chairman of the Committee of Arrangements, Hon. Chauncey I. Filley, and the Secretary, Mr. J. B. Gazzam, we tender our acknowledgments for tickets of invitation, and for valuable information received at various times during the past month; and to Mr. Martin Collins, Chairman of the Refreshment Committee, and A. A. Talmage, Esq., Chairman of the Excursion Committee, and to that committee generally for the attention received on board of the steamers.

To the ladies who added to the occasion by their presence, all expressed themselves gratified and pleased.

We cannot in an article like this, in the hurried trip of a steamer, take in at a bird's-eye view all the material interests. But we can recount and touch upon such prominent industries as necessarily come into view and mind, or recur to one and become the subject of conversation. St. Louis has abundant cause for satisfaction in the visit and excursion of our guests.

We have appreciated the matter ourselves from the start, and we now put it into such shape as to be appreciated by our citizens and the public. We have a city to be proud of; we have a great manufacturing city; we have solid wealth, and are increasing in handsome public and private dwellings. We have a city that in all its present bearings and future promise, invites population, invites capital, invites active business men. Our growth is rapidly going on, and the vast Southwest is a country which invites our attention and will bring each year millions of dollars to our trade.

COMMUNICATION FROM DELEGATES.

St. Louis, November 25, 1875.

Hon. Stanley Mathews, Chairman National Railroad Convention:

Dear Sir:—The impatience of the Convention yesterday to complete the work on which all so unanimously agreed, having cut off discussion and explanation upon the main question, viz., the passage of its resolutions, I beg leave, in behalf of the California delegation, the Nevada delegation and the delegation from Arizona, and as Chairman of the California delegation, to present the following reasons, in addition to those given in the resolutions offered by our delegation and published in the proceedings, why the great mass of the people of California desire the Texas and Pacific Railroad to be built as soon as possible, and to San Diego.

The opponents of this road upon our coast have succeeded in creating against it a spirit of opposition in some parts of California, and especially in San Francisco, on the ground that its construction to San Diego will seriously injure the city of San Francisco. But, sir, the mass of our people hold that its speedy completion will benefit San Francisco itself, as well as the people of all parts of the Pacific States.

Why, sir, San Francisco, the queen city of our coast, and upon a harbor acknowledged to be as fine as any in the world, has nothing to fear. Her permanent success and growth are assured. As a city, San Francisco is the pride of every Californian, and not one thing would any of us willfully do to injure her material and legitimate growth and prosperity. She is ever to be the chief mart of the Pacific States. Why, then, do we wish to connect with the Atlantic States by rail a new port on San Diego Bay, the second in excellence upon our California coast?

It is a sacred principle, dear to every American citizen, that *it endangers the liberties and interests of the people to allow too much power to be concentrated in one individual, or in a few individuals;* in one, because by an abuse of his power a tyranny may be established; in a few, because by abusing their power they may establish an oligarchy—either result being equally fatal to the principles of American freedom.

On this principle we want a competing road across the continent, that all the transportation interests of our coast may not be controlled by one great corporation, already grown too powerful. On this principle we want a second port upon our coast connected directly by rail with your Atlantic and Gulf cities, that all the vast and increasing trade interests of our Pacific coast may not be monopolized by one great city. In other words, to establish and maintain a modest rival to San Francisco four hundred miles to the southward, and on the safe harbor of San Diego, will have a strong tendency to keep the merchant princes and wealthy capitalists of San Francisco "upon their good behavior," and will, in more ways than one, result in the general good of all classes of our people. Besides this consideration, the building up of a thriving city at San Diego, in one of the most genial, healthful climates that the world can claim, will greatly benefit a large portion of Southern California, which is completely isolated, by the mountains and trade interests of our State, from San Francisco and Northern California. We doubt not, if the main trunk can be completed to San Diego, that lines connecting with San Francisco will soon be constructed, and the people of our State, to its extreme northern limits, will feel the benefits of the permanent competition which we are now satisfied will be secured by the speedy completion of the Texas and Pacific Railroad to San Diego.

The delegates of California, holding their credentials from Gov. Pacheco, and thus representing by their mode of appointment all portions and all interests of our State, desire, through you, to return their thanks for California to this truly National Convention for their decided and unanimous action in favor of the early completion of this much-needed highway and competing line to our coast.

      J. W. A. WRIGHT, of Borden, California.
      WALLACE LEACH, of San Diego, California.
      JOHN P. STEARNS, of Santa Barbara, California.
      D. FELSENHELD, of San Diego, California.
      GEORGE TURNER, Chairman Nevada Delegation.
      WM. G. BOYLE, Chairman Arizona Delegation.

THE MERITS OF THE TEXAS & PACIFIC RAILROAD.

[The following article was prepared by Prof. Waterhouse, of Washington University, and though it was not, for the reason given in the accompanying note, formally presented to the Convention, yet its array of facts and arguments is believed to be sufficiently relevant to a discussion of the 32d parallel route to warrant its insertion in the appendix of the proceedings of the Convention.]

Hon. Stanley Mathews, President Texas and Pacific Railroad Convention:

DEAR SIR:—Precluded by professional engagements from attending the sessions of the Convention, I submit the following paper on the advantages of the Texas and Pacific Railroad, with the earnest hope that its publication may contribute something, however little, to the furtherance of so grand an enterprise.

Very respectfully yours,
S. WATERHOUSE.

WASHINGTON UNIVERSITY, *November* 24, 1875.

The Texas and Pacific railroad has many advantages. It lies mostly on the 32d parallel. The mildness of the climate prevents the heavy snowfall of higher latitudes. During the late survey, hundreds of thermometrical observations were taken every month. Our inability, within the narrow limits assigned to this article, to follow in detail the course of the exploration, compels the selection of prominent and representative facts. On the 32d parallel the fall of snow is seldom more than one foot deep, even on the heights of the Sierra Madre and Nevada ranges. But even this slight obstruction is not lasting. In so mild a temperature, the snow soon melts and the obstacle disappears. The highest altitude at which the line of the 32d parallel—the one recommended by the St. Louis Convention—crosses the mountains is less than 5,000 feet above the level of the sea; still, even at this comparatively low grade, a light snowfall is an advantage of prime moment.

The road on the 32d parallel will escape the snowy barricades of more northern latitudes. In genial winters these highlands are hardly whitened with snow, and in the severest seasons the depth of snow is not sufficient to prevent cattle from getting their own living. With the exception of a narrow strip of sandy plains, grass is very abundant along the whole route; and, even on the arid wastes, there is said to be an adequate supply of forage for the animals necessary for the construction of the road.

On the 32d parallel the fall of rain is copious. Throughout most of the distance springs and streams are numerous. The engineers of the survey report that they found an abundance of water along the entire line of exploration. The distance to water was in no instance more than thirty miles.

Beds of coal have been found along the route of the Texas and Pacific railroad, but their extent and richness have not yet been developed. The regions traversed by this road abound in forests; oak, hickory, cedar, pine, hemlock, hackberry and cottonwood exist in quantities amply sufficient for all the uses of a large population.

The grades of the Texas and Pacific will be light. The road will, for the most part, traverse level bottom-lands, gently undulating savannas, or gradually ascending highlands. Even in the mountain passes, the grades are not nearly so heavy as those on the Central Pacific.

With exceptional detours, the Texas and Pacific railroad closely follows the 32d parallel of latitude. The distance by this route from Fort Worth to San Francisco is 1,851 miles. To San Diego or the Gulf of California, the distance would be several hundred miles less. It is claimed that this is the shortest practicable route to the Pacific coast. The Texas and Pacific will cross the Colorado river below the head of navigation. At the point of intersection, the Colorado is 19 feet deep and 600 feet wide. The water is always deep enough for large river steamers. The navigation is never obstructed by ice or sand-bars. The cheap conveyance of the materials of the road to intermediate points by water-carriage will greatly reduce the cost of construction. The completion of the railroad will induce an early settlement of the adjacent lands. The commercial necessities of the people will lead to a constant and ever-growing interchange of productions with other parts of the country. The transit of a large portion of this trade must necessarily be overland. These navigable streams will yet waft rich cargoes to the stations erected upon their banks. The commerce of the river will swell the freightage of the rail. Their co-operation will be a mutual benefit.

The Texas and Pacific will promote the development of a very important section of country. Missouri, the Indian Territory and Texas possess bottom-lands and rolling prairies of a richness that is a guarantee of speedy settlement and agricultural prosperity. This road crosses the sandy waste in its narrowest part. The extent of these barren plains has been greatly exaggerated. On the line of the Texas and Pacific railroad, the quantity of unproductive land, including the rocky slopes of the mountains as well as the arid desert, is only 18 per cent.

The explorations which have been made prove that New Mexico, Arizona and Southern California are rich in mineral deposits. There is a golden circulation in the veins of the Rocky Mountains. The lodes of the Sierra Madre glitter with precious treasure. Nature is here clad in brocade. Rich threads of silver have been deftly inwrought into the fabric of the mountains.

Southern California has few navigable rivers. The settlement of a region abounding in natural resources has been seriously delayed by want of communication. The construction of the Texas and Pacific will remedy this defect, afford facilities for commercial intercourse, and open to immigration the rich mineral lands of Southern California and New Mexico. The wants of Arizona and New Mexico demand the early completion of this railroad. According to the latest accessible estimates, the white population of Arizona is now 75,000, while New Mexico has 150,000 inhabitants, and an annual trade of $25,000,000.

The discovery of very rich mines of copper, silver and gold is rapidly attracting population to these Territories. The commercial embarrassments of the people increase with every accession to their numbers. The inadequacy of transportation is enhanced by every addition to the population. The existing tariff of rates was not attainable in season for our present use; but a few years ago, freight from the Pacific coast to the Colorado river was twenty cents a pound, and to the capital of Arizona thirty cents a pound. The cost of carriage to New Mexico would be still greater. The growth and prosperity of these Territories require the unremitting prosecution of a work whose completion would relieve their industry of such oppressive burdens.

The contrasts between the Texas Pacific and the Union and Central Pacific railroads are signally in favor of the former. The Texas Pacific has lighter grades and lower mountains to surmount. The Texas Pacific will never be obstructed by snowfall, but on the route of the Union and Central Pacific, massive blockades of snow sometimes arrest and frequently delay the passage of trains. The Union and Central Pacific run through vast reaches of sterile country.

Between the Rocky and Sierra Nevada mountains the line extends, with exceptional cases, through a verdureless alkaline waste. The sage-bush alone maintains a precarious and disheartened existence. Most of the region seems incapable of cultivation, and therefore of sustaining an agricultural population. Apparently this section of country can never be densely peopled. But the Texas Pacific will traverse a succession of fertile valleys nearly all the way to the Pacific coast. These valleys are susceptible of a tillage that will support a large population all along the line of the road. The construction of the Texas and Pacific railroad will induce the rapid peopling of adjacent lands, develop agricultural and mineral values, and create a taxable wealth, which, apart from strengthening the guarantee of repayment by the railroad, would soon reimburse the Government for all the obligations it would assume. The building of this road would, too, quicken the whole industrial life of the country. The amount of material, labor and money necessary for the construction of so extended a line is immense. Not only would the mechanical arts immediately employed in the work be benefited, but all the remoter vocations which support or equip the artisans would feel the enlivening impulse. The employment of thousands of laborers, not only along the line of the road, but also throughout the workshops of the land, and the disbursement of millions of money among the laboring classes would tend to relieve industrial depression and allay popular discontent. The Texas and Pacific railroad would confer large and immediate advantages upon the South, reviving its commercial activities and re-establishing its disturbed industries. It would benefit the North, not only by opening new channels of communication, but also by an annual economy of hundreds of thousands of dollars in the reduced freightage which competition would be sure to effect. But in order that the competition might be genuine and effective, the Texas and Pacific railroad should extend, as an independent line, all the way to San Diego. Any intermediate termination and connection with the Southern branch of the Central Pacific would prevent the national benefit to be derived from the rivalry of distinct roads. Irrespective of considerations of patriotism and national utility, an intelligent self-interest should lead the North to an active co-operation with the South in the construction of the Texas and Pacific railroad.

The Government, too, would be the recipient of important benefits. In the service of territorial mails, in the maintenance of frontier forts, in the transportation of soldiers, munitions and commissary stores, and in the reduction of border forces, which a rapid movement of troops by rail would render possible, it has been estimated by competent experts, on the basis of the known economies of the Union Pacific, that the Texas Pacific railroad would save the Government at least $5,000,000 annually.

The great increase in the population and business of Western Texas, New Mexico, Arizona, and Southern California, the large demands for heavy mining machinery and other industrial products, and the greater extent and costliness of the postal and military service on the frontier, urge the immediate construction of the Texas and Pacific railroad with an energy and eloquence that should at once command the favorable audience of Congress. There should be a reciprocity of benefits. In return for the great economy of men and means, which this road would enable the Government to practice in its territorial administration, the Government ought to be willing to further its completion by a loan of the national credit. For the rapid and cheap construction of the line, the Company need immediate funds. Without national indorsement, the bonds of the road in these times of financial depression could only be sold at depreciated prices, while the Company would have to pay interest on their face, and ultimately redeem them at par value. This would greatly increase the cost of the road and constantly burden the subsequent management with the unproductive payment of heavy interest. To avoid these embarrassments, to secure the prompt sale of their bonds without sacrifice, the Company ask the Government to guarantee the interest on their construction bonds at the extremely low valuation of $35,000 per mile of road. It is not at all probable that the Government would ever be compelled to pay one dollar of this interest, for it is scarcely possible that the profits of the road should not amount to five per cent. interest on $35,000 a mile. But, in any event, the earnings of the line, increasing from year to year, would soon repay the Government for the loan of its credit. As a still further protection of the national interests and as an additional reason for the Congressional indorsement of their enterprise, the Texas and Pacific Company propose to relinquish the vast tract of public lands which they now hold by Congressional grant. The ultimate value of these lands which the Company now offer to re-surrender will far exceed the sum which the Government will, in any possible contingency, be forced to pay by its guarantee of the interest on the bonds. To obtain Congressional aid it ought only to be necessary to secure the national interests from loss, and in this instance the rights of the Government have been protected by every defense which the law could erect. The legal safeguards which 'indemnify the Government for its indorsement of the bonds are a first lien on all the property of the road, the surrender of 30,000,000 acres of land already granted, the transportation of the mails, troops and supplies, and the deposit in the United States Treasury of $5,000 in bonds for each mile of road—to be sold by the Government if necessary to meet any possible deficiency during the period of constructing the road.'

But, in accordance with the traditional action of our Government in matters of great public improvement, in conformity with numerous railroad precedents, and in obedience to the dictates of sound sense and statesmanly wisdom, our Government ought, in any event, and irrespective of minor pecuniary considerations, to foster an enterprise so sectionally necessary and so nationally useful.

This road should be built so that the South as well as the North might have a cheap and convenient line of communication, and that the profits of interchange might not be consumed in unnecessary detours in transportation.

Then the Union, strong in the patriotic devotion of its citizens, would be bound in still closer alliance by the material ties of a community of interests and equal facilities of communication. Of the two great iron cinctures, the Southern will, in my judgment, be the more useful. The main reasons for this belief have already been given, but one point of superiority yet remains to be mentioned.

Japan and China, breaking through the reserve of centuries, are beginning to participate in the activities of Western nations. The Oriental merchants, naturally sagacious in business and fond of accumulation, are becoming impressed with the fact that their traditional policy of isolation is prejudicial to their commercial interests. The profits of foreign trade will lead to larger ventures, and soon the international commerce between the United States and the Orient will expand to vast proportions.

A recent trip to Japan and China strongly confirms these views. I am thoroughly convinced that our commerce with these countries will, if fostered by wise legislation and a just policy, soon become immense. There seems to be no good reason why the United States should not, by fair dealing, sagacious action and greater nearness, supplant England in the control of these profitable Oriental exchanges.

The distance from New York to Japan is probably 600 miles less via San Diego than it is by way of San Francisco. The Pacific Mail steamers sail from the Golden Gate due south almost to the latitude of San Diego before they turn their bows eastward. The Texas and Pacific railroad, saving 300 miles of water-carriage, and probably as much more of overland transportation, would by its economy of time and freight secure a monopoly of that Oriental trade which was destined to traverse the continent. San Diego will yet be the Western terminus of an Eastern line of steamships.

An enterprise so obviously national in its character and benefits should encounter no opposition; but if, unhappily, mistaken conceptions of local interest should array a sectional hostility against this railroad, still a concert of action on the part of the adjacent States would achieve success. The harmonious co-operation of the West and South is the essential condition and guarantee of victory. It would insure the Congressional legislation which alone is needed for the successful prosecution of the enterprise. But any diversion of forces, any undue pressure of minor issues, any overloading of the main line with branch roads will be sure to defeat the whole undertaking. Once secure the trunk, and the branches will grow of themselves. But if local jealousies, selfish interests and conflicting claims are allowed to thwart this enterprise, the States guilty of such grave misconduct are unworthy of the great benefits which the construction of the Texas Pacific would confer.

Printed in Dunstable, United Kingdom